HOW TO DRY FOODS

HOW TO DRY FOODS

Deanna DeLong

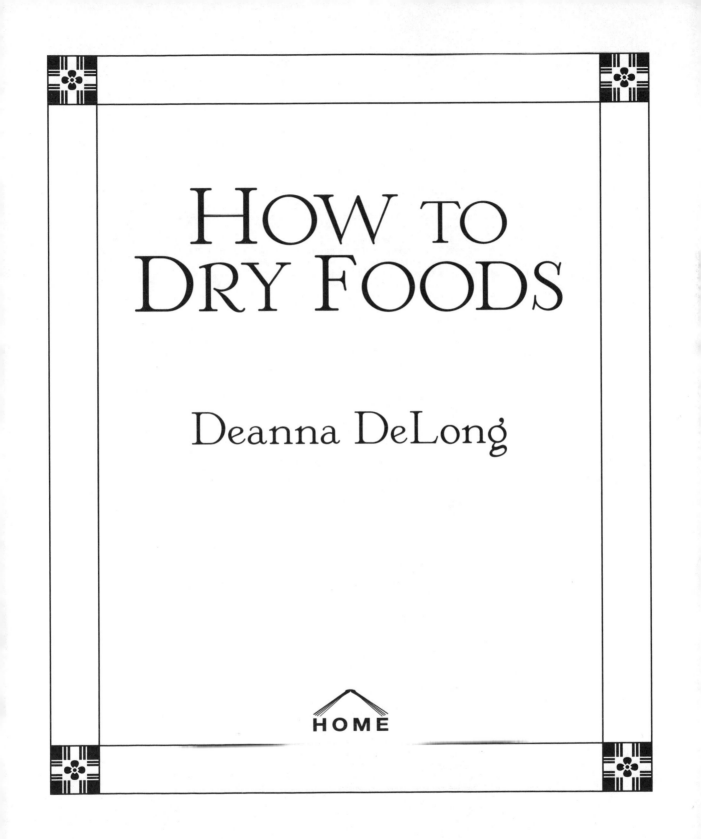

HOME

HOME BOOKS
Published by the Penguin Group
Penguin Group (USA) Inc.
375 Hudson Street, New York, New York 10014, USA
Penguin Group (Canada), 90 Eglinton Avenue East, Suite 700, Toronto, Ontario M4P 2Y3, Canada
(a division of Pearson Penguin Canada Inc.)
Penguin Books Ltd., 80 Strand, London WC2R 0RL, England
Penguin Group Ireland, 25 St. Stephen's Green, Dublin 2, Ireland (a division of Penguin Books Ltd.)
Penguin Group (Australia), 250 Camberwell Road, Camberwell, Victoria 3124, Australia
(a division of Pearson Australia Group Pty. Ltd.)
Penguin Books India Pvt. Ltd., 11 Community Centre, Panchsheel Park, New Delhi—110 017, India
Penguin Group (NZ), Cnr. Airborne and Rosedale Roads, Albany, Auckland 1310, New Zealand
(a division of Pearson New Zealand Ltd.)
Penguin Books (South Africa) (Pty.) Ltd., 24 Sturdee Avenue, Rosebank, Johannesburg 2196,
South Africa

Penguin Books Ltd., Registered Offices: 80 Strand, London WC2R 0RL, England

While the author has made every effort to provide accurate telephone numbers and Internet addresses at the time of publication, neither the publisher nor the author assumes any responsibility for errors, or for changes that occur after publication. Further, the publisher does not have any control over and does not assume any responsibility for author or third-party websites or their content.

PRINTING HISTORY
HPBooks revised edition / August 1992
Home Books revised edition / September 2006

Library of Congress Cataloging-in-Publication Data

DeLong, Deanna.
    How to dry foods / Deanna DeLong.— Rev. ed.
      p. cm.
    Includes index.
      ISBN 1-55788-497-8 (new edition)—ISBN 1-55788-050-6 (aug. 1992 edition)
    1. Food—Drying.   2. Dried foods.   3. Cookery (Dried foods)   I. Title.
TX609.D42 2006
641.4'4—dc22
                                      2006014037

PRINTED IN THE UNITED STATES OF AMERICA

10   9   8   7   6   5   4   3   2   1

PUBLISHER'S NOTE: The recipes contained in this book are to be followed exactly as written. The publisher is not responsible for your specific health or allergy needs that may require medical supervision. The publisher is not responsible for any adverse reactions to the recipes contained in this book.

To my patient and devoted husband, David, who always encourages my creativity and tirelessly supports me in my endeavors, even when it means being on his own while I'm off in some far corner of the earth.

To my incredible grown children, Alyson Whitaker, Isaac DeLong, and Shepard DeLong, who grew up peeling apples and preparing foods to dry without ever complaining—and who now dry foods with my grandchildren.

ACKNOWLEDGMENTS

I would like to thank the amazing people in the Republic of Georgia, Mozambique, Poland, Hungary, Guatemala, El Salvador, Costa Rica, and Honduras who touched and enriched my life as I taught them about food dehydration.

Many thanks to my dear friend and colleague Leon Cooper, who traveled with me on many of my projects to teach about food dehydration in developing countries, and who is always up for a new adventure. His positive attitude, ingenuity, and enthusiasm made even the most challenging projects successful . . . and fun!

There aren't words to express my gratitude to Dr. George York, retired professor from the University of California, Davis, who believed in me twenty-six years ago and encouraged me to write *How to Dry Foods*. Dr. York's expertise in food preservation was invaluable to the technical accuracy of this book.

I am grateful to my fantastic editor, Jeanette Egan, for her brilliant and insightful editing of this book. Her assistance was indispensable.

And most of all, I am thankful to my Father in Heaven for the divine inspiration that allowed me to write this book and share the experience of drying foods with enthusiastic people throughout the world.

CONTENTS

ADVANTAGES OF DRYING FOODS

Preserving foods is not a new idea. Many of us have preserved foods by canning or freezing. Drying is another method of preserving foods in season for use when they're not readily available. It also adds a new variety of snack food to your daily menus.

DRIED FRUITS ARE TASTY

Dried fruits and fruit rolls are delicious, and quite different from the same fruits when fresh. A dried peach tastes *peachier* than a fresh peach. The chewy texture and extra sweet flavor of dried fruits makes them a favorite of all ages.

DRIED FOODS ARE ECONOMICAL

Drying food at home is fairly inexpensive. A high-quality home food dehydrator can easily pay for itself in a summer or two. When comparing commercially dried foods to home dried, you'll notice that it is considerably less expensive to dry your own. When you dry your own, you're not paying for the expensive packaging and advertising that you pay for when purchasing commercially dried foods.

You can buy foods in season, go to U-Pick farms and local produce markets, or grow your own. Seasonal drying greatly increases the savings for your family.

Watch for specials at the supermarket for more savings.

DRIED FOODS ARE NUTRITIOUS

Dried fruits and fruit leathers are especially good replacements for sugar-laden snacks. However, there are more calories in dried foods on a weight-for-weight basis because the nutrients are concentrated. Be aware that 100 grams of fresh apricots have 51 calories, and 100 grams of dried apricots have 260 calories! Most dried fruits contain more than two times the calories of the same fruit fresh.

Nutritionally, drying compares well with other methods of preservation. For most foods, the nutritional value retained is about the same as with freezing. Drying has a lower heat exposure than canning and therefore destroys fewer vitamins. The nutrient losses during most drying processes are small in comparison to the loss during cooking. Using a pretreatment for apples, peaches, and pears lessens the loss of vitamins A and C.

The fiber and carbohydrates are not affected by drying. Neither are the minerals, such as potassium or magnesium, in some fruits.

If you're concerned about additives and preservatives, drying your own foods allows you to control what goes into the foods you eat.

DRIED FOODS TAKE UP MINIMAL STORAGE SPACE

Dried foods take from one-tenth to one-twentieth of the volume of frozen or canned, depending on how much water is in the fresh fruit.

If you store foods for emergencies or economy, the low volume of dried foods makes them very practical for your stored food supply. You can store twenty fresh tomatoes in a one-pint jar when they're dried, compared to three or four quarts for the same amount canned!

Their light weight and low volume are reasons why dried fruits are so popular with backpackers, campers, and people on the go.

DRYING FOODS AND CRAFTS AT HOME IS FUN

Because dehydrating most foods does not require a stove or boiling water, it can be a safe and fun family activity. Even small children enjoy taking the pits out of fruits or placing prepared fruits on trays.

Drying is so easy that even the beginner will have success if the simple instructions in this book are followed. If you're an experienced food preserver, be adventuresome and experiment with different combinations of fruits and vegetables.

If you love crafts, try making dried apple wreaths (page 138), potpourri (page 139), dried flowers (page 135), and even dried dough ornaments (page 140).

The good news about drying is that you rarely can make a serious mistake. Most dried foods are edible, even if you don't exactly follow all of the instructions in the book (the exceptions are fish and meat, which must be dried exactly as instructed).

THE SAFETY OF DRIED FOODS

Generally, the only food-safety issues you would have with dried foods are mold and fermentation, both of which are readily apparent, unlike with canned foods that may contain harmful bacteria while appearing to be unspoiled. You can see mold and you can smell fruits when they've fermented. If dried food is moldy or fermented, throw it away.

Jerky, other dried meats, and fish need extra-special care. If you choose to dry these products, read and follow the instructions in this book carefully.

Always observe good hygiene practices in the kitchen as you prepare foods for drying, or as you are packaging them. Wash your hands frequently with hot, soapy water, especially after touching something other than the foods. Keep your utensils and dehydrator trays squeaky clean. Use clean towels or dishcloths. Thoroughly wash all fruits and vegetables before preparing for drying.

HISTORY OF DRYING

Dried food has been used for survival from early nomadic days to modern times. Ancient Egyptians and Greeks are known to have dried food.

Early seagoing expeditions survived on dried fruit, grains, and meats. Columbus probably would never have discovered America if he hadn't fed himself and his crew with dried foods!

Drying was a necessity for the colonists and early settlers of the New World, or any place where homes had to be self-reliant during the winter. Fruits, especially apples, pears, peaches, and apricots, and some vegetables were dried for winter use. Quantities of fish and meat were dried and heavily salted to reduce spoilage. They were so salty that it's a wonder how they managed to eat them.

The first dehydrator used to dry fruits and vegetables by artificial means was introduced in France in 1795. It had a controlled temperature of 105°F (41°C) and a continuous hot-air flow. It was used to dry thinly sliced vegetables and fruits.

Drying on a large scale was not used until the beginning of World War I when tremendous quantities of food were needed to feed troops in the field. Considerable research on drying foods was conducted in countries involved in the war.

The Great Depression of the 1930s caused a surge in home drying in the United States. Canning equipment was expensive and often not available. Many homemakers began drying foods the way early settlers had.

During World War II, more than 160 vegetable dehydration plants went into operation in the United States alone, and the armies and navies used tons of dried foods. Dried food had the advantages of being lightweight, compact, and easy to transport.

DRYING TODAY

Almost every American family enjoys the convenience of prepared dried foods—from the morning breakfast juice powder to dehydrated instant soup mixes, main dish and dessert mixes, and dried fruit snacks.

Apricots, raisins, figs, prunes, apples, and other fruits are sun dried, with artificial help when the weather doesn't cooperate, and transported all over the world. Dried fruits, fruit rolls, and fruit finger foods are available on supermarket shelves around the country.

Molded fruit snacks are tucked into school and work lunchboxes and are nutritious alternatives to the traditional candy bar. The dried fruit industry is booming. The only problem is that these commercially dried fruits and fruit snacks are very expensive.

The advent of commercial dehydrators for home use has spawned a popular new hobby for families across the nation. Drying at home is now a practical, convenient, sanitary, and economical way to preserve foods for your family.

With a little guidance from this book and an efficient home dehydrator, or a series of very hot sunny days, you can make your own dried fruits and fruit snacks at a fraction of the cost of the ones on supermarket shelves.

THE DRYING PROCESS

Drying foods is really very simple and easy to learn. Increasing the temperature of food makes its moisture evaporate. Air moving over the food carries the moisture away. As the temperature is increased, the air can hold more water, and foods gradually dry. Each 27°F (16°C) increase in temperature doubles the moisture-carrying capacity of the air. Warmer air can carry more water off the food. However, you don't want to get the temperature so hot that you *cook* the food; you merely want to dry it.

Both of the terms *drying* and *dehydration* refer to the removal of water and are used interchangeably. *Rehydration* and *reconstitution* are interchangeable and refer to returning water to dried foods.

Controlling temperature and air circulation prevents food from spoiling while it is drying. If the temperature is too low or the humidity is too high, the food will dry too slowly, allowing the growth of microorganisms. If the temperature is too high, the food will *case harden*, or form a hard shell that traps moisture inside, and the food will spoil.

Certain microorganisms are present in all foods. When they encounter warm temperatures and water, which is naturally present in foods, they multiply and the food spoils. If sufficient water is removed from the food, these microorganisms cannot multiply and the food is preserved. Drying

FRESH WEIGHT TO DRIED WEIGHT

Twenty-five pounds of fresh-picked fruit such as apples, apricots, peaches, or pears will yield four to eight pounds of dried fruit, depending on the fruit and the weight loss from peelings, pits, seeds, or cores.

Twenty-five pounds of fresh-picked vegetables such as beans, carrots, onions, or peppers will yield three to six pounds of dried vegetables, depending on the vegetable and the weight loss from peelings and discarded stems or leaves.

temperatures do not kill the microorganisms, so they begin to grow again if water is added and the food again becomes perishable.

PRETREATMENT

All fruits and vegetables contain *enzymes*—naturally occurring substances that cause them to ripen. Drying slows the effect of these enzymes, but some enzymes continue to work even after the food has been dried, particularly in vegetables. This can lead to poor rehydration and loss of flavor. The action of enzymes can be stopped in vegetables by heating them (blanching).

Some fruits tend to *oxidize*—to combine with oxygen from the air—during drying and storage. This may cause browning, loss of vitamins, and loss of flavor. Pretreating with sulfites, sulfur dioxide, ascorbic acid mixtures, or heat can minimize oxidation in fruits.

Pretreatment is a matter of personal choice, but generally improves the quality and shelf life of dehydrated foods.

STORAGE OF DRIED FRUITS AND VEGETABLES

Packaging
Vacuum packaging is ideal for dried foods. Home vacuum-packaging appliances are very

---

FOR THE BEST-QUALITY DRIED FOODS

- Use only the freshest high-quality foods for drying.
- Only dry foods that will have a good quality when dried.
- Keep the storage time before drying to a minimum.
- Slice foods evenly and dry all the slices of one thickness at one time.
- Dry foods as quickly as possible, keeping the temperature at 150°F (66°C) for the first couple of hours and then 140°F (60°C) for the remaining drying time. (Some food, such as herbs, nuts, and mushrooms, should be dried at lower temperatures.)
- Do not overlap foods on the drying trays.
- Do not overload the dryer.
- Use the weather to your advantage. When it's hot, put your dryer outside. When it's cool, keep your dryer indoors. When possible, dry on days that have low humidity.
- Do not add fresh foods to a dryer full of partially dried foods.
- Cool foods before testing for dryness.
- Package dried foods properly, preferably vacuum packaged.
- Label with the name of the food, variety, date dried, pretreatment, and other helpful information.
- Store in a cool, dark, dry place, refrigerate, or freeze.
- Store in amounts that can be used at one time.
- Use dried fruits in less than one year, vegetables in less than six months.

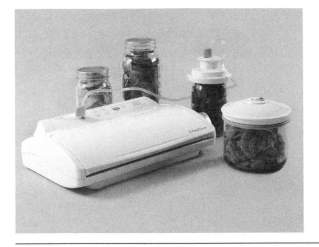

The FoodSaver Home Vacuum Packaging System has been the leader in home vacuum packaging for over fifteen years. The different models vary in convenience, design, and price, although all produce a good quality vacuum.

The most widely available model, the V2440 Advanced Design, is easy to use. It has a latch that keeps the lid closed, two speeds for ultimate vacuum control, and a built-in bag roll holder and cutter for making custom sized bags. It also has an accessory port, which is especially useful when you package dried foods in quart or half-gallon canning jars.

affordable and extend the shelf life of dried foods three to four times over containers that allow air.

The better the vacuum seal is, the better the quality and longer the storage time. Beware of heat-sealing devices that say that they vacuum package foods. A high-quality vacuum packaging appliance will pull a commercial-quality vacuum (fifteen to twenty inches mercury).

All kinds of dried foods benefit from vacuum packaging. Dried fruits and fruit leathers remain flavorful and pliable when vacuum packed. Dried vegetables, herbs, nuts, and trail mixes have a much longer shelf life when vacuum packaged. Vacuum packaging combined with low-temperature storage makes dried foods last longer.

Dehydrated fruits and vegetables are generally best stored in glass canning jars rather than vacuum packaged in bags, because dried vegetables tend to puncture bags and dried fruits and fruit leathers tend to clump together when vacuum packaged in a bag. Use Ball brand lids rather than Kerr brand lids for vacuum sealing in canning jars. They have a softer rubber and will keep the vacuum seal longer without heating the lid first.

All packaging materials should be airtight, moisture proof, and made of material that will keep out insects. Freezer bags should have as much air removed as possible, but plastic bags are not insect and rodent proof. If you are using metal containers, package in a plastic freezer bag prior to storing in the metal container. Always allow dried foods to cool to room temperature before packaging, to avoid condensation.

Packaging Materials

- Vacuum-packaging system such as the Food-Saver Advanced Design
  - Canning jars with Ball lids
  - Kitchen scissors
  - Heavy-duty freezer bags or freezer containers

METHODS OF DRYING

The method you use depends largely upon the quality you want in the food you're drying, and the time, effort, and money you're willing to invest. Each method of drying has advantages and disadvantages, and each gives different results. Foods dry best in a quality commercial dehydrator, although they can be dried in the sun or oven.

Totally natural methods, such as sun or room drying, can work in certain parts of the country where the weather is very hot, or under certain household conditions. The following discussion of each method should help you choose the best method for your purposes.

DRYING IN A DEHYDRATOR

A good-quality dehydrator is worth the investment. A food dehydrator will yield a better quality, more nutritious dried product than any other method of drying. Foods can be dried twenty-four hours a day and you don't have to worry about bad weather. Minimal time is needed for turning or rotating the food. Operating costs are reasonable.

Features to Look for in a Dehydrator
A variety of different features are available, but a good dehydrator must have a good heat source, an adjustable thermostat, and good, even air circulation.

Heat Source
- The heating element should be large enough for the drying area and is more cost-efficient if cycled by a thermostat.
- Different types of heating elements are used, ranging from 200 watts to 1,000 watts.

Adjustable Thermostat
- An adjustable thermostat allows varied temperatures for different products. It should be adjustable from 90°F to 160°F (32°C to 71°C) for the greatest versatility in use. You'll want the lower temperatures for nuts and herbs, and the higher temperatures to speed the drying process in the beginning of a batch of fruits and vegetables, or for meats or fish.
- It should be easy to adjust and read.

Fan or Squirrel Cage Blower
- A fan or blower removes moisture as it evaporates from the food, resulting in shorter drying time and thus a higher quality product.
- Circular fans and squirrel cage blowers are both popular. The circular fan is very efficient in a round dehydrator, and some box dryers use squirrel cage blowers.

Safety Features
- The UL label is your guarantee that the dryer has been tested for safety.
- Another excellent safety feature is a high-limit switch, which automatically shuts off the dehydrator should there be an electrical malfunction.

Sanitation
- A dehydrator should be easy to clean, preferably with dishwasher-safe trays.
- Walls should be nonflammable and easy to clean.

The Nesco/American Harvest Snackmaster Express features a top-mounted fan and 500 watts of drying power. The adjustable thermostat ranges from 95°F to 155°F (35°C to 68°C). It comes with four trays and is expandable to twelve trays.

All of the Nesco/American Harvest dehydrators have useful accessories. Fruit roll sheets allow you to dry fruit and vegetable roll-ups. Clean-A-Screen mesh screens keep small pieces of fruits and vegetables from falling through the trays. They also make cleaning and removal easy when you're drying sticky fruits.

Capacity and Design

- There are two main designs in dehydrators: round and rectangular.

- The round stackable dryers have the heat, fan, and thermostat either in the top or the bottom. The primary advantage of the round models is even drying and that they can be expanded by adding additional racks.

- The rectangular dryers have an external chamber that holds the heating element and fan. The air is then vented from the chamber through holes on each tray.

- The size of dryer you purchase depends on how much food you want to dry. Round stackable dryers can be expanded or contracted to the volume of foods you're drying, so they tend to be more energy efficient. Box dryers are limited to the size of the box and how many trays it contains. Because produce has to be sliced and dried in a single layer, the size and expandability of the dryer become quite significant. Two apples, sliced in ¼-inch slices, would take an entire tray.

- The newest round Nesco/American Harvest dehydrator has the heating element and fan in the *top*

of the dryer. It has an added advantage over the models with the elements in the bottom—drippings don't get trapped in the openings at the base.

- The walls of your dryer should be insulated to reduce heat loss. Double wall construction keeps heat loss to a minimum. Vents on each tray allow for even drying across each tray.

Trays and Tray Rotation

- The best trays are made of food-grade plastic. Some dryers require occasional rotation of the trays to ensure even drying. The vertically stacked Nesco/American Harvest has air vents on each tray, which provides for very even drying.

BEWARE!

Beware of commercial dehydrators that only have a heating element in the bottom and no fan or thermostat. They operate completely on convection, are very inefficient, and foods tend to mold. Fruit leather is impossible to make in this type of dryer without spoilage. This type of dehydrator is totally unsafe for meats or fish because the temperature is not high enough to dry safely.

- Box dryers tend to dry faster on the side with the heating element, requiring occasional rotation.

Tray Accessories

- Solid plastic or Teflon sheets allow you to make fruit and vegetable leathers.
- Plastic mesh screens keep foods from sticking and also keep small foods from falling through the trays. Nesco/American Harvest dehydrators have excellent solid sheets and plastic mesh screens.

Timer

- A timer can be a convenient accessory in a dehydrator.
- If it isn't an accessory on the dryer you have, purchase a timer and plug it into your dehydrator. When you estimate another four or five hours till a product is dry, it's nice to be able to go to sleep, knowing that a timer will automatically shut off the dryer.

Warranty

- What is the length of the warranty and what does it cover?
- Are replacement parts available and where would it be serviced should there be a problem?

DRYING IN THE OVEN

Oven drying is a good choice if you are a novice and just want to experiment and dry a little at one time before investing in a dehydrator.

One of the disadvantages of drying in an oven is the energy cost. Oven drying takes two or three times longer than drying in a dehydrator and more time is required to tend and rotate the food.

Food dried in an oven without convection is usually darker, more brittle, and less flavorful than food dried in a dehydrator, simply because it is very difficult to control oven temperature and the air circulation tends to be poor.

What Can You Oven Dry?

Most unsulfured fruits, fruit leathers, vegetables, meats, and fish can be oven dried. Sulfured fruits should not be oven dried because sulfur dioxide fumes may be irritating.

Do not attempt to oven dry foods with very high water content—more than 90 percent—such as rhubarb or tomatoes, or fruits with skins, such as prunes and cherries. Their skins prevent even evaporation.

Equipment
A Gas or Electric Oven, with or without Convection

- Test your oven with a thermometer for at least an hour before using it to dry food. It should maintain a temperature of 140°F to 150°F (60°C to 66°C). If it cannot be adjusted to this temperature, it is unsuitable for drying foods. Meats can be dried as high as 160°F (71°C) to 175°F (80°C).
- Convection ovens are best, because they are built with a fan to move the air, and have an outlet to remove moisture. Some electric ovens have an exhaust system, which circulates air through a venting system. This reduces heat loss and increases drying efficiency. If you have a convection oven or one with an exhaust system, you can leave the door closed.
- If you are using a conventional oven, prop the door open two to four inches to let moisture escape. In electric ovens, check to see that only the bottom element goes on.

Thermometer

- Check the oven temperature with a thermometer.
- Place the thermometer on the top tray toward the back of the oven for a representative temperature. Also check the temperature on the bottom tray.

Racks

- Oven racks are more practical than specially built drying trays. Sometimes you can find extra oven racks in stores selling used appliances.
- Cover them with four thicknesses of tightly stretched nylon netting. Sew the netting together like a pillowcase to fit over the racks. You can also use two layers of cheesecloth tightly stretched and pinned to the oven racks, but cheesecloth tends to sag more than nylon netting.
- Allow ¾-inch clearance between all edges of the trays and inside of the oven if using other types of racks.

Baking Sheets

- These give poor results because they do not allow air circulation. Those with nonstick surfaces are excellent for fruit leather.
- Uncoated metal or aluminum baking sheets may give the fruit leather a metallic flavor.

DRYING IN A MICROWAVE OVEN

Microwave ovens will dry small quantities of herbs, but only models that also use convection are suitable for drying other foods. Check with the manufacturer for dehydration instructions.

HOME-BUILT DRYERS

Dryers that you make yourself out of wood have numerous disadvantages over commercial dehydrators. All wood dryers are a potential fire hazard because of the nature of the appliance—heat and wood. No matter how well the dehydrator is constructed, there is always some danger. Wood can also be a source of harmful microorganisms, because it is difficult to clean.

Inefficient designs frequently require constant tending to keep food drying evenly and are costly to operate. Don't operate a wood dryer inside your home where it can cause a fire. Commercial models are less expensive over time because energy costs are less.

DRYING IN THE SUN

The majority of commercially dried fruits are sun dried. If you live in an area that has many consecutive days with temperatures in the nineties, relatively low humidity, and low air-pollution levels, sun drying may be a good choice for you.

Sun drying has several advantages. The cost is low, the only investment is in drying trays and protective netting, and large quantities of food can be dried at one time. The sun's ultraviolet rays have a sterilizing effect, which slows the growth of some microorganisms. Sun-dried fruit, particularly sulfured fruit, has an attractive sun-ripened color.

There are several disadvantages to sun drying. Sun drying requires considerable time and effort. Food that would be dried in six to eight hours in a dryer may take up to four or five days in the sun. You are entirely at the mercy of the weather. If it suddenly begins to rain, your hours of labor and the cost of the fruit may be lost if you can't get it indoors before it gets wet. More nutrients are lost from the lengthy exposure to the sun and air. Foods dried in the sun are dried under less sanitary conditions than those dried in a food dryer or oven.

What Can You Sun Dry?

Not all foods can be sun dried. They must have a fairly high sugar and acid content to prevent spoilage during the drying process because drying in the sun takes so long. Low-acid foods, such as vegetables, spoil rather quickly.

Most fruits can be dried in the sun because they are high in acid and sugar. Fruits chosen for drying should be high quality, ripe, and desirable for eating.

Fruit leather can be sun dried successfully in one or two days if the sun is hot and the humidity low. Protect fruit leather from insects or you'll wind up with bugs stuck to your fruit leather!

To successfully dry vegetables, you must have weekly temperatures above 100°F and very low humidity. Except for the desert Southwest, there are very few places with this kind of weather. Vegetables must be dried to a 5 percent or lower moisture to store well.

Red chili peppers may be sun dried when fully mature. If you visit Arizona or New Mexico, you'll see chili peppers hung from the sides of adobe houses.

Wash the chilies and string them on a strong thread through the stem ends, alternating the chilies so they hang in opposite directions. Hang them in a hot, sunny place to dry and protect them from dust and insects with a muslin or cheesecloth tent.

Sun drying is not recommended for herbs and spices because of the loss in aroma, flavoring oils, and color.

I don't recommend sun drying meats and fish.

When pioneers sun dried meat or fish, they used extremely high concentrations of salt as a preservative. We would find this high salt concentration unpalatable. The low acidity of meats and fish combined with low temperatures and long drying time presents a high risk of bacterial contamination, spoilage, and food poisoning.

Fruits Recommended for Sun Drying

Apples	Grapes
Apricots	Nectarines
Cherries	Peaches
Citrus peels	Pears
Coconut, shredded	Pineapple
Currants	Plums
Dates	Prune plums
Figs	

Fruits Not Recommended for Sun Drying

Avocados	Papaya
Bananas	Persimmons
Berries	Rhubarb
Cranberries	Strawberries
Melons	

Vegetables Recommended for Sun Drying

Chili peppers	Shell beans
Lentils	Soybeans
Peas	

Equipment

Drying Trays

- You can use commercial dehydrator trays, or build trays at home. Sometimes you can buy a broken dehydrator on eBay or at a garage sale and just keep the trays!

- If you build drying trays, use wood slats for stability and then cover with polypropylene food-safe plastic screening or stainless-steel screening. The mesh should be small enough so that finely diced produce will not fall through. Cleaning may be difficult on homemade trays because wood is not waterproof.

- Avoid screens made from *hardware cloth*. Hardware cloth is galvanized metal cloth that is coated with cadmium or zinc. These metals can oxidize, leaving harmful residues on the food. Also avoid copper and aluminum screening. Copper destroys vitamin C and increases oxidation. Aluminum tends to discolor and corrode.

Netting

- Use muslin, cheesecloth, or fine nylon netting to cover filled drying trays and protect the food from dust and insects.
- Wash netting after each use.

Procedure

The area used for sun drying should be conveniently located because you must turn the fruit two or three times a day. The location you choose should be free from dust and exhaust fumes and there should be adequate protection against insects, rodents, birds, and other animals. Cover the food with muslin, nylon netting, or cheesecloth. Sulfuring fruit also helps deter insects.

You will need direct sun for the first couple of days. You can move partially dried foods to the shade for the rest of the drying time. Good air circulation is nearly as important as sun.

OTHER EQUIPMENT AND UTENSILS

The proper drying equipment and utensils make the whole process of dehydration easier. These items are especially helpful:

- Apple peeler/corer/slicer
- Colander
- Cherry pitter
- Dehydrator
- Food processor or blender for pureeing fruits and vegetables
- Pear corer
- Knives (make sure they're sharp)
- Fruit roll trays (plastic or Teflon)
- Plastic mesh screens that keep foods from sticking and keep small pieces from falling through drying trays
- Sturdy vegetable scrub brush for cleaning vegetables and your dryer trays
- Thermometer
- Vacuum packaging machine

The top of the line, the **FoodSaver Pro III,** is the easiest of all models to use. It has a five-level heat-sealing adjustment, is completely automated, and has the added feature of being able to extend the vacuum time. This is especially useful when you package dried foods in half-gallon canning jars. The variable heat-sealing adjustment feature keeps the heat sealer from overheating when you are packaging lots of bags at a time. A bag storage compartment conveniently stores a roll of bags. The cutter makes it easy to custom make a bag to the right size.

DRYING IN A SOLAR OR HYBRIDIZED SOLAR DRYER

Using a solar dryer is a slightly better method than sun drying. A solar dryer collects the sun's rays and elevates the temperature 20°F to 30°F higher than the unaided sun. Higher temperature usually shortens the drying time.

Solar drying is best in areas with low humidity but still can be used in more humid regions, although length of drying time increases.

A solar dryer generally uses a portion of the dryer as a solar collector. Warm air is trapped in the solar collector and moves up by convection to the drying chamber where it elevates the temperature in the drying chamber above the ambient air temperature.

Solar dryers have a number of disadvantages. As with sun drying, you are at the mercy of the weather. There may be no effective way to control temperature, which usually means lower quality dried food. You must invest time and money in construction and the results are not guaranteed. Food must be turned and rotated to promote even and thorough drying.

A *hybrid solar dryer* combines an external heat source (electrical or gas generated) and fan with the natural warmth of the sun. In a hybrid solar dryer, a fan keeps the air constantly moving twenty-four hours a day. The fan greatly increases efficiency and shortens drying time.

The heating element is used at night when there is no heat from the sun. Ideally the dryer should have a thermostat, or at least a thermometer to monitor internal temperature in the chamber.

Depending on the dryer and its design, sanitation may be considerably better than with sun drying. The air outlets and intakes should be screened to prevent insects from sampling the drying food.

Hybridized solar dryers are useful in developing countries where energy resources are prohibitively expensive.

DRYING IN A WARM ROOM

Room drying is a natural method that was employed by the pioneers with a reasonable amount of success. The kitchen with a wood stove provided a fairly constant source of heat. The relatively low temperatures of modern thermostatically controlled cooling and heating systems usually make room drying difficult.

What Can You Dry in a Warm Room?

Confine room drying to herbs and nuts in the shell. Strings of red chilies, which have been partially sun dried or dehydrator dried, can be finished in a warm room. Make sure that the drying location has enough air circulation to prevent molding before the food is dried completely.

Equipment

Drying Trays

- See Drying in the Sun (page 13).

Fan

- Keep air moving over the drying food by placing a fan nearby.

How to Room Dry

You will need a room with a temperature of 80°F (27°C) or above, preferably exposed to the sun for part of the day, and relatively low humidity.

A sunny kitchen window, dust-free attic, or basement is a good place to dry. A furnace room can be used if there is no dust or soot from the furnace. Sometimes it is possible to dry in a car rear window or camper on a warm, sunny day if the windows are opened slightly so the moisture can escape. Even the space above a gas clothes dryer or water heater can be used if the pilot light remains on and the ventilation is good.

Place the foods to be dried on drying trays. You may stack the trays, allowing five to six inches of space between each tray to allow good air circulation. A fan can be placed next to the trays to increase air circulation.

Herbs may be hung root-end up inside a brown

DEHYDROFREEZING AND FREEZE-DRYING

There are two techniques for preserving food that combine drying and freezing. Dehydrofreezing can be done at home, while freeze-drying is a commercial process.

Dehydrofreezing removes some moisture, then products are frozen for long-term storage.

This is an increasingly popular method for preserving apricots and prunes, because they can remain as moist as commercially dried fruits without adding commercial preservatives.

To dehydrofreeze, dry the fruit or vegetable to about 30 percent moisture content (quite soft). Package the food in airtight containers and store in the freezer until ready to eat.

Freeze-drying is a commercial process combining freezing and drying, which causes a phenomenon known as *sublimation* to take place. Food is flash frozen, then placed in a vacuum chamber at low air pressure. Ice crystals go directly to a vapor, bypassing the liquid state. The vapor is removed and the dried product is packaged and stored without refrigeration. Freeze-drying equipment is very expensive and freeze-dried products must be packaged carefully because they crush easily and must be protected from light and moisture.

Freeze-dried foods reconstitute quickly and have a better taste, appearance, texture, and nutritive value than food dried by evaporation. Cell structure is maintained and foods after drying have the same volume as before.

paper bag with holes for ventilation as discussed in Herbs and Spices (page 97).

DRYING ON TOP OF THE STOVE OR RADIANT HEATER

During America's pioneer days, stovetop dryers were extremely popular and were in use continuously on top of wood-burning stoves during the harvest season.

A home-constructed stovetop dryer may be adapted to a gas or electric stove and give the same advantage as a solar dryer. It could also be placed above a radiant heater against a wall. A stovetop dryer is very limited in the quantity of food that can be conveniently dehydrated and would require an almost constant source of heat until the food is dried.

Take care if using a wood frame to prevent any open flame coming into contact with the wood.

CAUTION: MILK PRODUCTS

Milk and eggs are not recommended for home drying because of the high risk of food poisoning. Commercially dried milk and egg products are processed rapidly at temperatures high enough to prevent bacterial contamination. Home dryers cannot duplicate this process and the safety of home-dried milk and eggs cannot be guaranteed. However, cheese and yogurt, because they are on the opposite end of the pH scale (high in acid) from milk and eggs, can be dried in a dehydrator at 160°F (70°C).

FRUITS

Fruits are generally grouped according to the climate in which they grow. *Tropical fruits*, such as bananas, pineapples, papayas, and mangos, must have warm, humid climates to flourish. *Subtropical fruits* need a constant warm climate with moderate moisture. These include citrus fruits, figs, dates, and olives. *Temperate-zone fruits* include apples, apricots, berries, cherries, peaches, pears, and plums. With a few exceptions, fruits from all three groups may be dried. Most fruits that are dried in the United States are from the temperate-zone group. Imported tropical fruits are also readily available and, depending on the season, quite reasonably priced.

Fruits contain B complex vitamins, vitamin C, carbohydrates, and minerals such as iron, phosphorus, and calcium. Some vitamin C may be lost through the drying process, but other nutrients are relatively unaffected. The amount of vitamins retained by dried fruits depends largely on how they are processed, dried, and stored. In general, the longer the drying time (with temperatures less than 130°F [54°C]), the more nutrient loss in the food.

With an efficient dehydrator with a regulated temperature, there is little nutrient loss during drying. Dried fruits are nutritious snacks for lunch boxes or when you're on the go. All nutrients in fruits are concentrated by drying, leaving a higher density of nutrients by weight, including calories. Dried fruits are also a great source of fiber, which helps in digestion.

LETTING THE WATER OUT

Most fruits are covered with a skin, which keeps the fruit fresh and holds in the seed, juicy flesh, and incidentally, the flavor. For fruits to dry quickly enough to prevent spoilage or fermentation, that skin has to be perforated in some way to allow moisture to escape. There are various ways to do this, depending on the type of fruit and the drying method being used.

Cut some fruits in half. Fruits such as apricots and small peaches or pears may be cut in half. When the pits are removed, the fruit halves are dried skin-side down and the moisture gradually evaporates. The bottom portion of the skin prevents the juices from dripping out and helps keep in the flavor during drying.

Slice others so they are a uniform thickness. To speed drying of larger fruits, they should be peeled and cut into slices ¼- to ½-inch thick. The entire surface area of the fruit will dry in less time than fruits left whole or halved. Uniform slices will dry in the same amount of time.

With some fruits, such as pears or peaches, slicing them *lengthwise* will give you fewer, larger pieces than slicing crosswise, and they are all the same thickness, which promotes even drying. A very sharp, high-quality stainless-steel knife should be used to minimize the browning on the cut surfaces.

Some fruits can be checked. Small fruits such as plums, cherries, or grapes have a *waxy bloom* or thin, natural waxlike coating that keeps moisture in. This waxlike coating may be cracked or *checked* before drying so the moisture can escape. This will decrease the drying time. Checking is perforating the waxy bloom by chemical, heat, or mechanical means.

Commercially, fruits, such as plums, are checked by dipping the whole fruit in a lye solution. *This is not recommended for home drying because of the danger of handling lye and the possible retention of lye in the fruit.*

You can speed the drying process in whole and small fruits by dipping them in boiling water just long enough to crack the skins. This will hasten evaporation and shorten the time it takes them to dry. Fruits that have been dipped in boiling water are slightly less flavorful than those that are dried without dipping.

Pit fruits with stones. Any fruits with a pit or stone, such as cherries, should be pitted before drying. This shortens the drying time and produces a better tasting dried fruit. The pits tend to leave a flavor in the fruit if they are left in.

Larger fruits, such as plums, can be halved to remove the pits. You can also shorten the drying time of prunes or apricots by *flattening* them. Use your thumbs to press the rounded side in. This process, called *popping the backs*, exposes more drying surface to the air.

HOW DRY SHOULD THEY BE?

The final moisture content of home-dried fruits should be 15 to 20 percent. Because dried fruits are usually eaten without rehydration, some moisture is necessary for a chewy texture. Fruits that are overdried to a moisture level of 5 to 10 percent lose color, flavor, and nutrients and have a less palatable texture.

The dryness test for home-dried fruits is simply touching and tasting. The fruit should be chewy and leatherlike with no moisture pockets.

In order to keep several months without molding, home-dried fruits must be drier than those you buy in the grocery store. Commercially dried fruits are treated with chemical agents that inhibit the growth of mold and other microorganisms and slow browning during storage. With these additives, commercially dried fruits may contain as much as 30 to 35 percent moisture without spoiling, although they will still brown slightly during storage. If you want your home-dried fruits to be as moist as those from the store, keep them in the freezer until you are ready to eat them. See Dehydrofreezing (page 17).

APPEARANCE AND FLAVOR

Some fruits lend themselves to the drying process better than others. The flavor and texture of some fruits change when the fruit is dehydrated. The end result may be quite different from the fresh flavor. Personal preference will be your guide. With fruits such as oranges, cantaloupes, and watermelons, be prepared for a totally new flavor and texture, quite different from the fresh fruit, generally sweeter and chewier.

Variety. Some varieties of the same fruit have a stronger flavor and a higher sugar content or firmer texture. All these qualities produce a better product when dried. Although some varieties are listed in the instructions on how to dry specific fruits, you'll need to compare the varieties available in your area to select those best suited for drying.

Method of drying. The methods used for drying may alter the appearance and flavor of some fruits. The drying method you choose will depend on the climatic conditions where you live and the fruits you choose to dry. Fruits dried in a dehydrator differ in appearance from those dried in the sun. The sun's ultraviolet rays and the increased drying time affect the color and wrinkling in some fruits. Dark fruits, such as prunes or raisins, get much darker and more wrinkled when sun dried.

Pretreatment. The color in sulfured cut fruit tends to be much more pronounced when sun dried. Sulfured apricots dried in a dehydrator are a nice bright orange. However, when sulfured apri-cots are exposed to bright sunlight for even four to six hours during drying, that bright orange color changes to a very deep orange. Fruits to be dried in the sun need a considerably higher sulfur dioxide content, because they will lose a large amount of the sulfur dioxide in the lengthy sun-drying process.

Maturity. The maturity of a fruit when it is harvested and processed has a great deal to do with its quality when dried. If underripe fruit is dried, it will be less sweet, less flavorful, and lighter in color. Overripe fruit will have a slightly fermented flavor, mushy texture, and may darken excessively. Some fruits, such as pears, plums, or bananas, may be picked when still green and ripened under controlled conditions at home. Other fruits must be picked when they are at their peak ripeness because they will not continue to ripen satisfactorily during storage. Peaches and apricots, if picked green, will never develop the same full, sweet flavor as peaches or apricots allowed to ripen on the tree.

Many farmers and food processors forego the added sweetness and flavor and pick the perishable fruit slightly underripe so it won't be damaged during transportation, handling, or processing. You will find that maturity and natural sugar content are much more important in drying than in canning, because sugar is not added to dried fruits.

HOW TO DRY FRUITS

Sort and select the highest quality ripe, ready-to-eat fresh fruit. Fully ripe fruit should be firm and heavy for its size. If it's perfect for eating, it's perfect for drying. Handle fruits gently and process them quickly because when they are at the right stage for drying, they are also the most fragile.

WASH THEM GENTLY

Gently wash all fruits in cold water to remove dirt, bacteria, and insect larvae. Cold water will keep your foods fresher. Wash all of your foods just before processing. Don't let fruit stand in the water for long periods of time, because some of the nutrients will be dissolved and lost. Fruits with skins such as cherries or plums must be washed particularly well. Insect larvae cannot be seen on fresh fruit, but may hatch after the fruit has been dried and stored unless they are washed off before drying or killed by *pasteurizing* (heating or freezing after drying).

PREPARE FRUITS TO DRY

To prepare fruit for pretreatment and drying, remove stems and peels. Core or pit fruit and cut it into slices, halves, or quarters. Peels may be left on some fruit, but they tend to be tough and occasionally bitter. Trim away any bruised or soft spots. One soft spot can spoil an entire batch.

Prepare only as much fruit as you can pretreat and dry at one time.

KEEP CUT FRUITS IN A HOLDING SOLUTION

Place cut fruits that tend to brown in a weak ascorbic acid solution as soon as you cut them. This will reduce browning during preparation. Do not keep cut fruit in the holding solution for more than fifteen minutes. Longer holding causes the cut fruits to absorb water and increases the time needed to dry.

You can also use a sodium bisulfite holding solution consisting of ¼ teaspoon sodium bisulfite per quart of water until ready to pretreat.

Salted water is not a good idea. Do not hold cut fresh fruit in salted water or pretreat with salted water. This gives an undesirable flavor and a gray color to the fruit.

PRETREAT FRUITS THAT TURN BROWN

Oxidation and the continuous reaction of enzymes cause some fruits, such as apples, pears, peaches, and apricots, to turn brown when cut and exposed to the air. Unless these fruits are pretreated to slow oxidation and enzyme reaction, browning will continue during processing and storage. It isn't only the color, but you'll lose more vitamins A and C as well as the flavor.

Although pretreatment is generally recommended for apples, pears, peaches, nectarines, and apricots, it is certainly an individual preference. If you choose not to pretreat, store these dried fruits in the refrigerator or freezer to reduce deterioration.

Sulfiting, sulfuring, ascorbic acid solution, syrup blanching, and steaming are all methods of pretreatment to keep fruits from oxidizing. Sulfiting is the easiest, although it does not work very well on apricots. Apples, pears, peaches, and nectarines dry very favorably when pretreated with sodium bisulfite. Sulfuring or syrup blanching is preferable for apricots.

All other fruits require no pretreatment prior to drying.

Sulfiting

Sulfiting is soaking fruit in a solution of water and *sodium bisulfite, sodium sulfite,* or *sodium meta-*

FRUITS AT A GLANCE

FRUIT	QUALITY WHEN DRIED	SUITABILITY FOR LEATHER
Apples	Excellent	Excellent
Apricots	Excellent	Excellent
Avocados	Not recommended	Not recommended
Bananas	Good	Fair to good
Berries (seeds)	Not recommended	Excellent (seeds removed)
Blueberries	Fair	Only in combination
Cherries	Excellent	Excellent
Citrus fruits	Fair to good	Only in combination
Citrus peel	Excellent	Only in combination
Coconuts	Excellent	Only in combination
Crab apples	Not recommended	Only in combination
Cranberries	Fair	Only in combination
Currants	Good	Not recommended
Dates	Excellent	Only in combination
Figs	Excellent	Only in combination
Grapes	Excellent	Fair to good
Guavas	Not recommended	Only in combination
Kiwi fruit	Excellent	Excellent
Melons	Fair to good	Not recommended
Nectarines	Excellent	Excellent
Olives	Not recommended	Not recommended
Papayas	Good	Better in combination
Peaches	Excellent	Excellent
Pears (all)	Excellent	Excellent
Persimmons	Excellent	Excellent
Pineapples	Excellent	Excellent
Plums	Good	Good
Pomegranates	Not recommended	Not recommended
Prune plums	Excellent	Excellent
Quince	Not recommended	Not recommended
Rhubarb	Good	Fair
Strawberries	Excellent	Excellent

bisulfite. This releases sulfur dioxide and has the same general effect as sulfuring, but is not effective on apricots. When mixed with water and used as a soaking solution, sulfite penetrates the surface of the cut fruits, retarding browning and loss of vitamins.

It is fine for apples, pears, peaches, and nectarines. Sulfiting may be done in your kitchen. Drying time is a little longer than with sulfuring because of the water absorbed during the soaking period.

Use food-grade sodium bisulfite, sodium sulfite, or sodium meta-bisulfite. They are available from winemaking supply stores. You'll find sodium bisulfite more easily than the other two sulfiting products.

How to Sulfite

If you are using a holding solution before sulfiting, slice the fruit into a colander submerged in the holding solution. When the colander is full, transfer it to the sulfite solution. Set your timer. Soaking time varies with the type of fruit and its thickness. Sulfite should penetrate one to two millimeters deep to be effective during drying and storage.

The same variables apply to sulfite soaking as to sulfuring. Soak sliced fruit five minutes and halved fruit fifteen minutes.

Amount of Sulfite to Add Per Gallon of Water

Sodium bisulfite	1 to 2 tablespoons
Sodium sulfite	2 to 3 tablespoons
Sodium meta-bisulfite	3 to 4 tablespoons

After soaking in a sulfite solution, you may want to lightly rinse the fruit under cold running water. Rinsing improves the flavor of the dried fruit, but slightly lowers the sulfite content. Rinsing is optional. Try it both ways and decide which you like best.

Place the rinsed fruit on drying trays. Sulfited fruit generally takes 15 to 20 percent longer to dry than sulfured fruit, because of the water absorbed during soaking.

Sulfuring

Sulfuring exposes the fruit to sulfur dioxide (SO_2) fumes by burning flowers of sulfur in a closed container with the fruit. The fumes penetrate the sur-

---

WHEN YOU SULFITE, REMEMBER

- Keep dry granules in an airtight container. Sodium bisulfite has an indefinite shelf life as long as it is kept dry.
- Keep pretreatment solutions out of reach of children and pets.
- Discard pretreatment solution after use. The solution can only be used once. Make a new one for the next batch.
- Dry sulfited fruits in a well-ventilated area.
- If any adverse physical reaction is noticed, discontinue use of the pretreatment.

CAUTION

During drying, most of the sodium bisulfite dissipates into the air, leaving only a trace on the fruit. The U.S. Food and Drug Administration currently considers the trace concentrations found on properly pretreated and dehydrated fruit to be safe.

A few individuals, particularly those with asthmatic conditions, may have an unusually high degree of sensitivity to sulfiting. They may even be sensitive to airborne sulfite particles from the drying process.

If you have a respiratory or asthmatic condition, or are prone to allergies, do not use sulfiting as a pretreatment for your dried fruits.

If you use a sulfite pretreatment, be sure to label the fruit *pretreated with sulfites*.

face area of the fruit about one to two millimeters deep. Sulfuring must be done outdoors in the open because the fumes are harmful to people and animals when inhaled.

Sulfur dioxide treatments are the most effective for retarding oxidation and keeping dried fruits in prime condition and most flavorful. Sulfur dioxide is a combination of sulfur and oxygen. Sulfur is a solid nonmetallic element found in eggs and many strong-smelling vegetables, such as cabbage, horseradish, and onions. The small quantity of sulfur dioxide remaining in dried fruits is not harmful when consumed.

Although it is quite time consuming to construct the apparatus for sulfuring, once you have it, you can use it year after year.

Natural food advocates maintain that sulfured fruit is harmful and that sulfuring is done mainly for cosmetic reasons. There is currently no evidence to substantiate this claim. Research shows that sulfuring retards spoilage and darkening of fruits, lessens the contamination by insects during sun drying, and reduces the loss of vitamins A and C.

To Sulfur Fruits, You Will Need

Large box with two vents (wooden or cardboard)
Framed trays
Rack to hold the trays
Flat metal pan (pie tin)
Sublimed sulfur (flowers of sulfur)
Wooden matches

Equipment for Sulfuring
Large Box

- A box is needed to cover the fruit, trapping the sulfur dioxide fumes within the box. It should be made out of wood, but if you're a novice and don't want to invest the time or money in a wooden box, a heavy cardboard box will work just fine. A television or large appliance box is great because it is extra heavy.

- Seal any cracks with heavy packing tape and make two vents in the box. One vent should be in the bottom near where the sulfur will be placed, and the other vent at the upper edge of the opposite side on the top. If your box is cardboard, simply cut the vent, leaving one side intact so that it can be easily closed and taped.

- If the box is constructed of wood, the vents may be hinged or held in place by two pieces of wood on either side of the vent, so that the door of the vent can slide up and down.

- If you want to be extra fancy, insert a glass window in the top of the box to allow you to see the fruit. The more airtight the box is, the less sulfur is required, and the more effective the sulfuring treatment will be.

- Allow sufficient space in front of the trays to place the pan of burning sulfur on the ground. It should be at least six inches in front of the trays.

Framed Trays

- Framed trays are needed to hold the fruit during sulfuring. Screens allow the SO_2 to penetrate all sides of the fruit evenly. The screening should be Teflon-coated fiberglass, stainless steel, or plastic. Do not use aluminum or galvanized metal screening material because the SO_2 will corrode it.

- Plastic or fiberglass screens should be placed far enough away from the burning sulfur to keep them from melting. You will put the burning sulfur in front of, not under, the screens.

- Metal frames may be used and wiped thoroughly after sulfuring, although they will corrode with continued use. Plastic screens will also discolor. Stainless steel oven racks would work fine.

- Wooden slatted trays are much more likely to harbor bacteria, are difficult to clean, and do not allow the SO_2 to penetrate as evenly as plastic or stainless steel.

Rack to Hold the Trays

- It is easiest to have a wooden rack that fits comfortably inside of the sulfuring box to hold the trays.
- Wooden blocks or bricks in the tray corners can be used to elevate each tray, but care must be taken that they don't overturn because they can be quite unstable.
- Allow at least ten inches clearance from the ground to the bottom rack, and 1½ to 2½ inches between each tray.

Metal Pie Tin or Pan

- Use a flat metal pan to hold the sulfur.
- You will throw it away after use because the burning sulfur ruins it.

Sublimed Sulfur (Flowers of Sulfur)

- Use only sublimed sulfur, USP standard, for burning in your sulfur box. It is free of impurities, burns readily, and may be purchased at most pharmacies. You can also buy it in large quantities at a reasonable price from chemical supply companies.
- Garden-dusting sulfur has more impurities and is not recommended.
- It can be stored indefinitely in an airtight container.

How to Sulfur

- Prepare fruit by washing, cutting, and pitting.
- Spread fruit in a single layer on trays with the pit cavity or cut surface up.
- Do not overlap fruit.

- Select a good location outside for sulfuring. It should be away from people or pets and open windows. Place the box so that air can flow freely through the lower vent. The bottom tray should be at least ten inches above the ground.
- Place the sulfur in a clean, shallow metal pie tin. Use 1½ teaspoons of sulfur per pound of fresh-prepared fruit. Place the container of sulfur *in front of the trays*, not underneath them.
- Cover the trays with the box, leaving the vents open. If you are using a cardboard box, seal the bottom edges of the box with a towel.
- Light the sulfur. Use wooden matches. Light it in several places. It smolders, and doesn't ignite or flame. Do not leave burned matchsticks in the container because they will retard the burning.
- Take care not to inhale the sulfur dioxide fumes. They are harmful to your lungs.
- The fumes do the work, not the actual burning process. When about two-thirds of the sulfur is consumed, about ten minutes, close the vents and leave the fruit in the box for one to three hours or the recommended time. See the section on specific fruits for suggested times for sulfuring. Close the vents with heavy sealing tape.
- Sulfuring times vary with the type of fruit being sulfured, the size of the pieces, the condition and maturity of the fruit, and the efficiency of the sulfuring equipment.

CAUTION: DON'T INHALE SULFUR DIOXIDE FUMES!

Sulfur dioxide fumes must not be inhaled. They can cause damage to the delicate membranes of the lungs.

Sulfur fruit outside where there is a good flow of fresh air. Do not breathe the fumes and be certain that animals or children are not close by.

- Sulfuring is finished when fruit is bright and glistening and a small amount of juice appears in the pit cavity. The skin will peel off easily and the color will be even.
- Dry in the sun or in a dehydrator. Place the dehydrator in a well-ventilated place out of doors, or in an empty room that has windows that can be opened.
- Do not dry sulfured fruit in the oven.

When You Sulfur, Remember

- Freshly cut fruit absorbs SO_2 most rapidly.
- Immature fruit requires a higher concentration of SO_2 because it does not retain the SO_2 as long as fully ripe fruit does.
- Sun-dried fruit requires a higher SO_2 concentration than fruit dried in a dehydrator because much more of it is lost in exposure to sun and air.
- Fruit to be stored six months or longer, or at a temperature above 60°F (16°C), should have a higher SO_2 concentration.

Ascorbic Acid (Vitamin C)

Ascorbic acid mixed with water is another way to reduce browning and oxidation, but its protection does not last as long as sulfuring or sulfiting. There are several brands available in drugstores or grocery stores. One teaspoon of powdered ascorbic acid is equal to 3,000 milligrams of ascorbic acid in tablet form.

Ascorbic acid mixtures usually contain dextrose, an anticaking ingredient such as silicon dioxide, and ascorbic acid. They are sold in grocery stores for use on fresh fruits and in canning or freezing. They are more expensive and not as effective as using pure ascorbic acid.

How to Pretreat with Ascorbic Acid

- Mix 2 teaspoons powdered ascorbic acid in one quart of water.
- Place the fruit in the solution for five minutes.
- Drain the fruit and place on drying trays.
- After the solution is used twice, add another 1 teaspoon ascorbic acid.

How to Pretreat with Ascorbic Acid Mixtures

- Mix 1½ tablespoons ascorbic acid mixture with one quart of water and soak fruit for five minutes. Or lightly sprinkle dry mixture directly on the fruit.
- Drain the fruit and place on drying trays.
- After using the solution twice, add another 1 tablespoon ascorbic acid mixture.

Syrup Blanching

Syrup-blanched fruits have good color. They are sweeter and have a softer texture than sulfured and sulfited fruits. They also contain a little less of the vitamins A and C. Fruits that can be syrup blanched are apples, apricots, figs, nectarines, peaches, pears, and plums.

How to Syrup Blanch

- Prepare the fruit as you would for sulfiting.
- Prepare sugar syrup by mixing 1 cup sugar, 1 cup white corn syrup, and 2 cups water. Bring to a boil.
- Add 1½ pounds prepared fruit.
- Simmer for five minutes.
- Let the fruit stand in the hot syrup for thirty minutes.
- Remove with slotted spoon to a colander.
- Rinse lightly with cold water.
- Dry on drying trays.

Equipment and Ingredients for Syrup Blanching

- Large saucepan
- Slotted spoon
- Colander
- Sugar
- Corn syrup

Steaming

Steaming destroys the natural flavor and texture of fruit and some vitamins A and C. Steamed fruit doesn't have the full flavor of sulfured fruit or the sweetness of syrup-blanched fruit. It is the least effective way to pretreat fruits for drying, but can be used if you don't want to sulfite, sulfur, or syrup blanch.

How to Steam

- Prepare the fruit as you would for sulfiting.
- Place the fruit in the perforated section of a steamer without letting the fruit touch the water. Cover tightly and steam until heated through.
- To test for heat penetration, bite into a piece or break it and touch the center. It should be hot, but not cooked.
- Remove pieces of fruit with a slotted spoon and place on drying trays.

Equipment for Steaming

- Steamer
- Slotted spoon

DRY FRUITS IN A DRYER, SUN OR OVEN

Preheat the dehydrator. Arrange the prepared and pretreated fruit on the drying trays, leaving small spaces between slices or pieces so that the air can move freely between them. The pieces should not overlap.

Different fruits may be dried together because they do not have the strong flavor or odor of some vegetables. Dry similar-size fruit halves or slices on the same tray to save sorting near the end of drying. Smaller fruits, such as cherries and raisins, should be moved around on the trays occasionally to prevent them from sticking together and to promote even drying.

Leave your dryer on until all the pieces are dry. Turning it off at night may result in lower quality dried fruit. A timer attached to your dryer can allow you to have a peaceful night's rest without having to get up and check on your dried fruit. As you become experienced, you can guess about how much longer the dryer needs to remain on for the fruit to be sufficiently dried.

Do not add fresh moist pieces to a dryer filled with partially dried fruit. The increased humidity will greatly increase the drying time of the partially dried fruit.

Don't dry two foods that have quite different drying temperatures at the same time.

Occasionally, when the humidity is very high and you have overloaded your dehydrator, the fruits dry too slowly. Move the temperature higher if you suspect that this is happening. Fruits can sour or ferment when the temperature is too low and the humidity is very high.

Sun-dried fruit should be placed in direct sunlight for the first two or three days of drying. After that, put the trays in the shade for the remainder of the drying time. This will improve the flavor and cause less loss of color and nutrients.

Sun drying is slowed at night because the temperature drops or the fruit is brought inside. Low temperatures or interrupting the drying of fruits may result in fermentation or spoilage.

CHECK THE DRYING TEMPERATURE

The ideal temperature for drying most fruits is 140°F (60°C). However, you can increase drying temperature for the first couple of hours to 160°F (71°C) to remove surface moisture quickly. Lower the temperature back to 140°F (60°C) for the remainder of the drying time. Using a higher temperature at the beginning speeds drying without damaging the fruit. Check the section on specific fruits for any exceptions to these temperature guidelines.

TEST TO FIND OUT IF THEY'RE DRY

Watch and test the fruits carefully near the end of the drying period. It is easy to overdry. When fruits are dried too long, they are brittle, difficult to chew, and lose some of their wonderful flavor.

Let a piece of fruit cool to room temperature. Touch and taste it. It should feel pliable and leather-like and have no pockets of moisture. If it feels squishy in just one little part, put it back in to dry some more. Most fruits should contain between 15 and 20 percent moisture when properly dried.

If you want the fruits moister than suggested here, store them in the freezer to prevent them from molding.

CONDITION FRUITS TO DISTRIBUTE THE MOISTURE

When fruits are dry, some pieces may be a little moister than others because of the size of the pieces or their location in the dryer. *Conditioning* is a process used to distribute the residual moisture evenly in the fruit. It reduces the chance of spoilage.

After the dried fruit has cooled, loosely pack it in plastic or glass containers to about two-thirds full. Metal containers may give a metallic flavor to the fruit. Put the lid on tightly and let stand for two to four days. The excess moisture in some pieces will migrate to the drier pieces. Shake the containers daily to separate the pieces and check for signs of condensation on the lid. If condensation occurs, return the fruit to the dryer for more drying.

PASTEURIZE

Washing fruit does not always remove insect larvae, so fruits that are not peeled should be *pasteurized* to prevent insect infestation if you are going to store them at room temperature.

Freezer Pasteurizing

- After the fruit has been dried and conditioned, seal it in your packaging containers.
- Place the packaged fruit in a freezer set below 0°F (−18°C) for at least forty-eight hours before storing at room temperature.

Oven Pasteurizing

- You can also pasteurize fruit in the oven before it is packaged, but it will lose more of the heat-sensitive vitamins. Layer the fruit loosely in a roasting pan, not more than two inches deep.
- Place the pan in a preheated 175°F (80°C) oven for fifteen minutes or for thirty minutes at 160°F (71°C).
- Remove and allow the dried fruits to come to room temperature.

PACKAGE FOR STORAGE

Dried fruit should be cooled and conditioned before packaging. If you have a home vacuum-packaging machine such as the FoodSaver Advanced Design package the dried fruit loosely in canning jars.

If you use plastic freezer bags, remove any excess air. If you are going to store plastic freezer bags on the shelf and not in the freezer, remember that insects can chew through plastic bags. When storing food in plastic bags in a cupboard, place several smaller bags together inside of a large plastic or metal container.

Package your fruit in amounts that can be used within several days after opening. Every time dried fruit is exposed to air, there will be a slight deterioration in the quality.

Label Your Packaged Dried Fruits with the Following

- Fruit
- Variety
- Pretreatment
- Date dried

SHELF LIFE

The shelf life of dried fruits is dependent upon the moisture left in the fruits, their sulfur dioxide or sulfite content from pretreatment, exposure to light, type of packaging, and storage temperature.

Moisture Content

- The desired residual moisture in most dried fruits is 15 to 20 percent.
- Store fruits with higher moisture in the freezer to prevent mold.

Pretreatment

- The type of pretreatment will also influence shelf life. When fruits are sulfited or sulfured, they tend to keep longer with a higher quality.

- Warm temperatures and exposure to air result in increased loss of sulfur dioxide or sulfite, causing darkening and flavor loss.

Light

- Dried fruit colors tend to fade when exposed to light. Light also destroys vitamins A and C.
- Keep dried fruits in a dark cabinet or in the refrigerator or freezer.

Packaging

- Vacuum-packaged fruits will generally keep two to three times longer than those in plastic bags or nonvacuumed jars.
- Store dried fruits in freezer bags or freezer containers if you don't have access to a home vacuum-packaging machine with a vacuum jar sealer.

Storage Temperature

- Dried fruits stored in good packaging at room temperature will generally keep well for six months to a year.
- Dried fruit should be stored in the very coolest place available, preferably below 60°F (16°C). When fruits are well packaged and then refrigerated or frozen, they keep three or four times longer.

DRYING CANNED FRUIT

Fruit that has been canned in its own juice or in sugar syrup may be removed from the can or jar and dehydrated. This is an ideal way to use canned fruit that is older than a year that you want to recycle into your food supply.

Drain the canned fruit in a colander over a bowl so that you can catch the syrup. Reserve the syrup if you are making leather from some of the canned fruit. Add enough syrup back to the fruit to get the right consistency in the puree.

Rinse drained fruits lightly under cool water to remove the surface syrup and reduce the stickiness of the fruit pieces when they dry.

Dry fruit pieces until they are leathery with no visible pockets of moisture. Dried canned fruits resemble glacéed or candied fruits, make great lunch-box or hiking snacks, and can be used for candied fruit in most fruitcake recipes.

HOW TO USE DRIED FRUIT

Eat it! Most dried fruit is eaten as it is without reconstituting. It is the perfect lunch-box treat and is a nutritious snack for work or home. Dried foods are great for all outdoor activities because they are not perishable, are lightweight, and don't take up much room.

Rehydrate it. Most dried fruit is used in recipes as it is. However, you may wish to plump or soften the fruit slightly to make it more chewable. You can use one of these methods:

• Cover the dried fruit with hot or cold fruit juice or water. Let it stand for five to ten minutes, then drain. Hot liquid allows the fruit to rehydrate more quickly than cold. Fruit juice makes it more flavorful than water.

• Place the dried fruit in the top of a steamer over boiling water and steam for three to five minutes until the fruit is plump.

• Place dried fruits into hot cereal as it is cooking. Fruits will soften by the time the cereal is cooked.

Once moisture has been returned to dried fruits, they are quite perishable and should be used soon or refrigerated.

Use dried fruits in cooking. Dried fruit may be cooked in juice or water until it is tender. Soaking first, then simmering, gives a more tender fruit. Sugar and spices should be added near the end of the cooking time. Fruit juice always makes a more flavorful recipe than water, but you can also use water.

Many of your favorite recipes are tastier with the addition of dried fruit. In baked goods, partially rehydrating the fruit first will allow the liquid/flour balance to remain stable.

Use Dried Fruits to Reduce Fat in Your Recipes

Prepare purees in a food processor. When using fruit puree in your recipe, reduce the sugar in the recipe by at least one-third. As a rule, use only half of the specified amount of shortening, margarine, butter, or oil.

For example, if 1 cup margarine is called for, use only ½ cup. Replace the fat omitted with half that amount of puree.

When using pureed dried fruits to replace or reduce shortening or oil in baking, remember not to overmix or overbake.

Fruit Puree for Baking
Makes about 1½ cups puree

2 cups dried figs or prunes
¾ cup water
2 teaspoons vanilla extract

Cover dried fruit with water and allow to stand for 30 minutes to 1 hour. Puree the fruit, water, and vanilla in blender or food processor.

ALL ABOUT FRUITS

APPLES

Apples dry well and are healthy snacks. Apples contain vitamin C, a small amount of vitamin A and iron, and one-fifth of the recommended daily intake of fiber. A medium apple has about eighty calories. Apples are loaded with *pectin*, a soluble fiber that aids digestion. The high pectin in apples also makes them great to combine with other fruits that are low in pectin when you're making fruit leathers.

Dried apples can be soft and chewy or crisp, depending on your preference. Sprinkle with flavored gelatin powder or cinnamon and sugar before drying to add extra flavor and color.

Clever apple peelers/corers/slicers are available from several companies. These are simple to attach to your countertop. The real advantage is speed in preparation, as well as making uniformly thick slices, which means more even drying and less work for you.

HOW TO CHOP DRIED FRUIT

- Run the scissors or knife through hot water occasionally to prevent stickiness.
- Coat scissors or knife with vegetable oil.
- Before cutting, toss the fruit lightly with vegetable oil.
- Before cutting, toss the fruit lightly with some of the flour from the recipe you are using.
- Before cutting, toss the fruit with powdered sugar.
- If using a blender or food processor, freeze the dried fruit first and chop with the appropriate blade and speed.

Quality when dried: Excellent.

Varieties best for drying: More than 2,500 varieties of apples are grown in the United States. Tart, firm-textured varieties, such as Gravenstein, Granny Smith, Jonathan, Newton, and Northern Spy, are usually preferred over the sweet varieties. Sweet varieties such as Fuji and Golden Delicious can also be dried.

Selection: Apples should be mature but very firm and free from bruises or soft spots. They should have a good color for their variety.

Apples are usually *waxed* to keep them fresher. The wax replaces the *natural wax* that is removed when the apples are washed before they are shipped to produce markets. The wax is perfectly safe to eat.

Storage before drying: Cover with a cloth towel. Store at refrigerator temperature, 35°F to 40°F (2°C to 4°C), to maintain the highest quality until you're ready to dry them.

Water content before drying: 84 percent.

Preparation: Wash, peel if desired, core, and slice into ¼-inch slices or cut in quarters. They dry better in even slices. Hold in a solution of 1 teaspoon ascorbic acid per quart of water or ¼ teaspoon sodium bisulfite per quart of water until ready to pretreat.

Pretreatment: Soak slices or quarters for ten to fifteen minutes in a solution of 1 to 2 tablespoons sodium bisulfite per gallon of water. Rinse in clear water. Or you can sulfur ½-inch slices for forty-five minutes to one hour. Sulfur quarters for one to two hours. The least effective pretreatment is to steam blanch for three to five minutes. Steam blanching deteriorates the flavor.

Drying temperature: 130°F to 140°F (54°C to 60°C) until dry.

Dryness test: Pliable to crisp. Apples store best when they are slightly crisp. They should contain about 10 percent moisture when dry.

How to use: Rehydrate dried apples and use in granola, cookies, cobblers, and pies. Cook in apple dumplings or fritters.

Additional information: More information and recipes are available from:

U.S. Apple Association
8233 Old Courthouse Road Suite 200
Vienna, VA 22182
Phone: 703-442-8850
Fax: 703-790-0845
Email: sschaffer@usapple.org
Website: www.usapple.org

Michigan Apple Committee
13105 Schavey Road, Suite 2
DeWitt, MI 48820
Phone: 800-456-2753 or 517-669-8353
Fax: 517-669-9506
Email: Staff@MichiganApples.com
Website: www.michiganapples.com

New York Apple Association
P.O. Box 350
Fishers, NY 14453-0350
Phone: 585-924-2171
Fax: 585-924-1629
Email: pgregg@nyapplecountry.com
Website: www.nyapplecountry.com

APRICOTS

Because apricots are especially high in vitamin A, careful pretreatment and drying are important so vitamin loss is minimized. They also contain iron, fiber, vitamin C, and several B vitamins. Three medium apricots have about fifty calories.

California is number one in the nation for apricot production, and Washington State ranks second.

Dried apricots are so sweet and have such an intense flavor that they are a healthy way to satisfy your sweet tooth.

Quality when dried: Excellent.

Varieties best for drying: Blenheim/Royal is used most frequently for drying, although Tilton may also be used.

Selection: Apricots should be picked at their peak ripeness to have the best flavor when dried. They should be plump, well formed, and firm with a deep yellow or yellow-orange color. If they are yellow-green, they are not fully ripe. Although unripened apricots will soften and change color during storage, their flavor will not be as pronounced and they will tend to be tough and more shriveled. If you can pick them right from the tree when they're ripe, they will have the very best flavor.

Storage before drying: Cover with a cloth towel. Keep in a shallow box only one layer deep. When they're fully ripe, store them in the refrigerator at 35°F to 40°F (2°C to 4°C) to maintain the highest quality and keep them from deteriorating until you're ready to dry them.

Water content before drying: 85 percent.

Preparation: Apricots should be washed, halved, pits removed, and held in a solution of 1 teaspoon ascorbic acid per quart of water or a solution of ¼ teaspoon sodium bisulfite per quart of water until ready to pretreat.

Pretreatment: The most effective pretreatment for apricots is sulfuring. Sulfur halves skin-side down for two to three hours. If using a dehydrator, expose apricots to the sun for at least four to six hours after sulfuring to deepen the color and improve the flavor. If you choose not to sulfur, the next best alternative is syrup blanching.

Drying temperature: 130°F to 140°F (54°C to 60°C) until dry.

Dryness test: Pliable with no pockets of moisture.

How to use: Apricots are one of the most versatile of all dried fruits and may be used dried or rehydrated in meat dishes, salads, desserts, glazes, candies, or granola. In baking, apricots are a colorful addition in quick and yeast breads, coffee cakes, and Danishes. Use as a filling or topping for croissants, fruit-filled turnovers, or pies.

Additional information: More information and recipes are available from:

Washington State Fruit Commission
105 South 18th Street, Suite 205
Yakima, WA 98901
Phone: 509-453-4837
Fax: 509-453-4880
Email: info@wastatefruit.com
Website: www.nwcherries.com

BANANAS

More than 96 percent of American households purchase bananas at least once each month. Bananas are America's number one fruit and the average American consumes over twenty-eight pounds of fresh bananas each year! They are also great dried.

A cluster of bananas is called a *hand* and consists of ten to twenty bananas, which are known as *fingers*. Bananas are a good source of vitamin C, potassium, and fiber.

Bananas and plantains are grown today in every tropical region and are the fourth largest fruit crop in the world. They are not grown commercially in the continental United States. Most U.S. bananas are grown in Central and South America. They are available all year round.

Vary the flavor of dried bananas before drying them by sprinkling with flavored gelatin powder or dipping them in lemon juice or a lemon juice and honey mixture. After dipping, roll them in chopped nuts, sesame seeds, or shredded coconut.

Don't expect your home-dried bananas to taste the same as the banana chips from the store. Those are flavored with sugar, banana flavoring, and then deep-fat fried in coconut or palm oil. Home-dried bananas are much more nutritious!

Quality when dried: Good.

Varieties best for drying: Large, yellow, smooth-skinned varieties of bananas dry best. Smaller, red-skinned varieties such as Red Jamaica or Baracoa may also be dried. Ripe plantains may also be dried.

Selection: Bananas are one of the few fruits that ripen best off the plant. Bananas should be solid yellow with a tiny bit of green on the peel. When dried at this stage of ripeness, they will stay quite light without any pretreatment.

Avoid bruised or overripe bananas. As bananas ripen, the starch in the fruit turns to sugar. Bananas that are slightly brown flecked will have the sweetest, most pronounced flavor when dried. Solid yellow bananas will not be quite as sweet or as strong flavored. Dry both and decide which you like best.

Storage before drying: Bananas ripen rapidly at room temperature. Once ripe, they may be held for three to four days in the refrigerator, but expect the skins to turn dark when they're refrigerated.

Water content before drying: 65 percent.

Preparation: Peel and place your thumb into the stem end of the banana and push. The banana will naturally fall into three pieces. It is easiest to dry in lengthwise thirds because it will come off the trays easily and the pieces are easier to handle. You can also slice bananas ⅜- to ½-inch thick crosswise, although slices are more difficult to remove from the drying trays. Bananas tend to stick to the trays, so if you have the accessory plastic mesh screens, use them. The dried bananas will be easier to remove from the screens than from the trays because the screens flex.

Pretreatment: Bananas are best dried with no pretreatment. Because of their soft texture, bananas are not sulfited, steamed, or syrup blanched.

Drying temperature: 130°F to 140°F (54°C to 60°C) until dry.

Dryness test: Bananas should be pliable and leathery. You can also dry them until they are rock hard, but they are more difficult to chew. Plaintains should be dried rock hard. They can be ground in a food processor or blender to make plaintain flour.

How to use: Dried bananas are delicious snacks. They may be used in dry or cooked cereals, granola, or baby foods. Bananas may be rehydrated for use in banana breads, cakes, and cookies. Dried bananas are delicious dipped in melted chocolate and then in chopped nuts. If you dry them in thirds lengthwise, leave a couple of inches at the bottom without the chocolate to use as a handle.

Additional information: More information and recipes are available from:

International Banana Association
1901 Pennsylvania Avenue NW, Suite 1100
Washington, DC 20006
Phone: 804-379-1466
Email: info@eatmorebananas.com
Website: www.eatmorebananas.com

BERRIES

Blackberries, boysenberries, loganberries, raspberries, and huckleberries are not recommended for drying because they have too many seeds and dry slowly. However, when the seeds are removed, they make excellent fruit leather. You can remove the seeds with a juice extractor or sieve. For leather, these berries are better combined with applesauce because they have very little pectin.

BLUEBERRIES

Blueberries are grown in thirty-five states and more than 90 percent of all the blueberries in the world are grown in the United States.

Native Americans dried blueberries in the sun and taught the Pilgrims to use blueberries in many ways. Whole dried blueberries were added to soups and stews. They were ground into a powder and used in pudding and to season meat.

Blueberries are loaded with antioxidants, are full of vitamin C and fiber, and have a little vitamin A. One whole cup has only eighty-three calories. Blueberries are great to eat when fresh and best preserved by freezing. If you choose to dry them, they really should be sugar soaked. See the section on glacéed fruit (page 66).

Quality when dried: Fair to good, depending on whether or not they are glacéed.

Selection: Select large, firm, fully ripe berries that have a deep blue color all over.

Water content before drying: 83 percent.

Storage before drying: Cover with a cloth towel to keep them from shriveling. Store in the refrigerator at 35°F to 40°F (2°C to 4°C) to maintain the highest quality until you're ready to dry them.

Preparation: Wash berries in a colander with a gentle stream of cool water. Remove stems.

Pretreatment: Blueberries may be dried with no pretreatment, but will be puffy and hard. They are not like raisins unless they have been glacéed. During the glacé process, the sugar is absorbed into the berries over a period of days, and they become sweeter and more like raisins. See page 66.

Drying temperature: 130°F to 140°F (54°C to 60°C) until dry.

Dryness test: Leathery and pliable with no pockets of moisture.

How to use: Dried glacéed blueberries can be used in muffins, breads, and as a snack.

Additional information: More information and recipes are available from:

Ark-La-Tex Blueberry Growers Association
10268 FM 314
Edom, TX 75756
Phone: 903-852-6175
Email: info@bestberry.org
Website: www.bestberry.org

CHERRIES

Cherries were brought to America by ship with the early settlers in the 1600s. French colonists later planted cherry trees along the St. Lawrence River and throughout the Great Lakes area and in the Midwest.

Today, the U.S. cherry industry is concentrated in Michigan, Idaho, Utah, and the Northwest.

Look in your local cookware or gourmet shop for a cherry pitter, which pits a large quantity of cherries in a short time with little loss of juice or pulp.

There are two main types of cherries: sweet and sour. Sour cherries are lower in calories and higher in vitamin C and beta-carotene than sweet cherries. Both are good sources of fiber.

Quality when dried: Excellent.

Varieties best for drying: Bing cherries are the all-time favorite for drying. The stone is relatively small, while the fruit is crisp, firm, and juicy. Fresh Rainier cherries have a very sweet, delicate flavor with a golden pink-blushed skin color. If you want to retain the light color, these should be sulfured. Lambert and Van cherries are smaller than Bing and still quite flavorful. The tart or sour varieties such as Early Richmond or Large Montmorency dry well but are better used in cooking than as a snack.

Selection: Select large, plump and firm, fully ripe cherries with fresh-looking stems. Avoid small, underripe cherries with dark stems, dull color, or soft appearance.

Storage before drying: Place unwashed cherries in a large roasting pan to minimize bruising. Do not remove the stems. Cover with a cloth towel. Store in the refrigerator at 32°F (0°C) for up to five days. They are best dried right after harvesting.

Water content before drying: Sweet, 80 percent; sour, 84 percent.

Preparation: Wash cherries and remove stems. Remove pit with a cherry pitter and dry whole. You can also slice them in half, remove the pit, and dry the halves, but it is a lot of work!

Pretreatment: Cherries may be dried with no pretreatment, but the color will be very dark and the flavors more like raisins. Sulfured cherries hold their color and flavor better, especially for longer storage. Royal Ann cherries keep their rosy pink color when sulfured. Sulfur pitted cherries for one hour.

Drying temperature: 130°F to 140°F (54°C to 60°C) until dry.

Dryness test: Pliable and leathery with no pockets of moisture.

How to use: Dried cherries are excellent snacks. They may be substituted for or combined with raisins in cooking. The sweet varieties are a decadent treat when dipped in melted chocolate. They can be glacéed with good results.

Additional information: More information and recipes are available from:

California Cherry Advisory Board
P.O. Box 877
Lodi, CA 95241
Phone: 209-368-0685
Fax: 209-368-4309
Website: www.calcherry.com

Washington State Fruit Commission
105 South 18th Street, Suite 205
Yakima, WA 98901
Phone: 509-453-4837
Fax: 509-453-4880
Email: info@wastatefruit.com
Website: www.nwcherries.com

CITRUS FRUITS AND PEELS

Citrus fruits are one of those different fruits that you either like dried or you don't. In reality, most people dry only the peels and usually use them for convenient flavorings in recipes.

Oranges do not ripen after they are picked, but lemons do. Zest is the colored outermost skin layer of citrus fruits. Zest is rich in the flavoring oils and when dried, has numerous uses in recipes.

Citrus fruits are rich in vitamin C.

Quality when dried: Fair to good.

Varieties best for drying: The peels of citron, grapefruit, kumquat, lemon, lime, orange, tangelo, or tangerine may be dried. Thick-skinned navel orange peel is better for drying than thin-skinned Valencia peel. Dry only the sweetest oranges and grapefruits. Otherwise, they will be bitter when dried.

Selection: Select firm, juicy thick-skinned fruit with no signs of mold or decay.

Storage before drying: Wrap citrus fruits in paper towels, then in plastic bags. Store in the refrigerator at 35°F to 40°F (2°C to 4°C) to maintain the highest quality until you're ready to dry them.

Water content before drying: 86 percent.

Preparation: Wash well. To dry the peels, remove the outer 1/16 to 1/8 inch of the peel. The colored outer part of the peel contains the flavoring oils. Avoid the white bitter pith just under the peel. Citrus peels are also very nice when glacéed. If you want to dry whole slices, slice them in 1/2-inch-thick circles, keeping the peel intact.

Pretreatment: None.

Drying temperature: 120°F to 130°F (49°C to 54°C) until dry. Lower temperatures are suggested for citrus to avoid the loss of delicate flavoring oils.

Dryness test: Crisp. Peels will snap when broken. They will be leathery when glacéed.

How to use: Dried citrus peels should be stored in strips until ready to use. They can be chopped or powdered in a blender or food processor and substituted for grated lemon or orange peel in recipes. Dried peel has about twice the strength of fresh, so adjust the amount accordingly. Citrus peels that are glacéed can be used in cakes, puddings, or candies. Whole dried orange slices can be eaten as a snack. They can also be floated in summer punch or a hot tea. They can be hung on the Christmas tree as brightly colored, transparent ornaments.

COCONUTS

The coconut that you buy at the supermarket is generally sweetened. When you dry coconut at home, it is a totally different product. If you want to sweeten it, sprinkle with a little sifted powered sugar before drying, although our family finds it much more appealing unsweetened. Dried coconut is high in oil and keeps best in an airtight container in the refrigerator or freezer.

The coconut that you'll find in the supermarket is the dry coconut, with a hard brown shell surrounding firm coconut meat with liquid in the center.

Quality when dried: Excellent.

Selection: Select coconuts that appear fresh, are heavy for their size, and are full of coconut milk. Shake the coconuts to hear the milk slosh. Coconuts with moldy or wet *eyes* are not fresh.

Storage before drying: Store in the refrigerator at 35°F to 40°F (2°C to 4°C) to maintain the highest quality until you're ready to dry them.

Water content before drying: 51 percent.

Preparation: Pierce the eye of the coconut with an ice pick and drain the milk for drinking or to blend with other fruit juices.

Crack around the middle of the hard outer shell with a hammer and steam pieces thirty seconds to one minute to loosen the coconut meat or pry it out with a sturdy knife. You can also bake the shell at 350°F (180°C) for about twenty minutes. Remove, place the shell on a firm surface, and tap it with a hammer in several places to crack it.

Trim the dark outer skin. Grate or slice in chunks for drying.

Pretreatment: None.

Drying temperature: 110°F (43°C) until dry. Lower temperatures are suggested for coconut because it has such so much oil in it. Higher temperatures will increase rancidity.

How to use: Dried coconut is delicious eaten as a snack, added to cold or hot cereals, and as an addition to baked goods. It can be used in fruit smoothies, sprinkled on salads, or stirred into sautéed vegetables. It is commonly used in Thai and Indian dishes.

CRAB APPLES

Because of their small size and tartness, crab apples are not recommended for drying. However, the pleasant tart varieties may be combined with other fruits in fruit leather. Avoid bitter varieties.

CRANBERRIES

Cranberries are extremely tart and do not dry well unless they are sugar soaked over a period of several days. Commercially, you'll see them in the store called cran-raisins or Craisins. The commercially dried ones are all sugared, so are much sweeter than cranberries dried without the additional sugar.

Cranberries are an excellent source of potassium and are low in sodium. Dried cranberries have three times more fiber than fresh for the same weight.

Quality when dried: Fair, unless sugar soaked.

Selection: Either the large, bright red variety or the smaller sweeter dark cranberry may be dried. Select fresh, firm, glossy berries. Cranberries do not ripen after harvest.

Storage before drying: Store cranberries in the refrigerator at 35°F to 40°F (2°C to 4°C) to maintain the highest quality. They can keep up to two months in the refrigerator, but if you're going to dry them, dry them when they're the freshest.

Water content before drying: 88 percent.

Preparation: Wash to remove any traces or dirt or fungicide.

Pretreatment: Cranberries are best when sugar soaked over a period of several days (see Glacéed Fruit, page 66). If you prefer not to glacé, dip in boiling water to crack the skins. Otherwise, they will be puffy, very lightweight, and take forever to dry.

Drying temperature: 130°F to 140°F (54°C to 60°C) until dry.

Dryness test: Shriveled, lightweight, with no sign of moisture. Glacé cranberries will be leathery and a little sticky. The moisture content in dried cranberries should be only about 5 percent.

How to use: Dried glacé cranberries add a piquant flavor to spinach salad, cookies, baked items, and desserts. They can be used in any dish where you normally would use raisins.

CURRANTS

Dried currants are not the same as fresh currants. Dried currants are actually small raisins made from the Zante grape. Fresh currants are black, red, or pink and are the fruits of plants in the gooseberry family. Only the grape currants may be dried.

Quality when dried: Good.

Selection: Firm, ripe, seedless black varieties such as the Black Corinth and Zante may be dried, resulting in a dark raisin with a tart, tangy flavor.

Storage before drying: Store in the refrigerator at 35°F to 40°F (2°C to 4°C) to maintain the highest quality until you're ready to dry them.

Water content before drying: 81 percent.

Preparation: Do not remove the stems. Wash well to remove dirt or bacteria. Or they may be dried first and then lightly washed, stems removed, and dried again for a few minutes to remove the surface moisture.

Drying temperature: 130°F to 140°F (54°C to 60°C) until dry.

Dryness test: Leathery.

How to use: Substitute dried currants for raisins in cookies and breads. Dried currants are traditionally used in hot cross buns at Easter.

DATES

Dates are classified according to their fleshiness. Soft dates are rich in glucose and fructose. Drier dates have a larger percentage of sucrose. Up to 80 percent of the date flesh is sugar.

Dates have more sugar than any other fruit. There is a small amount of fiber, potassium, vitamins, and minerals. Dates have about twenty-four calories per date. One pound of dates is about 3 cups.

Quality when dried: Excellent.

Varieties best for drying: Fresh dates are classified as dry, semidry, or soft. Dry varieties are very high in sugar and contain only a small amount of moisture when ripe. They are nonperishable. Most soft or semidry varieties are perishable because they contain more water. Deglet Noor is the most popular dried date and accounts for 90 percent of California's crop.

Selection: Fresh dates should be plump with a rich red or golden color. Allow dates to ripen on the tree.

Storage before drying: Fresh, soft dates should be stored in the refrigerator at 35°F to 40°F (2°C to 4°C) to maintain the highest quality until you're ready to dry them. Dry varieties can be stored at 65°F (18°C) in an airtight container.

Water content before drying: 23 percent.

Preparation: Wash well.

Pretreatment: None.

Drying temperature: 130°F (54°C) until dry.

Dryness test: Leathery with a deep russet or brown color.

How to use: Dates may be eaten as a snack or added to cookies, cakes, granola, breads, and desserts. Use to sweeten fruit leathers or yogurt. To chop dates, use a pair of kitchen scissors instead of a knife. The dates clump less on scissors. To make *date sugar*, arrange the sliced dates on a baking sheet and bake at 350°F (180°C) for twenty to thirty minutes, or until very dry. Allow dates to cool. Process the cooled dates in a food processor until finely ground.

Additional information: More information and recipes are available from:

California Date Administrative Committee
P.O. Box 1736
Indio, CA 92201
Phone: 760-347-4510, 800-223-8748
Fax: 760-347-6374
Email: dates2000@earthlink.net
Website: www.datesaregreat.com

FIGS

Figs are the only dried fruit high in calcium and phosphorus, minerals necessary for bone building and body maintenance. They are low in sodium. Figs have more dietary fiber than prunes. Three pounds of fresh figs make one pound dried.

Figs are naturally sweet and 55 percent of the weight of dried figs is natural sugar. Figs are high in fiber, providing 20 percent of the minimum daily requirement, more dietary fiber per serving than any other dried or fresh fruit.

For sun drying, stack trays of partly dried figs. Overexposure to the sun toughens their skin and weakens their flavor.

Quality when dried: Excellent.

Varieties best for drying: The Black Mission variety is a deep purple that darkens to a rich black when dried, has rather small seeds and a pleasant flavor. White Adriatics are medium size, have high sugar, and have an attractive dried appearance. The all-purpose Kadota is relatively small, almost seedless, and a beautiful creamy amber color when ripe. The Calimyrna fig is very large, has a rich yellow color and large seeds, and is known for its nutlike flavor. All can be dried.

Selection: Figs mature slowly compared with most fruits and the sugar concentration also increases slowly while they mature. Figs should be picked just before they reach the fully ripe stage, but yield to soft pressure, usually indicated by small cracks in the skin. They should smell sweet. Handle them carefully because they bruise easily.

Storage before drying: Refrigerate figs if you're not going to dry them right away. Fresh ripe figs do not keep well, mold easily, and can be stored in the refrigerator for only two or three days.

Drying temperature: 130°F to 140°F (54°C to 60°C) until dry.

Dryness test: Leathery, no pockets of moisture.

How to use: Dried figs may be stewed or added to fruit compotes and garnished with yogurt or whipping cream. Chopped stewed figs may be combined with nuts and served as an unusual sandwich spread or used as a filling for cookies or pastries. Use them in fruit salads, cakes, puddings, breads, and cookies.

Dried figs can be stored for six to eight months. They are an excellent replacement for fat in baked goods. See Use Dried Fruits to Reduce Fat in Your Recipes on page 31.

Additional information: More information and recipes are available from:

California Fig Advisory Board
7395 N. Palm Bluffs, Suite 106
Fresno, CA 93711
Phone: 559-440-5400
Fax: 559-438-5405
Email: info@californiafigs.com
Website: www. californiafigs.com

GRAPES

Raisins are among the very first dried fruits recorded in history. In 1490 B.C., history books first note that raisins were sun-dried grapes. In 1876, the Scottish immigrant William Thompson grew a seedless grape variety that was sweet, tasty, and thin skinned. Ninety-five percent of California raisins are made from Thompson seedless grapes.

About four and a half pounds of grapes yield one pound of raisins. Raisins are high in iron and contain about 70 percent natural sugar. One-fourth cup of raisins is one serving of fruit.

Stored in the refrigerator at 40°F (4°C), raisins will retain their color, flavor, and nutritional value for about six months. Raisins freeze well for long periods of time in airtight containers and can be thawed quickly at room temperature.

Quality when dried: Excellent.

Varieties best for drying: The Thompson Seedless is best for drying. Sultanas and Red Emperor are also very flavorful. It isn't practical to dry varieties with seeds because it is too difficult to remove them. Stay with the seedless varieties.

Selection: Select fully ripe, sweet, seedless grapes that are still attached to the stems. Grapes do not continue to ripen after they have been picked. They should be smooth, plump, well colored, and firmly attached to the stem.

Storage before drying: Store grapes wrapped in paper towels in loosely closed plastic bags in the refrigerator at 35°F to 40°F (2°C to 4°C). If grapes are harvested during rainy periods or following slight freezes, store for a very short time.

Water content before drying: 81 percent.

Preparation: Wash carefully right on the drying trays to remove dirt. Remove from stems once they're on the trays or after they're dried.

Pretreatment: For *golden raisins*, sulfur the Thompson variety for one hour before drying. Another method to keep them light in color is to steam them until the skin cracks, which decreases the drying time and retains the light color, but they are less flavorful.

Drying temperature: 130°F to 140°F (54°C to 60°C) until dry. Expect them to take eighteen to twenty-four hours or more to dry in a dehydrator, three or four days in the sun.

Dryness test: Leathery with no pockets of moisture.

How to use: Raisins are a treat alone or combined with other dried fruits and nuts. They add texture and flavor to baked goods, pancakes, or muffins and in cold or hot cereals. Include raisins in a peanut butter and jelly sandwich. Try raisins in cream cheese on bagels. Add chopped raisins to chicken, turkey, ham, or tuna salad sandwiches. Always add raisins with nuts and other dried fruits for a naturally good trail mix. Liberally sprinkle raisins over green salad to add a new texture.

Raisins are a great *kid food*. Make sandwiches into spaceships and fruit salads into happy faces.

When raisins become dry or when a recipe calls for *plumped* raisins, cover them with very hot juice or water and soak for two or three minutes.

Additional information: More information and recipes are available from:

California Raisin Marketing Board
3445 North First Street, Suite 101
Fresno, CA 93726
Phone: 559-248-0287
Email: info@raisins.org
Website: www.calraisins.org

KIWI FRUIT

Originally called the Chinese gooseberry, the kiwi fruit was introduced to the United States from New Zealand. The sparkling green flesh is hidden underneath the fuzzy brown exterior of this two-inch oval fruit. When kiwi fruit are cut crosswise, the emerald-green flesh has a ring of small black edible seeds. With a flavor and seeds similar to strawberries, this fruit dries very well.

One kiwi fruit contains about fifty calories. Kiwi fruits have twice the vitamin C of oranges, as much potassium as bananas, and are good sources of magnesium, fiber, and vitamin E.

Quality when dried: Excellent.

Varieties best for drying: Hayward kiwi fruit are fuzzy, brown, and oblong in shape and are the primary variety grown commercially. This variety is primarily grown in California's Central Valley and will not survive the cold in the Midwest. The flesh is tart-sweet and tastes like a combination of citrus, melon, and strawberry. Hardy kiwi fruits are also good for drying and are considerably sweeter than the Hayward variety.

Selection: Select kiwi fruit with no bruises or soft spots, wrinkles, or signs of exterior damage. Kiwi fruit should be soft as a ripe peach, free from decay, internal injury, or broken skin.

Storage before drying: Ripen kiwi fruit at room temperature for three to five days. They can be stored for about one week in the refrigerator at 32°F (0°C). If refrigerated while they are still green, remove them from the refrigerator several days before you want to dry them so they can ripen.

Water content before drying: 82 percent.

Preparation: Wash and remove outer skin. Slice ½- to ¾-inch thick, either crosswise or lengthwise.

Pretreatment: None.

Drying temperature: 130°F to 140°F (54°C to 60°C) until dry.

Dryness test: Leathery and pliable with no pockets of moisture.

How to use: Eat dried kiwi as a candylike snack. It makes a colorful addition to trail mix.

Additional information: More information and recipes are available from:

California Kiwifruit Commission
1183 Manning Drive
El Dorado Hills, CA 95762
Phone: 916-933-3477
Fax: 916-933-7394
Email: info@kiwifruit.org
Website: www.kiwifruit.org

MANGOES

Mangoes are the *apples* of the tropics and one of the most popular fruits in tropical countries around the world. The mango is a member of the cashew family of flowering plants and can range from two to ten inches in length. Mangoes originated in Southeast Asia, and India is still the major producer, growing more mangoes than all other fruits combined. Mangoes were introduced into Mexico in 1775 and are now an important export crop from Mexico. California and Florida supply U.S. markets, along with Mexico and Central America.

The flesh of a mango is flavorful, sweet, and very juicy, much like a peach with a hint of pineapple. It has a single large kidney-shaped seed in the center, which is attached to the fruit with thin fibers. Fibers are more pronounced in fruits grown with hard water and chemical fertilizers. The leathery skin is waxy and smooth, and depending on the variety, may be pale green or yellow marked with red.

Mangoes are a nutritional bargain with 50 percent more beta-carotene than a same size serving of apricots, and 20 percent more than cantaloupe. They are also high in fiber, vitamin C, and potassium. An average-size mango has 110 calories.

Most of the dried mango available in supermarkets has been highly sugared, with about 60 percent of the water replaced with sugar. When you dry your own at home, the added sugar isn't necessary, since the fruit has an aromatic, delicious sweet flavor, without the additional sugar.

Quality when dried: Excellent.

Selection: Mangoes have the best flavor if allowed to ripen on the tree. Mangoes should remain on the tree until they begin to color and then they should be harvested. Never buy completely green mangoes, as they won't ripen and have an unpleasant chemical taste.

Ripening fruit turns the characteristic color of the variety (red, yellow, green, orange, or any combination) and begins to soften to the touch, much like a peach. The ripeness of a mango can be determined by either smelling or squeezing. Use your nose! A ripe mango will have a full, fruity aroma emitting from the stem end. No fragrant aroma most likely means no flavor. Mangoes are ready to dry when they yield to gentle pressure and are slightly soft to the touch.

Storage before drying: The ideal storage temperature is 55°F (13°C). Mangoes will store at this temperature for one to two weeks. Mangoes should not be refrigerated during the ripening process. The fruit ripens best if placed stem-end down in trays at room temperature. Cover with a damp cloth to prevent shriveling.

Water content before drying: 80 percent.

Preparation: The skin of the mango is not edible. Cut off both ends of the fruit with a sharp, thin-bladed knife. Place the fruit on the flat end and cut away the peel from top to bottom along the curvature of the fruit. Cut the fruit from the pit by carving lengthwise along the pit. There will be two large slices on the "cheek" side and two smaller slices on the other sides. When you've taken all the flesh off for drying, just nibble the rest off the pit. It is messy, but delicious.

Mangoes may be sugar soaked over a period of several days (see Glacéed Fruit, page 66).

Pretreatment: None.

Drying temperature: 130°F to 140°F (54°C to 60°C) until dry.

Dryness test: Leathery and pliable with no pockets of moisture. Mangoes tend to create little "air bubbles" in pieces as they dry. During drying, you can occasionally *pop* those bubbles with your fingers to ensure even drying.

How to use: Dried mangoes are terrific in all combinations of trail mix. Use in salsa, chutney, and baked goods.

MELONS

Melons arrived in America with the slave trade. Pictures of watermelons have been discovered in Egyptian tombs that are more than 5,000 years old.

Today, the country's major producers are Arizona, Florida, Texas, Georgia, and California.

Melons are one of the few fruits that are never cooked, but they can be dried. Choose the ripest melons for the sweetest dried flavors. Melons are a good source of vitamin C and have trace amounts of potassium, calcium, and iron. Melons with a deep orange or red flesh are rich in vitamin A. One-half cantaloupe has about eighty calories. A wedge of honeydew has about fifty calories.

Quality when dried: Fair to good.

Varieties best for drying: All varieties of melons can be dried, each with its own distinctive flavor. Green- and orange-fleshed honeydew, cantaloupe, casaba, and watermelon can all be dried. Yellow-meated watermelons are just as sweet as the red varieties and have an almost identical taste.

Selection: Melons should be picked when they are mature, firm, and heavy for their size. The underside of a ripe watermelon is yellow and the rind has a healthy sheen. Melons will not get any sweeter after they are picked, although they will soften. Choose a symmetrical melon that is free of bruises, cuts, and dents. Seedless varieties are simpler to dry because you don't have to remove the seeds.

Except for watermelons, the blossom ends should be slightly soft and when you smell the end, it should have an aroma.

Storage before drying: Unripe whole melons may be kept in a paper bag at room temperature between 65°F to 75°F (18°C to 24°C) for two or three days. Wrap cut ripe melons in plastic wrap and refrigerate up to five days.

Water content before drying: 81 percent for most melons. Watermelons have a whopping 92 percent water.

Preparation: Wash and remove outer skin, any fibrous tissue, and seeds. Slice ½-inch thick.

Pretreatment: None. Dipping in lemon juice before drying can enhance the flavor of dried melons.

Drying temperature: 130°F to 140°F (54°C to 60°C) until dry.

Dryness test: Leathery and pliable with no pockets of moisture.

How to use: Eat as a snack. The strong, distinctive flavor prohibits mixing with other fruits. Dried melon doesn't work well in recipes.

NECTARINES

Nectarines are a cross between a peach and a plum and are even better as a dried fruit. Nectarines have smooth skins and are missing the fuzz found on peaches. The amount of red color varies by variety and is not an indication of ripeness or quality. Although the skin is a little tough when dried, most people prefer to leave it intact.

One nectarine has sixty calories and is fairly high in vitamins A and C, potassium, niacin, and fiber.

Quality when dried: Good.

Selection: Pick mature nectarines for flavor and sweetness. They do not increase in sugar after harvesting. They should be fully colored, firm, and plump with a slight softening along the seam and a sweet aroma.

Storage before drying: Place in a shallow pan to avoid bruising, cover them with a towel, and store in the refrigerator at 35°F to 40°F (2°C to 4°C) for short periods before processing to maintain highest quality.

Water content before drying: 82 percent.

Preparation: Wash and cut into ½-inch slices. Nectarine flesh usually clings to the pit, so you will remove pieces to dry by cutting vertical slices to the pit. Remove the pit.

Pretreatment: Soak for ten to fifteen minutes in a solution of 1 to 2 tablespoons sodium bisulfite per gallon of water. Lightly rinse in clear water. You can also sulfur slices for forty-five minutes to one hour. Sulfur halves or quarters for one and a half to three hours.

Drying temperature: 130°F to 140°F (54°C to 60°C) until dry.

Dryness test: Pliable or leathery with no pockets of moisture.

How to use: Pack dried nectarines in lunch boxes. They can be added to most recipes for baked goods or granola.

PAPAYAS

The enzyme papain is extracted from the papaya. Papain is used in treating digestive ailments and is the main ingredient in meat tenderizers.

Papayas contain more beta-carotene than carrots and more vitamin C than an orange. Papayas also contain the minerals potassium, magnesium, and calcium.

You'll find glacé dried papaya in the bulk foods section of your supermarket, dehydrated by replacing most of the water with sugar. It is much thicker than papaya that you would dry without soaking in sugar. If you want to try it yourself, see Glacéed Fruits, page 66.

Quality when dried: Good.

Selection: Papayas are round to oblong, yellow to dark orange, and can weigh five to thirty pounds. Most of the papayas in U.S. supermarkets are small compared to those in tropical countries, where they frequently weigh twenty or thirty pounds.

Select smooth-skinned mature fruit that has a slight give when you touch it. Do not buy hard green papayas because they will not ripen properly.

Storage before drying: Store fully ripe papayas in the refrigerator at 35°F to 40°F (2°C to 4°C) to maintain the highest quality.

Water content before drying: 89 percent.

Preparation: Wash the outer skin well, cut in half, and remove the black seeds attached to the walls of the inner cavity along with any fibrous material. Peel thinly and cut lengthwise into ¼-inch slices. If you want a sweeter fruit, papayas may be sugar soaked over a period of several days (see Glacéed Fruits, page 66).

Pretreatment: None.

Drying temperature: 130°F to 140°F (54°C to 60°C) until dry.

Dryness test: Leathery and pliable with no pockets of moisture.

How to use: Try a trail mix combined with pineapple, mango, and bananas.

PEACHES

There are two categories of peach—clingstone and freestone, distinguished by the ease with which the edible area pulls away from the stone (pit).

The Spanish introduced peaches into Florida in 1513. Peach farming slowly spread throughout the thirteen colonies and then migrated westward. California gold miners were the first to commercially farm cling peaches.

Peaches contain beta-carotene (vitamin A), vitamin C, vitamin E, and fiber. A medium-size peach has about forty calories.

Quality when dried: Excellent.

Varieties best for drying: Both freestone and clingstone varieties may be dried. Freestone peaches usually have a softer texture than clingstone and do not dry as well, but their stones are easier to remove. Clingstone tend to have a fuller flavor.

Selection: *Peaches must ripen on the tree if they are to be full flavored and sweet.* Their delicious flavor and sugar will not develop once they are removed from the tree, even though they change color and get soft. Green or underripe peaches will dry into a grayish product with poor flavor and woody texture.

Select firm, ripe fruit that is heavy for its size, firm-textured rather than pithy, and with the most pronounced flavor.

Storage before drying: If you must wait to process ripe peaches, store them in the refrigerator at 35°F to 40°F (2°C to 4°C) for the best quality.

Water content before drying: 89 percent.

Preparation: Wash and scald in boiling water to remove skins. Immediately plunge into cold water to cool. You can leave the skin on, but it tends to become quite tough when dried. Hold cut peaches in a solution of 1 teaspoon ascorbic acid per quart of water or a solution of ¼ teaspoon sodium bisulfite per quart of water until ready to pretreat.

Pretreatment: Soak for five to fifteen minutes, depending on the thickness, in a solution of 1 to 2 tablespoons sodium bisulfite per gallon of water. Lightly rinse in clear water. Or, you can sulfur halves or quarters for two to three hours.

Drying temperature: 130°F to 140°F (54°C to 60°C) until dry.

Dryness test: Leathery and pliable with no pockets of moisture.

How to use: Peaches may be eaten dried or slightly plumped in breads, chutney, cobblers, cookies, dumplings, granola, and pies.

PEARS

In the eighth century B.C., Homer referred to pears as a "gift of the gods." The early Romans developed more than fifty different varieties and introduced the cultivated pear to other parts of Europe.

Bartlett pear trees came out West in the covered wagons of forty-niners that were heading for the Great California Gold Rush. The Bartlett is America's favorite pear, and it is outstanding for drying.

California grows 60 percent of the nation's pears. They are available July through November.

A medium pear has about 100 calories. It also contains vitamin C, a healthy amount of fiber (about four grams), potassium, and small amounts of calcium and iron.

Quality when dried: Excellent.

Varieties best for drying: Bartlett are the best variety for drying, although other varieties may be dried.

Selection: Pears ripen to perfection only when they are removed from the tree. Unlike most fruit, pears are better when picked hard and unripe. They improve in both texture and flavor after they are picked. They ripen from the inside out. Look for pears with smooth, unblemished skin.

Storage before drying: They should be picked while still green and stored in the refrigerator at 35°F to 40°F (2°C to 4°C), until ready to ripen.

Place a thick cloth or towel in the bottom of a shallow pan. Place the pears in a single layer in the pan. Cover with a clean cloth. Ripen for two to three days in a dark place at room temperature, between 65°F to 75°F (18°C to 24°C). When ready for drying, the pears should be golden yellow but not soft or mushy. Handle gently to avoid bruising.

Depending on the stage of ripeness, ripe Bartletts can hold in the refrigerator for three to four days.

Water content before drying: 83 percent.

Preparation: The dried peel tends to be tough and grainy, so gently wash pears and peel thinly. Remove the core with a spoon or pear corer and cut lengthwise into ½-inch slices. Pears may also be halved or quartered, although they do not dry evenly.

Hold in a solution of 1 teaspoon ascorbic acid per quart of water or a solution of ¼ teaspoon sodium bisulfite per quart of water until ready to pretreat. Do not prepare large quantities at a time because the soft texture will begin to deteriorate in the holding solution.

Pretreatment: Soak in a solution of 1 to 2 tablespoons sodium bisulfite per gallon of water for five to fifteen minutes, depending on the thickness. Rinse in clear water and place on drying trays.

Or sulfur ½-inch slices for forty-five minutes to one hour. Sulfur halves or quarters for three to six hours, depending on the size. Pears do not readily absorb sulfur fumes, hence the longer sulfuring times.

Drying temperature: 130°F to 140°F (54°C to 60°C) until dry.

Dryness test: Leathery and pliable with no pockets of moisture.

How to use: Dried pears are one of the great luxuries of life. Just eat them as is. They can be added to almost any baked good and granola and are delightful in salads.

Additional information: More information and recipes are available from:

California Pear Advisory Board
1521 I Street
Sacramento, CA 95814
Phone: 916-441-0432
Fax: 916-446-1063
Email: info@calpear.com
Website: www.calpear.com

PEARS (ASIAN)

The Asian pear is juicy like a pear and crisp like an apple. It is a true pear and not a hybrid of an apple and pear. Asian pears must be carefully handled to minimize bruising and brown marks. California produces about 80 percent of the Asian pears grown in the United States.

Asian pears are a good source of the B-complex vitamins and also contain vitamin C and a small amount of phosphorus and iodine.

Quality when dried: Excellent.

Varieties best for drying: There are three types of Asian pears and all are suitable for drying:

- Round or flat fruit with green to yellow skin
- Round or flat fruit with bronze-colored skin or a light bronze-russet color
- Pear-shaped with green or russet skin

Selection: Asian pears are picked from the tree before they fully ripen and are allowed to ripen in storage. Cold retards ripening and heat speeds it.

Skin color is a fairly reliable guide to ripeness. They are usually sold ripe and ready to eat. Green-skinned varieties are at their best for eating when they turn yellow-green in color.

Storage before drying: Ripen for two to three days in a dark place at room temperature, between 65°F to 75°F (18°C to 24°C). When ready for drying, the pears should be firm and not soft or mushy. Handle gently to avoid bruising. Depending on the stage of ripeness, ripe Asian pears can hold in the refrigerator for almost a week.

Water content before drying: 81 percent.

Preparation: Wash and remove skin. It tends to be tough when dried. Core and slice crosswise into ½-inch thick circles. You can also leave the core in, although it tends to toughen when it dries.

Pretreatment: Soak in a solution of 1 to 2 tablespoons sodium bisulfite per gallon of water for five to fifteen minutes, depending on the thickness. Rinse in clear water.

Drying temperature: 130°F to 140°F (54°C to 60°C) until dry.

Dryness test: Leathery and pliable with no pockets of moisture. You can also dry them fairly crisp if you like them that way.

How to use: Eat as a candylike snack or use in recipes as you would dried pears.

PERSIMMONS

Persimmons are a most interesting fruit. In their underripe state, some varieties contain a strong mouth-puckering *astringent*. It goes away when the fruit is ripened.

The firm-ripe varieties (nonastringent) can be eaten or dried while still firm and behave much like an apple. They are edible and can be dried in their crisp firm state. However, they will have their best flavor if allowed to rest and soften slightly after harvest.

Persimmons are a very popular fruit in Japan and the Republic of Georgia (part of the former Soviet Union). In these countries, they are generally air dried whole. A firm string is wrapped around the stem end and they are looped together, each string holding ten to fifteen persimmons. They are hung under the eaves of houses and air dried over a period of four to six weeks. They turn brown and then white as the sweating sugar crystallizes on the surface of the fruit.

Persimmons are second only to dates in the amount of natural sugar they contain.

Persimmons are an excellent source of vitamin A. One persimmon has about ninety-five calories and will supply one-half of the daily requirement for vitamin A, one-fifth of the requirement for vitamin C. They are also a fair source of iron.

Quality when dried: Excellent.

Varieties best for drying: Fuyu or Hachiya are the two most common varieties available in the United States. Fuyu are *firm-ripe*, medium size, and oval shaped like a flattened apple. They range from pale orange to deep red-orange and are nonastringent when firm-ripe.

Hachiya are classified as a *soft-ripe* persimmon and generally are left on the tree until fully colored, although they are still quite firm when harvested. They have a high tannin content and are extremely astringent and unpalatable while immature. The tannin gradually disappears as the fruit matures.

Selection: Persimmons are round or egg shaped and two to four inches in diameter. They are usually yellowish or orange, but may be streaked with red. Some varieties are a bright orange-red when fully ripe.

Persimmons should be cut from the tree with handheld pruning shears, leaving the stem intact.

Astringent varieties, such as Hachiya, must be handled very carefully to avoid bruising. They will soften and develop an almost thick jellylike interior within a week to two weeks after harvesting. Jelly ripe is prime condition for drying. Hachiya varieties are also the best for fruit leather. Combined with orange juice, persimmon leather made from Hachiya varieties is irresistible.

Nonastringent persimmons, such as Fuyu, can be dried when they are crisp as an apple.

Storage before drying: Stored in a cool, dark place, firm-ripe persimmons will keep for two to four months. Before processing, ripen in a dark place at room temperature, between 65°F and 75°F (18°C to 24°C). When astringent varieties are ready for drying, the astringency will be totally gone and they will be soft to the touch.

Water content before drying: 79 percent.

Pretreatment: None.

Preparation: Wash carefully and remove the stem cap. The edible tomato like skins tend to be tough. Skins are best removed by blanching persimmons in boiling water for two to three minutes. Transfer immediately to cold water, as you would to peel a tomato. Slip off the skins when the fruit is cool enough to touch. You can also peel firm persimmons with a sharp knife or apple peeler, although it takes a lot longer than blanching.

Using a serrated knife, slice the peeled persimmons into ½- to ¾-inch rounds. In seeded varieties, gently remove the seeds with your hands.

Drying temperature: 130°F to 140°F (54°C to 60°C) until dry.

Dryness test: Dried persimmons are light to medium brown. They should be tender and pliable but not sticky.

How to use: Dried persimmons may be eaten as a snack, made into fruit rolls, or used in sweet breads or cookies.

PINEAPPLES

Because of the high acid content and the enzyme bromelain, large quantities of fresh or dried pineapple eaten at one time may give some people canker sores. If you plan to dry more than two to three pineapples at one time, wear rubber gloves during preparation to protect your hands from the acid.

Most commercially dried pineapple comes from Taiwan, Thailand, or the Philippines and is highly sugared. When it is dried, it is soaked in a sugar syrup solution for up to three weeks. Each day the sugar content is increased. About 60 percent of the water is replaced with sugar.

When you dry pineapple at home, you don't need to have the added sugar. Fully ripened pineapples are very naturally sweet and the sugar concentrates when the water is removed.

Pineapple is a good source of vitamin C and fiber. It is also a fair source of thiamine. Two ½-inch-thick slices of fresh pineapple contain about sixty calories.

Quality when dried: Excellent.

Selection: Dry only fully ripe pineapples with a yellowish-brown shell. They should be heavy and symmetrical. Pineapples may be harvested when partly green, and although the color changes during transportation, pineapples will not actually ripen after they are picked. The natural sugar does not increase after picking.

Large pineapples are a better buy for drying than small ones. Fresh, deep crown leaves indicate freshness. Smelling the bottom of the pineapple is a good indicator of how sweet it is or if it is overripe and has begun to ferment. No smell means poor taste. A full, rich pineapple smell usually indicates a properly ripened, flavorful pineapple.

Overripe pineapples may be slightly decayed at the base and the sides may have dark, soft, watery spots.

Water content before drying: 86 percent.

Storage before drying: Store fully ripe pineapples in the refrigerator at 35°F to 40°F (2°C to 4°C) to maintain the highest quality. They can remain at room temperature for one to two days when ripe.

Preparation: Wash, and remove the top and bottom. Remove the rough outside peel by slicing vertically from the top to the bottom. Cut out the eyes by making diagonal cuts around the pineapple. If you want to dry in circles, cut crosswise into ½-inch slices. If you want to dry in spears, slice lengthwise and remove the small core. Cut lengthwise into ½-inch spears. You can also cut crosswise into ½-inch slices without removing the core. When dry, the core will raise and be a little tough, but it is still quite edible.

Drying temperature: 130°F to 140°F (54°C to 60°C) until dry.

Dryness test: Leathery, but not sticky.

How to use: Dried pineapple is best as a snack or in trail mix. It can be added to any baked good. Do not use dried pineapple in gelatin because the enzyme will prevent the gelatin from setting.

PLUMS

Early settlers brought the European plum to the United States. All prunes are plums, but not all plums are prunes. Plums with cling pits are less desirable for drying, because the pits are more difficult to remove than "prune plums." Most varieties of plums will ferment if dried with pits in. California produces more than 90 percent of the nation's plums. Plums are high in vitamin C.

Quality when dried: Good.

Varieties best for drying: There are more than a dozen varieties of plums, most of which can be dried satisfactorily. They may be as small as a cherry or as large as a small peach and are red, blue, purple, green, or yellow. Prune plums (see opposite page) are grown especially for drying because they are richest in sugar and solids.

Selection: Select fully mature, fresh, sweet fruit, free from soft spots and blemishes. Look for a slight "give" when squeezed and a fragrant plum aroma. Plums come in a large range of colors that vary by variety, so a good smell and slightly soft texture are better indicators of ripeness than color.

Storage before drying: Ripen plums by placing them in a paper bag. Fold the top over loosely and keep it at room temperature for one to three days. Never use a plastic bag; it may cause decay and can produce off flavors. Ripe plums may be stored in the refrigerator at 35°F to 40°F (2°C to 4°C) for one to three days.

Water content before drying: Between 80 and 90 percent, depending on the variety.

Drying temperature: 130°F to 140°F (54°C to 60°C) until dry.

Dryness test: Pliable and leathery.

How to use: Dried plums are excellent as a snack, although the skins are slightly tough. Use them in cookies, muffins, breads, cakes, granola, and puddings.

PRUNE PLUMS

Prune plums are characterized by their sweetness and pronounced flavor. They are used primarily for drying, but can also be canned, frozen, and made into jams and jellies.

They are one of the few fruits allowed to fully ripen on the tree before they are picked for drying. California is the world's largest producer of prunes, supplying 70 percent of the world's supply and 99 percent of the prunes sold in the United States.

Three pounds of fresh fruit make one pound of dried prunes. Prunes are an excellent source of fiber, antioxidants, and iron and contain potassium, calcium, phosphorus, vitamin A, thiamine, riboflavin, and niacin. They supply the soft bulk necessary for good elimination and are very high in natural sugar.

Quality when dried: Excellent.

Varieties best for drying: High-quality prune plums should be sweet with a good flavor, be medium to large in size, and have a fine texture and smooth small pits. The Prune d'Agen makes up to 99 percent of the commercial production of California prunes. Other good varieties for drying include Imperial, Robe de Sergeant, Sugar, Burton, Brooks, and Italian.

Selection: Prune plums should fully ripen on the tree before being picked to ensure the highest natural sugar content. Pick only the plums that come off very easily. They should be slightly soft but not mushy, very sweet, and have a lustrous color.

Storage before drying: Before processing, store prune plums in the refrigerator at 35°F to 40°F (2°C to 4°C) to maintain the highest quality.

Water content before drying: 79 percent.

Preparation: Wash well to remove dirt or insect larvae. Halve, remove stone, and flatten by pushing in the cupped side with your thumbs. This will greatly reduce drying time by increasing the drying surface. Dry skin-side down to keep the juice in the prune and keep it from dripping to the floor of your dehydrator. Prunes may be dried whole, but the drying time will be about four times longer. To dry whole, dip in boiling water to crack or *check* the skins. This hastens drying time. Prunes dried whole tend to drip more during drying.

Pretreatment: None.

Drying temperature: 130°F to 140°F (54°C to 60°C) until dry. Expect them to take at least eighteen to twenty-four hours or more to dry.

Dryness test: Leathery and pliable with no pockets of moisture. Because no preservatives are added to inhibit mold growth, the moisture content should be about 18 percent to store satisfactorily. If it is higher, the prunes will mold during storage at room temperature. If you like prunes that are quite soft, store them in the freezer to prevent molding.

How to use: Dried prunes are excellent snacks. To plump, steam for two to three minutes or soak in fruit juice. To stew, simmer for a few minutes, season with allspice, cloves, cinnamon, lemon, nutmeg, orange, sherry, or vanilla. Prunes can be used in cookies, muffins, brownies, breads, coffee cakes, strudels, and pies. They are delicious in candies, salads, puddings, stuffing, gelatin desserts, and meat dishes.

See Use Dried Fruits to Reduce Fat in Your Recipes (page 31) for ideas on cutting fats in baking recipes with prune puree.

Additional information: More information and recipes are available from:

California Dried Plum Board
P.O. Box 348180
Sacramento, CA 95834
Phone: 916-565-6232
Fax: 916-565-6237
Email: pconine@cdpb.org
Website: www.californiadriedplums.org

RHUBARB

Rhubarb is technically a vegetable, but it is usually served in desserts as a fruit and is rarely eaten raw because it is so tart. Its unique taste makes it a favorite in pies and desserts and it dries quite well.

It originated in Asia more than two thousand years ago and was initially cultivated for its medicinal qualities. In the eighteenth century, rhubarb was grown for culinary purposes in Britain and America.

Rhubarb is rich in vitamin C and fiber. One cup of fresh rhubarb contains about twenty-six calories.

The leaves of rhubarb contain poisonous oxalic acid salts and should not be eaten. Oxalic acid salts cause the tongue and throat to swell, preventing breathing.

Quality when dried: Good.

Varieties best for drying: The bright-red sweeter varieties dry best. There are also speckled pink varieties with good flavor. Green varieties can also be dried.

Selection: Rhubarb stalks should be *pulled* (not cut) soon after they reach full size and should be firm, straight, crisp, glossy, and brightly colored.

To harvest, remove the larger outside stalks, pulling them firmly from the base. Leave at least one-third of the inner plant stalk intact, as rhubarb is a perennial plant and will continue to produce for five to eight years.

Storage before drying: Wrap in paper towels, then in plastic bags. Store in the refrigerator at 35°F to 40°F (2°C to 4°C), to maintain the highest quality.

Water content before drying: 95 percent.

Preparation: Do not trim or cut the stalks until you are ready to dry them. Wash, trim and discard leaves, and trim the ends. Cut into 1-inch cubes. Optional: To decrease acidity and the amount of sugar needed to sweeten, pour boiling water over the pieces and let stand for three to five minutes. Drain before placing on the drying trays.

Drying temperature: 130°F to 140°F (54°C to 60°C) until dry.

Dryness test: Tough to crisp.

How to use: Rhubarb is incredibly versatile and may be combined with strawberries or apples in pies or used as a filling for strudels, tarts, and other baked goods. It can be made into delightful jams, pickles, conserves, and sauces.

STRAWBERRIES

The average strawberry has 200 tiny black seeds, but they don't interfere with the delicious taste of a dried strawberry and you don't really notice them in strawberry leather.

Strawberries are nutritionally power packed, low in fat and calories, and naturally high in fiber, vitamin C, potassium, and antioxidants. Eight medium-size strawberries have only forty-five calories.

California grows 88 percent of America's strawberries and most varieties dry well.

Quality when dried: Excellent.

Varieties best for drying: Sweeter varieties, which have a full red color and firm texture, dry best. The softer varieties are better in leather.

Selection: Choose firm, ripe, red berries with a solid color. They should be picked when fully ripe. They will not develop flavor and natural sugar if picked when slightly green and will not continue to ripen off the vine. Do not remove the stems until you are ready to process them.

Water content before drying: 90 percent.

Storage before drying: Cover strawberries with a cloth and store in the refrigerator at 35°F to 40°F (2°C to 4°C) to maintain the highest quality.

Preparation: Gently wash strawberries in a colander under cold running water, a pint at a time. Remove the cap and cut in half lengthwise.

They are best dried on plastic mesh screens, which are placed on top of the drying racks. Dry skin-side down to keep them from sticking to the

---

HOW MUCH DOES YOUR DRIED FRUIT COST?

Determine the cost of electricity per kilowatt-hour in your area. Your utility or monthly electric bill can give you this information. The following formula will give you the cost per pound of dried fruit.

$$\frac{\text{Cost per kWh} \times \text{Hours to dry}}{\text{Weight of dried fruit}} + \frac{\text{Cost of fresh fruit}}{\text{Weight of dried fruit}} = \text{cost per pound of dried fruit}$$

For example, if you can load ten pounds of apples (at \$.39 per pound) in your dryer and it takes five hours to get two pounds of dried apples, at \$.075 per kWh (cost in the Northwest), the cost would be:

$$\frac{.075 \times 5}{2} + \frac{\$3.90}{2} = 2.14 \text{ per pound of dried apples}$$

Dried fruits cost a lot more in the supermarket because the price includes the cost of the fruit, drying, packaging, distribution costs, advertising, and the retailer's markup.

trays. Smaller berries may be dried whole. If berries are too thin, they will stick to the drying trays.

Pretreatment: None.

Drying temperature: 130°F to 140°F (54°C to 60°C) until dry.

Dryness test: Strawberries should be pliable and leathery, with no pockets of moisture.

How to use: Dried strawberries are a great snack. They may be sprinkled on dry or cooked cereals, combined with granola, or used in ice cream, milk shakes, or yogurt. Do not rehydrate because they will lose their firm texture.

Additional information: More information and recipes are available from:

California Strawberry Commission
P.O. Box 269
Watsonville, CA 95077
Phone: 831-724-1301
Fax: 831-724-5973
Email: info@calstrawberry.com
Website: www.calstrawberry.com

HOW TO DIP DRIED FRUITS IN CHOCOLATE

Two different types of chocolate are used for dipping: *real chocolate* or *confectioner's coating*. Confectioner's coating does not have cocoa butter; it is replaced with vegetable oil. It looks like real chocolate and can be molded without tempering.

If you want the taste, flavor, and texture of real chocolate, it must be *tempered* by cooling it after it is heated.

Tips for Perfect Chocolate Dipping

- Prepare a baking sheet by covering it with waxed paper.

- Make sure dried fruits are at room temperature prior to dipping.

- Place chocolate to be melted in a double boiler or a metal bowl placed in very warm water over a shallow saucepan. Do not boil the water.

- Take care to keep water out of chocolate. Even one drop of water will ruin an entire batch of chocolate.

- Stir mixture constantly with a rubber spatula until chocolate is melted and the mixture is smooth, about twenty minutes. Do not rush the melting process.

- If necessary, replace the water with more very warm water.

- Remove the chocolate from the water bath and continue stirring until the chocolate cools slightly, two to three minutes. You can also add more grated or chopped chocolate to cool it.

Facts to Know about Dipping Chocolates

- You can use whatever type of chocolate you want, but the better the chocolate, the better the end result.

- Do not dip chocolate on humid days.

- Chop chocolate into small pieces for smooth and even melting.

- Some brands of dipping chocolate can be melted in the microwave. Check package directions.

- Avoid all types of moisture when melting chocolate. Steam or drops of water causes chocolate to *seize* or become very firm, crumbly, and grainy. If this occurs, it may be corrected by stirring in 1 teaspoon shortening for each 2 ounces of melted chocolate.

- If chocolate is melted at too high a temperature, it will become crumbly and grainy.

- Real chocolate should be *tempered*. Tempering forms the hard candylike chocolate shell that stays shiny. If it is not tempered, when the chocolate cools, the exterior may *bloom*—meaning the cocoa in the chocolate separates—turning the shiny dark chocolate to a dusty brown.

- *Tempering* involves melting the chocolate, cooling it slightly, and then reheating it as needed during the dipping process.

- Store chocolate tightly wrapped in a cool, dry place. Do not refrigerate.

Chocolate-Covered Dried Fruits

These are for true chocolate lovers.

    16 ounces dipping chocolate, milk chocolate,
        dark, white, or yogurt dip, chopped into small
        pieces
    30 pieces dried fruit

Place two-thirds of the chocolate in the double boiler over very warm water, 100°F to 110°F (38°C to 43°C). Melt the chocolate until it is smooth. Remove the top of the double boiler containing the melted chocolate and place it on a towel on the counter. Beat in the remaining one-third of the chocolate, which slightly cools the chocolate. The mixture should be smooth and glossy. Hold at that temperature by moving the container on and off the hot water while you are dipping.

Using a fondue fork, set a piece of dried fruit firmly on the tines. Dip into the melted chocolate. Gently tap the fork against the side of the bowl to remove excess chocolate. Invert the chocolate-covered fruit onto waxed paper and pull off the fork with another fork. You can use your fingers, but it's a lot messier.

Surprise Dried Fruit Inside of Molded Chocolate

Fill chocolate molds about halfway with properly melted chocolate. Add a piece of dried fruit to each mold when it is slightly hardened.

Chocolate-Dried Fruit "Still Life"

Fill a small paper muffin cup with about ⅜ inch of melted chocolate. Arrange a selection of small dried fruits into the chocolate so that they are half submerged. When the chocolate solidifies, remove the paper cup. You'll have a dried fruit *still life* in a pool of chocolate.

FRUIT LEATHER ROLLS

Fruit rolls (also called fruit leathers) are chewy, taffylike fruit pieces or rolls made from pureed fruit that has been dried. It gets the name *leather* because the dried pureed fruit is shiny and has the texture of leather. To make leather, fresh, cooked, canned, or frozen fruit is pureed into a smooth thick liquid and then poured onto a flat surface. As the puree dries, it takes on a translucent leather-like appearance and texture. When dry, fruit leather can be pulled off the drying surface and still hold its shape.

Fruit leathers are a delicious snack, perfect for lunch boxes during the winter when fresh fruit is expensive or unavailable. Cut small pieces of fruit rolls and add to cereals, puddings, and desserts for a fresh fruit flavor.

No one knows where the idea for fruit leather originated. It has been made for several hundred years by the people of Hunza, a small state in the Himalayan Mountains in northwest Pakistan. Apricots are one of the most important foods to the long-living Hunzakuts, who use primitive methods to make them into leather. They first pound the apricot pulp until it is smooth and then spread it on smooth, flat surfaces to dry in the sun.

Fruit rolls and dried fruit snacks are one of the most popular supermarket commodities and you'll find a variety of brands and flavors. They're expensive, often costing eight to ten dollars a pound, with attractive, colorful, kid-friendly packaging. Making them at home will save money and you can also control what goes into them. They really don't need the dyes, preservatives, and added sugar you will find in the commercial ones. They are fun to make and a great complement to the fruits you dry. Save the less than perfect pieces of fruit for your leathers.

FRUITS THAT CAN BE MADE INTO LEATHERS

Most fruits make good leathers. Some are better when combined with another fruit because they don't have enough pectin to make stable leather or they may be too watery. See Fruit Leather at a Glance (page 62) for guidelines and some ideas for combinations.

Fresh Fruits

- Use fresh fruits in season. Fruit leather is ideal for using the culls and slightly bruised or overripe fruit unsuitable for canning or drying.

- Cut away any bruised or spoiled portions, then puree.

- Citrus fruits should only be used in combination with other fruits because they are mostly liquid and have little pulp.

Frozen Fruits

- Thaw frozen fruits and puree and follow directions for leather.

- You can also puree some of the fruit in the blender, cook if necessary, and freeze it in airtight containers. When you aren't pressed for time and your dryer isn't full, thaw the puree and dry as you would fresh puree. Frozen fruits frequently have a better texture when combined with canned applesauce. Freezing tends to make them watery.

Cooked Fruits

- Some fruits such as apples may be better when cooked first.

- Steaming is an ideal way to cook fruit, because it doesn't require adding water.

- You can also cook fruits in juice to add extra flavor.

Canned Fruits

- You can make fruit leather from fruit that has been home or commercially canned. Drain the syrup, reserving it, and puree the fruit in the blender.

- Add back some of the syrup to get just the right consistency for leather.

- For a fresher flavor, add 1 tablespoon fresh lemon juice per quart of puree or blend the pureed canned fruit with a puree of fresh fruit such as pineapple or applesauce.

HOW TO MAKE FRUIT LEATHER

Prepare your trays. Line a drying tray with a solid plastic sheet that comes with your dehydrator. You can also use Mylar or food-grade 4mil plastic. Kitchen plastic wrap is too fragile and tends to tear and blow over the drying fruit leather.

Do not use waxed paper or aluminum foil. The leather tends to stick and you may have to eat the wrapping with the leather. Lightly coat the plastic solid sheets with a nonstick vegetable spray. Teflon-coated baking sheets also work well and generally do not need the nonstick vegetable spray. Vegetable oil tends to cause the leathers to stick.

Wash, peel, or take out the seeds. Wash and prepare the fruit according to the directions in Fruit Leather at a Glance (page 62).

When making leather from seeded fruits such as raspberries, blackberries, loganberries, marionberries, or boysenberries, the seeds make the leather unpalatable when dried. A centrifugal juicer or juice extractor can work very well to puree the pulp and eject or remove the seeds. You can also put the puree through a colander or mesh strainer with small holes. These berries tend to be very low in pectin and make better leathers when combined with applesauce.

Cut or halve the fruit and put it in the blender.

Puree in the blender. Puree the fruit in the blender until it is very smooth. You will need about 2½ cups of puree to make an 18 × 14-inch tray of leather ¼-inch thick. In some blenders, you may have to add a small amount of water or fruit juice to start the blending process. Add as little water or juice as possible.

Pretreat the puree in fruits that oxidize. Apples, apricots, cherries, pears, peaches, nectarines, and strawberries tend to oxidize when pureed for fruit rolls. A tiny pinch of sodium bisulfite in a blender full of puree will slow the oxidation and darkening of the leathers. You can also heat fruit purees to prevent darkening and cool them before drying or combining with other purees or flavorings. Heating puree tends to change the flavor of the leather.

Combine different kinds of fruits. Puree each individual fruit alone. Then combine two or more purees together, adding sweetening, spices, or flavorings. Taste the puree to decide on the right balance. Remember the flavor will concentrate when it dries.

Sweet enough? Fruit that is fully ripe produces the best-flavored leather and usually needs no sweetening. If the puree is too tart, add 1 tablespoon light corn syrup or honey for each quart of puree. Repeat until puree is sweet to the taste, remembering that it will concentrate as it dries. The honey flavor may be too strong for some fruits. Granulated sugar added to fruit puree may crystallize during storage, resulting in brittle leather. Brown sugar tends to add a more pronounced flavor. You may also use artificial sweeteners.

Add spices or flavorings. Spices or flavorings will concentrate when dried, so use them sparingly. Experiment with spice and fruit combinations. Add one spice or flavoring at a time in small amounts and taste to determine if you like it.

Different spices can totally change the flavor of your leather. Start with just a pinch of spice or ¼ teaspoon per quart of puree. Taste the puree before adding more. You should be able to tell that something has been added, but not what. If the flavor shouts at you, you have used too much. Try these flavors:

- Allspice
- Cinnamon
- Cloves
- Coriander

- Ginger
- Mace
- Mint
- Nutmeg
- Pumpkin pie spice

Extracts, fresh juices, and citrus peels add an extra zip to leathers. Extracts are more concentrated than fresh juices, so begin with ¼ to ½ teaspoon per quart of puree. To use fresh citrus juice, begin with 1 tablespoon per quart of puree.

If you want to use grated lemon, lime, or orange peel, try 1 teaspoon per quart of puree. Just use the thin outer covering since the pithy white part tends to be bitter.

- Almond extract
- Lemon extract, juice, or peel
- Lime juice or peel
- Maple flavoring
- Orange extract juice or peel
- Peppermint extract
- Root beer concentrate
- Vanilla extract

Prepare drying trays. Spray lightly with non-stick cooking spray. Vegetable oils do not work well and may cause the leathers to stick to the tray.

Try some dried fruits in your leathers. To add some extra texture and variety to your fruit rolls, try adding tiny bits of previously dried fruits.

- Chunky Cherry: Add pieces of dried cherries to apple, apricot, or grape leather.
- Berry Boysenberry: Add pieces of dried strawberries to an apple-boysenberry combination.
- Great Grape: Add raisins to any fruit leather or fruit combination.
- Marvelous Mango: Add slivers of dried mango to a tropical mix with any combination of apples, pears, pineapple juice, orange juice, passion fruit, grapefruit, or lemon.
- Scrumptious Strawberry: Add tiny bits of dried apple slices to strawberry leather.
- Amazing Apricot: Add small chunks of dried apricots to an apple, apricot, and lemon combination.

Add a garnish. Sprinkle garnishes on fruit leather before drying or while the leather is still quite moist so the garnish will stick. You can also mix some of the garnishes with the puree before pouring it out to dry; just don't blend it with your blender.

You can use a garnish alone or combine two or more for a special flavor blend.

- Coconut, shredded or flaked
- Dates, chopped
- Dried fruit, finely chopped
- Granola
- Miniature marshmallows
- Nuts, finely chopped
- Raisins, finely chopped
- Poppy seeds
- Sesame seeds
- Sunflower seeds, plain or honey roasted

Pour the puree onto the drying tray. Pour the puree onto the prepared drying tray. Slightly tilt the tray to spread the puree evenly. Commercial fruit leather sheets made by Nesco/American Harvest have a ¼-inch lip that keeps the leather from running over the edge. Puree should generally be about ¼-inch thick across the entire surface of the drying tray. Spread the puree to the edges of the tray with a rubber spatula. Leave at least a 1-inch border on flat trays to allow for spreading during drying.

The **Nesco/American Harvest Gardenmaster** is designed with the serious food preserver in mind. It is expandable to thirty trays. Between twenty and thirty trays, it loses a little efficiency, but still dries extremely well. It operates on 1,000 watts of power and has a quiet 2,400 RPM motor with a specially designed 4½-inch fan. The adjustable 90°F to 150°F (30°C to 66°C) thermostat gives the flexibility to dry a variety of foods. It dries four times faster than dryers without a fan or motor.

If you want to dry a lot of food at once, two of the Nesco/American Harvest Gardenmasters can work very efficiently together. Fill both dryers with as many trays as you have. After about four to six hours, the volume of the dried foods is decreased by about 60 to 70 percent. Transfer the partially dried produce on both dehydrators to one dehydrator and begin a new batch on the second one. This versatile feature of being able to transfer trays from one dryer to the next makes your drying much more energy efficient.

Make some fun-shaped leathers. If you want to make shaped leathers, use cookie cutters that are open at the top and the bottom. Place the cookie cutter on the top of the prepared fruit-roll sheet. Pour puree into the inside of the cookie cutter until it is about ¼-inch thick. Gently lift the cookie cutter straight up. The puree will spread a little during drying, but will generally maintain the shape of the cookie cutter. It is helpful if the puree is a little on the thick side. You can also leave the cookie cutter in place for the first part of drying, adding additional puree to the inside until you reach the desired thickness.

Make some crazy designs with your leather. Prepare puree separately for two or three different colored fruits. Make interesting designs as you pour the purees onto your drying tray. Use a poultry baster to add each new flavor to keep very distinct lines. A bull's-eye with concentric circles or different colors is very easy to do. Make a smiley face or a clown. Stripes and polka dots are fun.

Try some molded fun fruits snacks. These molded dried fruits that you can make yourself are similar to the fruit snacks that you find in the supermarket. Purchase chocolate molds that are made out of strong plastic. They are available online or from specialty cookware shops.

Fill each cavity to the top with fruit puree and tap the filled mold on the counter to settle the fruit puree and release any air bubbles. A poultry baster makes filling very easy. Place the filled mold on drying trays. When dry to the touch, add more puree. It generally takes three to four fillings to produce a firm piece of molded fruit.

It's best to make these when your dryer is already in use with other fruits. Add a new layer to the mold each time you begin a new batch of fruits.

To release the fun fruits, reverse the mold over a flat surface and tap it firmly. The molded pieces of fruit should just fall out. If they don't immediately fall out, chill for a few minutes in the refrigerator or freezer.

The molds should never be washed. Soap scum can remain on the molds, which will give a taste to the fruit snack or molded chocolate. Use a soft, dry cloth to wipe out the cavities after each use.

Dry at the right temperature. Dry your fruit rolls at 130°F to 140°F (54°C to 60°C) until dry. If they're dried too slowly, they have more of a tendency to stick. If dried at too hot a temperature, they'll tend to be brittle.

Is it dry? With clean hands, touch the top of the leather in several different places. It should be translucent, feel like leather, and not be soft to the touch. When the leather is sufficiently dried, you will be able to pull it up, beginning at the edge of the tray. If it sticks in the center and some of the puree underneath is still moist, return it to the dehydrator for another hour or so.

Fruit leather dried in a dehydrator is usually dry in four to eight hours, depending on the thickness, the consistency of the puree, the type of fruit, the efficiency and temperature of your dehydrator, and the outdoor humidity. Sun-dried leather may take one to two days, depending on the temperature, humidity, and breeze. Oven drying may take up to eighteen hours.

Oops! It's overdried! You were busy and forgot to check your fruit leather and it is now brittle and cracks when you try to peel it off. Don't despair! Add a layer of prepared applesauce to the top of your overdried leather and return it to the dryer. The top layer will rehydrate the overdried bottom layer, resulting in two-toned fruit leather. Just watch it more carefully during the second drying.

Your other choice is to chip off the brittle pieces and use them as leather chips for toppings and flavorings on cereals and in puddings. Add them to yogurt, ice cream, milk shakes, and baby cereal.

Remove leather from the trays. Remove the leather from the tray while it is still warm and roll it up. Cooled fruit leather does not roll as easily and may crack. Roll into long rolls and cut with kitchen scissors. Then cut the long rolls into shorter pieces. Lunch box–size rolls are about four to six inches long. You can also cut rolls into bite-size pieces.

Garnished leather is more difficult to roll. Cut it into bite-size pieces using kitchen scissors.

You can dry leather in the sun. Fruit leather can be sun dried successfully in one day if the sun is hot and the humidity is low. The only problem is protecting the leather from insects. They usually find it as delicious as we do! Fruit leathers do not have the protection of sulfuring as fruits do to keep away the bugs.

Nonstick baking sheets are ideal for sun drying leather since they usually do not need to be sprayed with a nonstick vegetable spray. These types of trays need to be seasoned before use by rubbing generously with vegetable oil, then wiping away the excess with a paper towel.

Place a small cup or glass outside the baking sheet on each corner to elevate the protective cheesecloth. Secure cheesecloth or nylon netting over the leather and stretch it under the baking sheet to protect it without touching it. Be sure the screening is anchored at the corners. If it blows into the drying leather, you'll have a very sticky mess.

If not completely dry, some of the fruit puree will stick to the baking sheet. Occasionally the top surface may be dry to the touch, but when you lift it up, some puree will stick to the baking sheet. As soon as it is dry enough to peel it from the baking sheet, flip the leather over and dry the bottom until it is no longer sticky.

Store your fruit leather. For one- to two-week short-term storage, cut the fruit leather rolls into bite-size pieces and shake them in a container with powdered sugar or cornstarch, or a combination. Store them in an airtight container in a cool, dry place.

To store in glass canning jars, cut the rolls into four- or five-inch pieces, position them upright inside of a wide-mouth one-pint canning jar. Vacuum seal if you have a home vacuum-packaging machine, such as the FoodSaver. If not, secure the top with a lid and screw band. If you want the individual rolls in plastic wrap, wrap them before putting them in a jar. Do not roll the plastic wrap inside with the fruit rolls, as the leathers will stick to the wrap.

For storage up to a year, your fruit rolls will keep the highest quality when stored in the refrigerator or freezer. Leathers containing nuts or co-

conut should always be stored in the freezer and eaten within two to three months.

You can also fill fruit leathers. Filled leathers are festive treats and are more nutritious than candy. Unroll leathers that have already been dried and spread them with fillings. Then roll again, jelly-roll fashion, and cut the rolls into bite-size pieces with a very sharp knife or kitchen scissors.

Filled leathers can't be stored, so eat them right away. Try the following fillings:

- Chocolate, melted
- Cream cheese, softened
- Process cheddar cheese spread
- Fruit fillings
- Fruit jam or preserves
- Marmalade
- Marshmallow cream
- Peanut butter, smooth or crunchy

Label so that you can remember what, how, and when. It is helpful to label fruit rolls clearly so you can decide what you like and don't like for next season. Label your containers clearly with a permanent marker or stick-on labels. Include the date, type and variety of fruit, and any spices, flavorings, or garnishes.

Use fruit rolls as snacks. Replace vending machine snacks with healthy fruit rolls at work and school. Keep them in your child's sport bag or backpack for a pick-me-up at after-school sporting events. Keep some in the car for an energy boost while you're driving. Fruit rolls are lightweight and are perfect for camping, hiking, and backpacking. With the goodness of homemade, they're ideal gifts for birthday party favors. Keep some in

---

CAUTION: DRYERS USING ONLY CONVECTION HEAT CAN'T BE USED FOR DRYING FRUIT ROLLS AND SOME OTHER FOODS

The stackable convection dryers do not work well for making fruit rolls because of the poor air circulation across each tray. Unless your dryer has a double-walled construction, which allows even airflow up the sides and across each tray, *you can't dry leathers in it.* When the air is blocked, as it is in a single-wall-constructed dryer, the leather will mold.

They're poor for drying fruits as well and should *never* be used for meats or fish because temperatures aren't high enough.

FRUIT LEATHER AT A GLANCE

FRUIT	PREPARATION	COMBINE WITH OTHER PUREES	SPICES OR FLAVORINGS AND SWEETENING
Apples	Wash and core. Puree with or without skins in blender in a small amount of water or juice. Or apples may be cooked, then pureed.	All fruits	Allspice, cinnamon, cloves, coriander, lemon, mint, nutmeg, orange, vanilla, white corn syrup, honey
Apricots	Wash and pit. Puree with skin in blender. To retain light color, heat to almost boiling, or add 1/16 teaspoon sodium bisulfite to 1 quart uncooked puree.	Apple, pineapple, plum	Allspice, cinnamon, cloves, coriander, lemon, nutmeg, orange, white corn syrup, honey, brown sugar
Bananas	Peel. Puree in blender.	Apple-berry, lemon-walnut, orange-pineapple	Cinnamon, cloves, coriander, lemon, nutmeg, orange, vanilla, white corn syrup, honey, brown sugar
Blackberries, loganberries, marionberries	Wash. Puree in blender. Sieve to remove most of seeds.	Combine with apples to improve texture.	Cinnamon, lemon, white corn syrup
Blueberries	Wash. Puree in blender.	Too bland alone; combine with apple or peach.	Cinnamon, coriander, lemon, white corn syrup
Cherries	Wash and remove stones. Puree in blender. Add 1/16 teaspoon sodium bisulfite to 1 quart uncooked puree or heat to almost boiling. Cool.	Apple, apple-pineapple banana, pineapple, raspberry, rhubarb	Almond extract, cinnamon, lemon, orange, white corn syrup
Cranberries	Wash. Puree in blender.	Apple, apple-date, apple-orange, apple-pear	Cinnamon, cloves, ginger, lemon, orange, white corn syrup, honey
Figs	Wash fruit and remove stems. Peel if desired.	Apple, apricot, peach	Lemon, orange, white corn syrup
Grapes	Wash. Puree in blender. Sieve to remove seeds. Cook to thicken. If using leftover pulp from grape juice, put through food mill to remove seeds and skins; add juice for desired consistency.	Apple, raspberry	Lemon, white corn syrup
Mangoes	Wash fruit and cut off ends. Peel and cut away from stone lengthwise, as close to the stone as possible without fibers.	Apple, apricot, peach, pineapple	Lemon, orange, white corn syrup, honey, cinnamon, nutmeg, cloves

FRUIT LEATHER AT A GLANCE

FRUIT	PREPARATION	COMBINE WITH OTHER PUREES	SPICES OR FLAVORINGS AND SWEETENING
Nectarines, peaches	Boil 2 minutes to remove skins. Halve fruits; remove stones. Puree in blender. To retain light color, add $\frac{1}{16}$ teaspoon sodium bisulfite to 1 quart uncooked puree, or heat to almost boiling.	Apple, blueberry, pineapple, plum, raspberry	Cinnamon, cloves, ginger, almond, nutmeg, white corn syrup, honey
Pears	Peel and core. Puree in blender. To retain light color, heat to almost boiling, or add $\frac{1}{16}$ teaspoon sodium bisulfite to 1 quart uncooked puree. Puree tends to be watery when not mixed with another puree.	Improved when combined with: apple, apple-cranberry, pineapple, rhubarb	Cinnamon, cloves, coriander, lemon, mace (dash only), nutmeg, orange, white corn syrup, honey
Persimmons	Wash fruit and blanch to remove peels easily. Peel. Cut to remove seeds.	Apple, apricot, orange, peach, pineapple	Lemon, orange, white corn syrup, honey
Pineapples	Remove outer skin, eyes, and core. Puree in blender.	Apple-orange, apricot, cherry, rhubarb-strawberry	Lemon, orange, white corn syrup
Plums	Wash fruit and remove stones. Puree in blender. Add $\frac{1}{16}$ teaspoon sodium bisulfite to 1 quart puree.	Apple, apricot, peach, pear	Cinnamon, coriander, lemon, orange, white corn syrup
Pumpkin	Cut into large pieces, peel, and remove seeds. Steam until soft. Puree in blender.	Apple	Cinnamon, ginger, nutmeg, pumpkin pie spice, white or dark corn syrup, honey
Raspberries	Wash. Put through juice extractor to remove seeds or puree in blender and sieve to remove seeds.	Apple	Lemon, mint, orange, white corn syrup
Rhubarb	Wash, cut into pieces, and steam until tender.	Improved when combined with cherry, raspberry, strawberry, strawberry-pineapple	Lemon, orange, white corn syrup
Strawberries	Wash. Puree in blender. Add $\frac{1}{16}$ teaspoon sodium bisulfite to retain color and flavor.	Apple, apple-rhubarb, peach, pineapple, rhubarb	Lemon, orange, white corn syrup

FRUIT LEATHER TROUBLESHOOTING TIPS

PROBLEM	CAUSE	PREVENTION OR SOLUTION
Puree is too thin.	Very juicy fruits.	Combine with thicker fruit puree.
	Too much water added during blending.	Slowly cook the puree over low heat to evaporate some of the water before drying.
Puree is too thick.	Type of fruit—apple or pumpkin.	Add fruit juice or water to thin to pouring consistency.
	Using leftover pulp from making juices or jellies—apple, apricot, cherry, grape, or plum.	Add fruit juice or water to thin to pouring consistency.
Insects are attracted to leather during sun drying.	Insects find fruit leather delicious!	Cover with cheesecloth or nylon net during drying, using blocks or spools to elevate. Be sure covering is secure and will not blow into the sticky leather.
Leather sticks to drying surface.	Drying surface is not suitable for drying leather. Waxed paper or foil does not work.	Lightly coat surface with nonstick vegetable spray.
	Puree is too thin.	Pour puree ¼ inch thick.
	Fruits low in natural pectin—black-berry, cranberry, loganberry, marionberry, raspberry—stick more than fruits higher in pectin.	Combine low-pectin fruits with fruits containing more pectin such as apple.
Leather is brittle around the edges and still sticky in the middle.	Puree was thicker in center.	Tilt drying surface before drying to distribute puree evenly or pour puree a little thicker around the edges.
	Uneven air flow in oven or dehydrator.	Rotate shelves more often. Sun dry if weather permits.
Leather becomes brittle during drying or storage.	Type of fruit—pear, pineapple, or rhubarb.	Combine with other fruits.
	Insufficient air circulation as in oven drying.	Rotate trays or sun dry.
	Too high heat; leather dried too quickly.	Check temperature during drying. It should not exceed 140°F (60°C).
	Overdrying.	Watch carefully near end of drying. Use brittle leather chips as dessert toppings, in baked goods.

FRUIT LEATHER TROUBLESHOOTING TIPS

PROBLEM	CAUSE	PREVENTION OR SOLUTION
Leather is grainy.	Peelings were left on fruit when pureed, especially pear.	Peel fruit for leather. Combine pears with other fruits such as apples.
Leather is too seedy.	Failure to sieve out enough seeds.	Sieve puree through strainer to remove as many seeds as possible before drying.
Leather turns excessively dark.	Enzymatic browning occurs in some fruits—apple, apricot, nectarine, peach, pear, and strawberry.	Add a pinch of sodium bisulfite to a quart of puree during blending or heat puree almost to boiling to retard browning.
	Improperly wrapped for storage—light, air, and moisture tend to darken fruit leather.	Wrap securely in plastic wrap, then store in moisture-proof containers in a dark place.
	Storage location is too warm; heat tends to darken.	Store in cool place or freezer.
Leather molds during storage.	Leather was insufficiently dried before packaging.	Be sure leather has no moist or sticky areas before packaging.
	Improperly packaged so moisture is absorbed by the leather.	Wrap securely in plastic wrap, then store in moisture-proof container.

your seventy-two-hour kit for emergencies. Be sure to rotate them every six months.

CAMPING AND TRAIL FOODS

Dried foods are ideal for backpacking and camping because they keep well without refrigeration and are low in volume and weight. Meat and fish jerky are high-protein snacks. Dried nuts and seeds are also high in protein, fat, and other nutrients, making them great for the trail. Dried fruits, fruit leathers, and vegetable leathers will appeal to a camper's sweet tooth and are quick energy foods.

If you start with supermarket convenience foods and dress them up with home-dried foods, you will add flavor and nutritive value to outdoor meals and save quite a bit of money.

Try a ready-to-cook soup base with your own dried vegetables. Add dried meats and vegetables to packaged rice or potato dishes. For dessert, stir dried fruits into prepared puddings.

Dried foods are easy to carry and use if you package them in individual plastic bags. Group the small bags in larger bags according to the meals they will be used for. Then label the large bags: *Breakfast, Lunch, Dinner,* or *Trail Food* so the dried foods needed for each meal will be easily accessible in one bag.

Allow enough time to reconstitute dried foods. An hour or two before you plan to cook, add water to the fruits or vegetables in the plastic bags. To prevent leaks, place the bags in a second plastic bag. Let the food rehydrate while you set up camp and start the fire.

GLACÉED OR CANDIED FRUIT

Glacé is the French word for *glazed*, and refers to fruits that are preserved in sugar syrup. Glacé or candied fruit is made by removing 50 to 60 percent of the water in the fruit and replacing it with sugar. The fruit is then dried some more in a dehydrator. The process can take from four days to three weeks, depending on how sugared you want the fruit to be. These instructions are for a moderately sugared fruit. Glacé fruit has a much higher sugar concentration than natural fruit dried without this process.

See the section (pages 32 to 54) on individual fruits for proper selection and preparation. When you prepare apples, apricots, peaches, and pears, hold the cut pieces in a solution of 1 teaspoon ascorbic acid per quart of water to preserve their fresh color and texture until you're ready to begin the glacé process. Do not use sodium bisulfite as a holding solution.

FRUITS THAT GLACÉ WELL

- Apples
- Apricots
- Blueberries
- Cherries
- Citrus peel
- Cranberries
- Mangoes
- Papayas
- Peaches
- Persimmons (only Fuyu)
- Pears
- Pineapple
- Prune plums

PREPARING FRUIT FOR GLACÉ

Blueberries
Preparation: Wash blueberries and remove stems.

Cherries
Preparation: Wash cherries and remove stems and pits. Prick cherries several times with a pin to perforate the skin.

Cranberries
Preparation: Wash cranberries.

Persimmons (Only Fuyu)
Preparation: Wash, peel, and slice ⅜-inch thick. Remove seeds.

Prune Plums
Preparation: Wash, cut in half, and remove stone. Prick skin side several times with a pin to perforate the skin. Flatten by pushing in the cupped side with your thumbs.

How to Glacé Fruit

The following directions are for 1½ pounds of prepared fruit. To glacé citrus peel, use ¾ pound of peel and halve the remaining ingredients.

FIRST DAY

2 cups water

⅔ cup sugar

½ cup white corn syrup

1½ pounds prepared fruit

Combine all of the ingredients, except the fruit, in a large saucepan. Bring to a boil. Add the fruit. Heat the syrup-fruit mixture to 180°F (82°C) on a candy thermometer. Remove from the heat. Allow the mixture to cool. Cover and let it stand at room temperature for eighteen to twenty-four hours.

SECOND DAY

1¼ cups sugar

Carefully remove the fruit from the syrup with a slotted spoon. Add the sugar to the syrup in the saucepan. Bring to a boil. Remove from the heat. With a large metal spoon, skim the foam from the surface of the syrup and discard. Add the fruit to the hot syrup and heat the syrup-fruit mixture to 180°F (82°C) on a candy thermometer. Remove from the heat. Allow the mixture to cool. Cover and let it stand at room temperature for eighteen to twenty-four hours.

THIRD DAY

2 cups sugar

Repeat the process of the second day, adding the sugar to the remaining syrup after removing the fruit, then heating, and let stand.

FOURTH DAY

1 cup sugar

Repeat the process of the second day, adding the sugar to the remaining syrup after removing the fruit, then heating, and let stand.

After the final eighteen to twenty-four hour standing time, remove the fruit from the syrup. Place the fruit in a colander and rinse lightly with cold water. Transfer the fruit to drying trays and dry at 130°F to 140°F (54°C to 60°C) until the fruit is leathery and has no pockets of moisture. Drying time for glacé fruit will be one-fourth of the drying time for fresh fruit because so much of the water has been replaced by sugar.

Fruit-Flavored Pancake Syrup

The fruit-flavored syrup that is left from making glacé fruit is delicious on pancakes or waffles.

Bring the leftover syrup to a boil and boil about 1 minute. Remove from the heat and skim the foam from the surface of the syrup.

Pour the syrup into hot, sterilized canning jars. Fill the jars to within ¼ inch from the top and wipe the jar rims. Put sterilized lids and screw bands on top of the jars.

Process for 5 minutes in a boiling water bath canner. Remove and place the hot jars on toweling to cool. Keep for up to a year. After opening, store in the refrigerator.

VEGETABLES

Vegetables are the edible parts of plants. They can be grouped by the part of the plant we eat. In one group of vegetables we eat the *fruit of the plant*, such as cucumbers, eggplant, melons, peppers, squashes, and tomatoes. Some foods, such as tomatoes and cucumbers, are really fruits, but are eaten as vegetables.

Another category consists mainly of *leaves and stems* of plants. These include asparagus, cabbage, lettuce, rhubarb, spinach, and other leafy greens.

Another group contains *root* or *tuber* vegetables, such as beets, carrots, onions, parsnips, potatoes, rutabagas, and turnips.

When we eat beans, sweet corn, peas, and soybeans, we are eating *seeds*.

When drying, the fruit of the plant, the root or tuber portions, and the seeds dry and rehydrate better than stems and leaves. Exceptions are listed in the information on specific vegetables.

Vegetables are excellent sources of vitamins A and C, thiamine, and niacin. They also contain minerals such as calcium, phosphorus, and iron. Vegetables generally contain a lot of fiber, which aids the digestive process. Peas and beans are good sources of protein.

The only nutrients affected by drying are vitamins A and C. Depending on how carefully vegetables are dried and stored, their nutrient loss can be minimized.

YOU NEED TO KNOW

Drying is one of the *least practical* ways of preserving vegetables. The quality of most vegetables is excellent when frozen and marginal when canned or dried. If you have a freezer, it just makes more sense to freeze them because it's easier to freeze them and the quality is better. Frozen asparagus, cauliflower, and broccoli are far superior to dried ones. Other vegetables, such as carrots and potatoes, are available fresh at reasonable prices all year. I don't recommend drying these.

You'll find *instant* dried vegetables at the supermarket in a variety of products such as mixes, salad sprinkles, and instant soups. These *instant* vegetables have been *freeze-dried*, a different process than what you can do at home. Their quality is superior to home dried, and they rehydrate instantly because of the way in which they are processed.

Drying vegetables at home requires extra effort for a good-quality product that will be stable in storage and be tasty and tender when cooked.

Many dried vegetables that have been rehydrated and cooked are tougher than fresh or frozen ones. This can be caused by the physical characteristics of the specific vegetable, the maturity and quality of the fresh vegetable when it is processed, the pretreatment before drying, the method used to dry, or the storage time and temperature. The fresher the vegetable when it is processed and dried, the better it will taste when rehydrated and cooked.

VEGETABLES ARE BEST WHEN THEY'RE TENDER

Tenderness is usually influenced by the quality and freshness of the vegetable when it was dried. Green beans may be kept in the refrigerator for one or two days after picking and still taste quite fresh when cooked and eaten. If those same beans are refrigerated two or three days and then dried, they will be much less tender than beans dried the day they were picked.

- Harvest only fresh and tender mature vegetables.
- Don't store vegetables before drying.

- If you cannot process vegetables immediately after picking, refrigerate them.
- Do not wash vegetables until just before you are ready to process them. Water speeds up deterioration and nutrient loss.

Pretreat. Pretreat by steam or water blanching to soften vegetable tissues so that water can escape more readily during drying and reenter more easily during rehydration. Most vegetables are not edible if they are not blanched prior to drying.

Pay attention to drying time and temperature. Because vegetables are lower in sugar and acid than fruits, they must be dried under more controlled conditions than fruits to prevent spoilage. Drying time and temperature are critical to the safety and tenderness of dried vegetables. The longer the drying time, the less tender the dried vegetable.

Dry pieces of the same size together. Drying time is proportional to the thickness squared. If a ¼-inch dice dries in two hours, a ½-inch dice will take eight hours, or four times longer.

With a few exceptions (see Vegetables Recommended for Sun Drying, page 14), vegetables should not be sun dried because it takes too long and spoilage is likely.

Shelf life is short. Most vegetables will not keep in good condition for more than a few

DRYING FROZEN VEGETABLES

If you're in a hurry and need some dried vegetables for a camping or backpacking trip, buy some frozen vegetables. Since commercially frozen vegetables have already been blanched, they can be put directly on the trays to dry. You don't even have to thaw them first because they will thaw in the dryer in the first few minutes.

months, unless they are stored in the refrigerator or freezer. As a rule, use all dried vegetables within six months. Properly dried and packaged vegetables will not spoil, but will rapidly deteriorate in flavor and nutrition. Vacuum packaging will generally double the storage life of dried vegetables.

HOW TO DRY VEGETABLES

Sort and select the highest quality fresh vegetables. Most vegetables dry best when they're young and tender. If vegetables are immature, they tend to have weak or poor color and flavor. Overly mature vegetables are tough, woody, or fibrous.

WASH THEM GENTLY

Wash vegetables just before processing because water left on vegetables increases deterioration. Use cold water because it helps preserve freshness. Do not soak vegetables because vitamins and minerals dissolve in water and will be lost by soaking. If vegetables are covered with garden dirt, wash them under cool running water so the dirt doesn't resettle on the vegetable.

PREPARE VEGETABLES TO DRY

Peel, trim, core, cut, and slice or shred your vegetables. Peeling some vegetables is optional, but be aware that peels tend to be tough when dried. Remove any fibrous or woody portion and core when necessary. Cut away any decayed or spoiled spots because one spot can contaminate an entire batch of dried vegetables.

Prepare only as many vegetables as you can dry at one time. Keep pieces a uniform size so they will dry at the same rate.

PRETREAT VEGETABLES TO KEEP THEM TOP QUALITY

Vegetables deteriorate much more rapidly than fruits during storage because of continued enzyme action. Enzymes are chemicals in all fruits and vegetables that cause them to ripen. The higher sugar and acidity of fruits counteract this enzyme action. Pretreating vegetables by *blanching* decreases the chances of spoilage and increases the quality and storage life.

Blanching is heating in steam or boiling water before drying. Without blanching vegetables, enzymes will continue to react, resulting in tough, flavorless, light-colored vegetables that do not rehydrate well.

Blanching sets the color and shortens the drying and rehydration time by relaxing the tissue walls so moisture can escape or reenter more rapidly. It also kills organisms on the surface that may cause spoilage. Blanched vegetables take less time to cook than a similar fresh vegetable because they are already partially cooked.

In *steam blanching*, the vegetables are suspended above the boiling water in a colander or wire basket and heated only by the steam. In *water blanching*, the vegetables are placed in a wire basket and submerged in boiling water. Steam blanching is preferred because fewer water-soluble vitamins and minerals are lost.

If you plan to keep dried vegetables longer than a couple of months, some vegetables benefit from a small amount of sodium bisulfite added to the steaming water or some other type of pretreatment. See All About Vegetables (page 78) for specific information on each vegetable.

How Long to Blanch?

A general rule for blanching is that the vegetables should be heated all the way through, but should not be cooked enough to eat. They should still taste undercooked and feel firm. A great way to test is to actually take a bite from the steaming basket.

At higher altitudes, above 5,000 feet, increase *steam-blanching time* by about two minutes and *water-blanching time* by about a minute.

Slightly under-blanching is preferred because you can put the hot vegetables directly into a preheated dryer, assuming that they will continue to cook slightly just from the residual heat within the vegetable.

Serious under-blanching may cause deterioration in storage, poor rehydration, or bad color. When vegetables are over-blanched, they lose color, flavor, and nutrients and have poor texture when rehydrated. It's tricky to blanch just the right amount of time and takes constant watching so you get it just right.

Steam blanching. A steamer is perfect for steam blanching. It is like a double boiler, except the upper pan is perforated, which lets the steam circulate freely without water touching the vegetables. It needs a tight-fitting lid to prevent steam from escaping. If you don't own a steamer, use a steaming basket, which sits above the water in a covered pan.

Place one to two inches of water in the bottom of the steamer or pan and bring it to a rolling boil. Layer the prepared vegetables in the upper perforated part no more than 2½ inches deep. They should be loosely packed. Cover tightly with the lid and steam for the specified time. Begin timing

from the moment the lid is replaced. Small pieces of vegetables may need occasional stirring to expose all their surfaces to the steam.

Sulfiting during steam blanching. Sulfiting is suggested for vegetables that tend to deteriorate rapidly during storage, such as green beans or corn. Sulfiting increases shelf life, holds the color, and lessens vitamins A and C loss, and is recommended if you plan to store these vegetables longer than three months. These fragile dried vegetables also keep better in the refrigerator or freezer than on the shelf.

To sulfite, add 1 teaspoon sodium bisulfite per cup of steaming water. Do not add sodium bisulfite when water blanching vegetables. The vegetable will absorb the sulfur taste from the water.

Draining on a paper or cloth towel and then transferring to the drying tray is unnecessary handling of the tender vegetables. Pour blanched vegetables directly from the steamer or blanching pot onto your drying trays that are placed over the sink. If there is excess water on the drying tray, wipe the underside with a clean dishtowel. The heated vegetables will begin drying immediately because they are already warm.

Water blanching. Fill a pot two-thirds full of water and bring it to a rolling boil. Place the prepared vegetables in a wire basket and submerge them in the boiling water. After putting the vegetables in the water, bring it to a boil again before beginning timing. If it takes longer than a minute to come to the second boil, you probably have too many vegetables in the pot.

DRY VEGETABLES IN A DEHYDRATOR

Preheat the dryer. Arrange the prepared and pretreated vegetable pieces on drying trays, leaving a little space between for air circulation. Dry pieces of similar size on the same tray. Layer diced or small vegetables such as corn or peas in thin layers to allow good air circulation. They are best dried on a plastic mesh screen over the tray so that they don't fall through. Nesco/American Harvest dryers have these screens. Stir them occasionally during drying.

All vegetables except garlic, onions, and peppers may be dried together. Garlic, onions, and peppers may be dried with each other, but tend to flavor milder vegetables. Do not dry extremely thin vegetables, or herbs such as parsley or greens, in a dryer heavily loaded with larger, moist fruits or vegetables.

CHECK THE DRYING TEMPERATURE

You can begin drying as high as 160°F (71°C) for the first couple of hours when the dryer is fully loaded and the vegetables are very moist. The actual temperature of the vegetables may be as much as 20°F to 30°F cooler than the air temperature because of the cooling effect of moisture evaporation. Most fruits and vegetables can be started out at higher temperatures in the beginning due to this evaporative cooling effect.

After a couple of hours, lower the temperature to 140°F (60°C) and maintain that temperature until the vegetables are dry.

If you dry vegetables below 130°F (54°C), the low temperature encourages the growth of bacteria.

TEST FOR DRYNESS

Near the end of drying, check vegetables frequently and remove those that appear dried. Remove a piece, let it cool, feel it, and taste it. Most vegetables when dry are tough, brittle, and crisp or cracking hard. Some would shatter if hit with a hammer.

Because vegetables are dried to such a waterless state, the *conditioning* process, which is used to evenly distribute moisture in fruits, is unnecessary.

The less moisture that dried vegetables contain, the longer they will keep. Generally, they should have no more than 4 or 5 percent moisture when fully dried, compared to 15 to 20 percent in fruits.

FOOD SAFETY

Unlike home-canned vegetables, there is no danger from botulism in home-dried vegetables. Once a vegetable is dried, spoilage will occur only if moisture is reabsorbed. Too much residual moisture in the vegetables can cause spoilage.

If vegetables were not completely dry when removed from the dryer or were not packaged properly, mold and a spoiled smell will tell you they are unsafe to eat.

Long storage time, heat, or exposure to air may cause some vegetables to develop a strong unpleasant taste and odor. They are safe to eat, but their nutritional value may be poor and they really don't taste good. It's better to toss them.

Vegetables do not need to be pasteurized unless they are exposed to insects. To pasteurize, place packaged dried vegetables in the freezer for forty-eight hours to kill any insect larvae.

PACKAGE FOR STORAGE

Cool vegetables before packaging to prevent any remaining moisture from condensing in the package. Place only enough dried vegetables in one bag or jar to be used within one week. Every time a container is opened and the food is exposed to air, humidity reenters, causing deterioration.

If you have a home vacuum-packaging machine

such as the FoodSaver, package dried vegetables in glass pint jars and vacuum seal. Vacuum packaging retards oxidation, one of the primary reasons for quality and nutritive loss. The vacuum packaging bags do not work well for dried vegetables because the bags tend to puncture.

If vacuum packaging is not available, dried vegetables should be stored in canning jars or freezer bags with as much air removed as possible.

LABEL PACKAGED DRIED VEGETABLES

Always label the dried vegetables so you'll know what they are.

- Vegetable
- Variety
- Pretreatment
- Date dried

SHELF LIFE

The shelf life of dried vegetables is dependent upon the moisture left in the vegetables, how they were pretreated, exposure to light, the type of packaging, and their storage temperature.

Store in the coolest place possible, preferably the freezer or refrigerator. If space isn't available in your freezer, store in the coolest, darkest place in your home.

Since light fades vegetable colors and decreases their vitamins A and C content, dried vegetables should always be protected from the light.

HOW TO USE DRIED VEGETABLES

Dried vegetables usually need to be rehyrated before they are cooked.

Rehydrating Vegetables

- Home-dried vegetables rehydrate slower than fruits because they have lost more water. They are much slower to rehydrate than the commercial freeze-dried vegetables.

- Dried vegetables are usually more tender if they have been soaked long enough to reabsorb most of their lost water. If they are placed directly into a boiling soup or stew and are cooked without given time to plump, they will be tough.

- Use only as much water as necessary to cover vegetables when you're rehydrating them. Rehydration water contains some dissolved nutrients, so use it in soups, stews, or sauces.

- Rehydrating may take fifteen minutes to two hours, depending on the vegetable, thickness of pieces, and temperature of water used. The hotter the water, the quicker dried vegetables will rehydrate. Do not let vegetables stand in water more than two hours without refrigerating them. Holding them at room temperature longer than two hours gives bacteria a chance to grow, just as it would in fresh or thawed frozen vegetables.

Cooking

- After they're rehydrated, vegetables are ready to be cooked. In a fully rehydrated vegetable, the cooking time is about the same or slightly longer than it would be for the same frozen vegetable.

- Simmered vegetables are more tender than those cooked over high heat.

- If the vegetable is used in a baked food, it may be reconstituted, drained, and used in the recipe without further cooking.

- Because most dried vegetables do not have the same eye appeal or color as fresh or frozen, it helps to dress them up a bit. Combine them with fresh or frozen vegetables, use them in soups, stews, casseroles, or sauces or give them extra flavor and color with seasonings. Add salt or seasonings after rather than before they're cooked.

GOURMET DRIED TOMATOES

Gourmet grocery stores, specialty food outlets, and many supermarkets are featuring sun-dried tomatoes. They range from ten to twenty dollars per pound and you'll find them sliced, minced, powdered, halved, or chopped. They may be packaged dry or in a seasoned or unseasoned oil.

The Italians first introduced this delicacy to the American market and are still one of the primary sources of dried tomatoes found on U.S. supermarket shelves. Made from *Roma* or *paste* tomatoes, the majority are lightly salted and dried in the sun.

The prime variety used in drying is the plum-shaped Roma tomato. They are used in making tomato paste and for drying because of their robust sweet flavor and low water content. Most varieties of tomatoes only have about 6 percent solids and 94 percent water. The Roma varieties may contain as much as 15 percent solids, with 85 percent water. Higher solids content means that you have more tomato left after the water is removed.

Not all tomatoes can be successfully dried. Low acid tomatoes may develop black spots during drying. The black spots are not spoilage, but don't taste very good and are certainly not as appetizing

as the fully ripe, robust red dried tomato. There is no way to tell beforehand if tomatoes are high or low acid, although some varieties of seeds state *high* or *low acid* on the package.

Be sure that plum tomatoes are fully ripe before harvesting. Tomatoes picked ripe are richly colored. Those picked before ripening are lighter in color. Tomatoes picked early and commercially ripened may have a rich red color, but are not as flavorful as a vine-ripened tomato.

You can dry tomatoes with or without skins. The skins are easily removed and tend to be tough when dried. Blanch tomatoes in boiling water for two to three minutes. Remove with a slotted spoon and submerge immediately in cold water. Remove skins and core.

Halve tomatoes lengthwise. Place the halves on drying trays with the rounded sides down, cut sides up, close together, but not overlapping. Plastic mesh screens keep the tomatoes from sticking to the trays and make them easier to remove after they're dried.

Roma tomato halves will take about ten to fifteen hours to dry in a dehydrator at 140°F (60°C).

If you're drying round tomatoes, blanch, peel, and slice ¾- to 1-inch thick. When dry, they will be paper thin. If you slice them thinner than ¾ inch, they will be difficult to remove from the drying trays. When possible, dry tomatoes of the same size so they'll be done at the same time.

The amount that you can dry at once depends on the surface area of your dehydrator, the drying temperature, and the outside humidity. If you overload a dryer and it is very humid, tomatoes can sour before they dry. Take care if the humidity is high, and don't dry too many at once.

If you live in a very hot, arid climate, you can

successfully sun dry tomatoes by lightly salting them and protecting them from insects with screening.

When dry, they are quite crisp or tough. The surface should not feel tacky to the touch. Watch them near the end of drying and remove the dried ones, leaving those that need more drying.

Proper storage of dried tomatoes is critical if you want them to maintain good quality. If left out at room temperature, or in a container that is not airtight, they will deteriorate rapidly and absorb moisture from the air.

Ideally, they should be vacuum packaged and stored in the freezer. If this isn't practical for you, package inside of airtight glass jars. Store in a refrigerator or freezer until you use them.

Do not chop or flake them until you're ready to use them. When making tomato flakes or chunks, put the dried tomatoes in a food processor or blender and *quick chop* to the desired size. Chopping a few at a time results in a better texture. Too many at once will gum up the blades of the blender or food processor.

If you want to marinate them in olive oil for use in Italian or other dishes, store them in the refrigerator in a sterile glass container.

Dried tomatoes are a flavor booster to any pasta. Chop them in the blender for tomato flakes and sprinkle them on salads, pasta dishes, a sandwich, or as seasoning in a soup. Add them to softened cream cheese as a spread for bagels. Sprinkle them on the top of pizza at the end of baking. Add them to rice, couscous, or pasta salad recipes. Bake them in rustic bread along with chopped chunks of garlic.

VEGETABLE CHIPS, FLAKES, AND POWDERS

Thinly sliced dried vegetables, or vegetable chips, are a nutritious low-calorie snack. Sometimes they are a nice change from sweet snacks.

A food processor makes quick work of slicing firm vegetables. Try tomato chips, cucumber chips, zucchini chips, or paper-thin carrot or parsnip chips with your favorite dip. Mix dried vegetable chips on a plate with fresh vegetables and dips.

Use your blender or food processor to chop dried vegetables into flakes or a fine powder. Flake or powder them before using or store in a tightly sealed container in the freezer for a month or so.

The shelf life and nutritional value of powdered or flaked dried vegetables is much less than that of sliced or whole dried vegetables, so do not chop more than you will use within a month.

Flaking dried vegetables

- Flake or powder different vegetables separately and then blend together to make mixed flakes or powder. Because dried vegetables have different textures, they will take different times to chop.

- Dried vegetables should be very dry and crisp before chopping. Be sure the blender or food processor is completely dry. If any moisture is present, the vegetables will clump instead of flaking.

- Process about ½ to 1 cup of dried vegetable pieces at one time. Larger amounts will not powder or flake evenly. Put the dried vegetable pieces in the blender. Set the speed on chop for several seconds or pulse it if it has a pulse setting. Turn it off, scrape down the sides with a rubber spatula, and chop again for several more seconds.

VEGETABLES AT A GLANCE

VEGETABLE	QUALITY WHEN DRIED	VEGETABLE	QUALITY WHEN DRIED
Artichokes	Fair	Okra	Fair
Asparagus	Poor	Onions	Excellent
Beans, green	Fair to good	Parsley	Good
Beans, lima	Good	Parsnips	Good
Beets	Fair	Peas	Fair
Broccoli	Not recommended	Peppers, chili	Excellent
Brussels sprouts	Not recommended	Peppers, green or red	Good
Cabbages	Fair	Popcorn	Excellent
Carrots	Good	Potatoes	Not recommended
Cauliflower	Not recommended	Potatoes, sweet	Excellent in leathers
Celery	Poor	Pumpkins	Not recommended
Collard greens	Not recommended	Radishes	Not recommended
Corn, sweet	Good	Rutabagas	Not recommended
Cucumbers	Poor	Spinach	Not recommended
Eggplant	Not recommended	Squash, summer	Not recommended
Garlic	Excellent	Squash, winter	Not recommended
Horseradish	Good	Sweet potatoes	Excellent (in leathers)
Kale	Not recommended	Swiss chard	Not recommended
Kohlrabi	Not recommended	Tomatoes	Excellent
Legumes	Good (air dried)	Turnips	Good
Lettuce	Not recommended	Turnip greens	Not recommended
Mushrooms	Good	Zucchini	Not recommended
Mustard greens	Not recommended		

Repeat until the vegetables are the right size for your use.

Storing flaked and powdered vegetables

- Store vegetable flakes and powders in airtight containers with as little air as possible. Vacuum packaging is ideal. Select the right size container for the amount that you're processing.

- Keep them in the refrigerator or freezer and use within a month or two.

- Flakes and powders made from unblanched vegetables will not keep as long as those made from blanched vegetables and should be used within two weeks. They develop an unpleasant flavor during longer storage.

How to Use Them

- Dried vegetables are great *salad sprinkles*. They don't need to be reconstituted because they will absorb moisture from the salad and dressing. Coarsely chop dried carrots, cucumbers, zucchini, onions, celery, or tomatoes to add flavor and texture to salads.

- Combine dried vegetables and herbs for your own special seasonings. Because home-dried vegetable seasonings and herbs have no anticaking additives, make small quantities and store them in airtight containers in the freezer. Make seasoning salts by mixing vegetable and herb powders with table salt. The addition of salt decreases the tendency of the powder to cake.

- Vegetable flakes and powders make excellent seasonings for soups and sauces. For soups and sauces, combine 1 tablespoon vegetable powder and ¼ cup boiling water for each cup of soup or sauce. Let the mixture stand for ten to fifteen minutes before adding to the soup or sauce base.

- Dried tomatoes are extremely concentrated. One tablespoon of tomato powder is equivalent to one medium fresh tomato. Use sparingly so as not to overpower a prepared dish.

Shelf life is increased with vacuum packing and cooler storage. To keep the best quality, they should be stored in the refrigerator or freezer. Most vegetables will taste good for two to four months, depending on the type of vegetable and storage conditions. Vegetables stored at higher temperatures or without vacuum packaging *will not spoil* after four months. However, there will be a gradual deterioration in taste and nutrition.

ALL ABOUT VEGETABLES

Because many vegetables have a poor quality when dried and rehydrated, I have not listed them here or given instructions on how to dry them. If they're in the *not recommended* list (page 77), it doesn't mean that they can't be dried. It's just that the quality is very poor. If your garden is brimming with vegetables, your freezer is full, your neighbors have all they can use, and you don't know what to do with the rest, then dry them. Just know that they may not taste as good as you'd like.

ARTICHOKES

Artichokes are a most interesting vegetable. They are actually classified as a *thistle* because of their thorny chokes. The edible part is actually the flower bud.

One large artichoke contains only twenty-five calories, no fat, and is a good source of vitamin C, potassium, magnesium, and dietary fiber. Artichokes are best eaten fresh, but the *hearts* can be dried.

Quality when dried: Fair.

Varieties best for drying: Green Globe.

Selection: Dry only the tender hearts of fresh young artichokes.

Storage before drying: Wrap in paper towels and place in loosely closed plastic bags. Store only briefly in the refrigerator at 35°F to 40°F (1°C to 3°C) to maintain highest quality.

Water content before drying: 87 percent.

Preparation: Wash artichokes thoroughly under running water, spreading the petals. Pull off lower leaves that are small or discolored. Cut off the stem close to the base so the artichoke sits flat on your cutting board. Cut off the top quarter and the tips of the leaves. Sprinkle with a mixture of lemon juice and garlic. Steam until the petals are tender. Remove the leaves and eat. Remove and discard the fuzzy choke. Cut the heart in half to dry.

Pretreatment: Steam blanch whole artichokes for twenty-five to thirty-five minutes, or until a petal is tender and pulls off easily.

Drying temperature: 130°F to 140°F (54°C to 60°C) until dry.

Dryness test: Brittle.

How to use: Soak dried artichoke halves in a mixture of ¼ cup water, ¼ cup olive oil, 2 tablespoons vinegar, 1 teaspoon lemon juice, and one minced garlic clove. Use as you would canned marinated artichoke hearts.

Additional information: More information and recipes are available from:

California Artichoke Advisory Board
P.O. Box 747
Castroville, CA 95012
Phone: 831-633-4411
Fax: 831-633-0215
Website: www.artichokes.org

ASPARAGUS

Asparagus is a member of the lily family and grows from a crown that is planted about a foot deep in sandy soil. An asparagus spear can grow as much as ten inches in a twenty-four-hour period! The larger the diameter, the better the quality.

Asparagus is high in folic acid, potassium, fiber, vitamins A, B6, and C, and thiamine.

Quality when dried: Poor; if you want to preserve it, it is much better frozen.

Selection: Select bright green asparagus spears with closed, compact, firm tips.

Storage before drying: Dry as soon as possible after harvesting. If you store asparagus, stand spears upright in two inches of cold water in the refrigerator. Place a paper towel over the top of the spears and a plastic bag over the paper towel. Tuck the plastic bag under the container. They will keep for three to five days.

Water content before drying: 92 percent.

Preparation: Wash spears thoroughly in cold running water. Trim stem end. You can also peel the skin from the stalk, especially toward the base, for more tender asparagus. Sort according to stalk thickness and cut in 2-inch lengths.

Pretreatment: Steam blanch two to three minutes.

Drying temperature: 130°F to 140°F (54°C to 60°C) until dry

Dryness test: Very tough to brittle.

How to use: Rehydrate asparagus, cook until tender, and serve it in a cream sauce seasoned with lemon juice or Parmesan cheese and paprika. Chop in the blender or food processor and use in cream of asparagus soup.

Additional information: More information and recipes are available from:

California Asparagus Commission
311 E. Main Street, Suite 204
Stockton, CA 95202
Phone: 209-474-7581
Fax: 209-474-9105
Email: ccwatte@hotmail.com
Website: www.calasparagus.com

Michigan Asparagus Advisory Board
P.O. Box 550
DeWitt, MI 44820
Phone 888-669-4250
Fax: 517-669-4251
Email: maab@voyager.net
Website: www.asparagus.com

BEANS, GREEN

Green beans (also known as snap beans) are the immature pod and beans of legumes. As they mature, they will produce fat seeds and tough, inedible pods. Green beans are a good source of carbohydrates, have a moderate amount of dietary fiber, vitamin C, and beta-carotene. There are only fifteen calories in ½ cup of fresh beans.

Often dried green beans are not tender and tasty when rehydrated. It takes a little extra effort to help them retain their tenderness and flavor.

Green beans are warm-season vegetables and rank second only to the tomato in popularity in home gardens.

Bush beans stand erect without support. Pole beans climb supports and are more easily harvested.

Quality when dried: Fair to good.

Varieties best for drying: Bush bean varieties that dry well are Blue Lake, Bush Kentucky Wonder, and Derby. Pole varieties good for drying are Blue Lake, Kentucky Blue, and Kentucky Wonder. The bean plant continues to form new flowers and produces more beans if pods are continually removed before the seeds mature.

Selection: Harvest fresh beans before they become tough and stringy. Dry only fresh tender beans with a vibrant green color and bright appearance. They should have thick walls and small seeds and be free from strings.

Storage before drying: Store only briefly in the refrigerator at 35°F to 40°F (2°C to 4°C) to maintain highest quality.

Water content before drying: 90 percent.

Preparation: Wash pods and snip off pod ends. Slice lengthwise for French cut, or crosswise into 1-inch segments, slanting knife diagonally to expose more surface area for drying.

Pretreatment: Steam blanch for two to three minutes or water blanch for three to four minutes. If steam blanching, use water containing 1 teaspoon sodium bisulfite per cup of water. Place on drying tray and freeze solid, thirty to forty minutes before drying, to tenderize.

If steamed and frozen before drying, beans will dehydrate faster and be more tender when rehydrated. Sulfiting lengthens their storage life.

Drying temperature: 130°F to 140°F (54°C to 60°C) until dry.

Dryness test: Brittle or crisp.

How to use: Serve rehydrated green beans in a cream of mushroom sauce with almonds, or in soups, stews, or casseroles.

BEANS, LIMA

You probably won't be able to find fresh lima beans unless you grow your own. Most lima beans are dried, canned, or frozen. The lima bean is named after Lima, Peru, and is a very popular bean with its buttery flavor and creamy texture.

The outer skin on lima beans lengthens the drying time and the rehydration process, lowering the quality of rehydrated limas.

An easy way to dry limas is to vine dry them. Leave the pods on the vine in the garden until the beans inside rattle. When the vines and the pods are dry and shriveled, pick the beans and shell them. If they are still moist, finish drying in your dehydrator.

Quality when dried: Good.

Selection: Use dark green pods that are well filled. The beans should be plump, with tender skins and a light green color.

Storage before drying: Hold the unshelled pods for only a brief period at 40°F (22°C) before processing to maintain the highest quality.

Water content before drying: 68 percent.

Preparation: Wash pods and shell, then wash again.

Pretreatment: Steam blanch lima beans for two to four minutes or water blanch for three to five minutes.

Drying temperature: 130°F (54°C) to 140°F (60°C) until dry.

Dryness test: Hard or brittle.

How to use: Use rehydrated lima beans in soups, stews, or in a cream sauce with other vegetables.

BEETS

Beet tops are an excellent source of vitamin A and calcium. The roots are good sources of vitamin C. Beets also contain folic acid, fiber, and a little potassium.

Beets contain a powerful red pigment that stains dishtowels, wooden cutting boards, and sinks. Salt easily removes stains from your hands.

Quality when dried: Fair.

Varieties best for drying: All varieties dry equally well. The tops do not dry well. Use them fresh.

Selection: Harvest beets when they are about 1½ inches in diameter, the best size for cooking, pickling, or drying. As they get bigger, they may become tough and fibrous. Dry those with a uniform dark red color, smooth skins, and minimal light and dark color rings.

Storage before drying: Use tops immediately. Store the roots in a loosely closed plastic bag up to one week in the refrigerator at 35°F to 40°F (1°C to 3°C) to maintain highest quality.

Water content before drying: 87 percent.

Preparation: Wash beets and remove tops, leaving an inch of stem on the beet. Select beets that are uniform in size to prevent overcooking.

Pretreatment: Steam until almost tender. Prick with a fork to check for doneness. Peel and cut into ¼-inch strips or ⅜-inch dice.

Drying temperature: 130°F (54°C) to 140°F (60°C) until dry.

Dryness test: Crackling brittle.

How to use: Flake dried beets in a blender or food processor to use in dry salad dressings, soups, and stews or rehydrate to use in borscht or to boil. Rehydrate by soaking in a small amount of water overnight in the refrigerator. Beets are tasty when seasoned with fresh dill, bay leaves, cloves, nutmeg, or mint.

CABBAGE

Although they don't look alike, cabbage, kale, broccoli, kohlrabi, cauliflower, and Brussels sprouts are all from the same family of plants.

Cabbage only requires three months of growing time, and one acre of cabbage will yield more edible vegetables than any other plant. Dried cabbage readily reabsorbs moisture from the air. It will keep only if extremely dry.

Cabbage is rich in beta-carotene, vitamin C, vitamin K, and fiber. There are only sixteen calories in 1 cup.

Cabbage contains isothiocyanates that break down into smelly sulfur compounds during cooking. Do not use aluminum pans because it causes an even stronger reaction.

Quality when dried: Fair.

Varieties best for drying: Green, Savoy, and red.

Selection: White varieties do not dry as well as green or red. Cabbage should be solid, firm, round, and heavy for its size.

Storage before drying: Wrap in a paper towel and store only briefly in a plastic bag in a refrigerator at 35°F to 40°F (2°C to 4°C) to maintain the highest quality.

Water content before drying: 92 percent.

Preparation: Wash cabbage and trim outer leaves. Cut cabbage in half, core, and shred into ¼- to ⅜-inch-wide pieces.

Pretreatment: Steam blanch for two to three minutes.

Drying temperature: 130°F to 140°F (54°C to 60°C) until dry.

Dryness test: Crisp.

How to use: Cook with ham in soups.

CARROTS

The first carrots were white, purple, and yellow. The Dutch developed orange carrots in the 1600s.

Carrots belong to the parsley family. Carrots are the highest in carotene (the source of vitamin A) of any vegetable, and high in fiber and sugar. One cup of diced fresh carrots has only thirty-five calories.

Quality when dried: Good.

Varieties best for drying: Chantenay, Danvers, Imperator, and Nantes

Selection: Choose smooth, well-formed, deep orange carrots that are slightly more mature than for table use and without woody fiber or a pithy core. Carrots with green areas or yellow tops are old or sunburned. Most carrots are sold without the tops because the tops draw moisture from the roots.

Storage before drying: Cut off the tops one inch above the root, wrap in a paper towel, and store only briefly in a plastic bag in the refrigerator at 35°F to 40°F (2°C to 4°C) to maintain the highest quality.

Water content before drying: 88 percent.

Preparation: Wash, trim tops, and peel. If you do not remove the peelings, it adversely affects the taste when dried. Slice crosswise or diagonally no thicker than ⅜-inch or cut into ⅜-inch dice.

Pretreatment: Steam blanch for two to three minutes. Remove and dip in a cornstarch solution of 2 tablespoons cornstarch to 2 cups water. Drain and place on dryer trays. The cornstarch solution helps the keeping quality.

Drying temperature 130°F (54°C) to 140°F (60°C) until dry.

Dryness test: Very tough to brittle.

How to use: Chop dried carrots in the blender or food processor for carrot flakes to use as salad sprinkles, in dry soup mixes, in cookies or carrot cake. They are nice when seasoned with dill, coriander, chervil, and tarragon.

CELERY

Celery is a member of the carrot family. Two medium stalks of celery have only twenty-five calories and 10 percent of your daily requirement for vitamin C.

Quality when dried: Poor.

Varieties best for drying: Pascal.

Selection: Dry only tender, yet mature, long, crisp stalks with fresh leaves. The stalk should feel smooth on the inside rather than rough or puffy. The leaves should be fresh with no signs of wilting. Light green stalks have a better flavor than those that are dark green. Scratch the root end of a stalk of celery with your fingernail. A sweet or bitter smell means a sweet or bitter flavor.

Storage before drying: Wrap in a paper towel and store only briefly in a plastic bag in the refrigerator at 35°F to 40°F (2°C to 4°C) to maintain the highest quality.

Water content before drying: 94 percent

Preparation: Trim base and wash stalks and leaves. Cut crosswise into ½-inch slices.

Pretreatment: Water blanch for 30 seconds to 1 minute in a baking soda solution of ½ teaspoon soda per cup of water to preserve the green color. Celery should still be quite crisp after blanching. Place on plastic mesh screens for drying so that it doesn't fall through the trays.

Drying temperature: 130°F to 140°F (54°C to 60°C) until dry.

Dryness test: Crisp.

How to use: Add to soups and stews with fresh vegetables. To make celery flakes, chop both dried leaves and stalks in the blender and use for salad seasoning. To make celery salt, add one part salt to one part powdered dry celery.

CORN, SWEET

The corn plant is native to the Americas. Sweet corn, a mutation of field corn, appeared in the mid-1800s.

There are about 600 kernels on each ear of corn. The best dried corn is simply the freshest corn and it should be dried immediately after harvesting. During storage, the sugar quickly turns to starch and the flavor and sweetness are lost.

One ear of yellow sweet corn has about eighty-four calories and is high in fiber, niacin, and some vitamin A.

Corn is the main ingredient in most dry pet food.

Quality when dried: Good.

Varieties best for drying: Both white and yellow sweet corn varieties dry very well.

Selection: The husks should be fresh looking and bright green, and the silk ends free of decay or worm damage. Pull the husk back and poke one of the kernels at the tip of the silk end with your fingernail. If juice squirts out and is only slightly cloudy, it's fresh. If the juice is thick, the corn is too old.

Tender, fresh, young ears with plump kernels dry best. The kernels should be large enough so there are no spaces between rows.

Storage before drying: Do not store corn. Process it right after harvesting and do not husk it until you're ready to dry it.

Water content before drying: 73 percent.

Preparation: Husk ears by pulling the husks down the ear. Snap off the stem at the base. Under cold running water, rub the ear in a circular motion to remove the silk or use a stiff vegetable brush.

Pretreatment: Steam blanch ears for three to five minutes over water containing 1 teaspoon sodium bisulfite per cup of water. With the large end down on a cutting board, cut the kernels off the half of the cob closest to the cutting board. Turn it upside down and cut the remainder of the kernels. Do not cut too closely; leave about one-fourth of the kernel on the cob.

Drying temperature: 130°F to 140°F (54°C to 60°C) until dry.

Dryness test: Crisp and crunchy.

How to use: Mix with peppers and onions on the drying tray and sprinkle with seasoning salt for a delicious dried snack. Rehydrate dried corn to use in fritters, chowders, and soups or to make creamed corn. To make cornmeal, grind dry corn in a blender or food mill.

CUCUMBER

Fresh cucumbers are a garden delight. They should only be dried for novelty or when your garden produces so many that you've run out of the energy to eat them fresh.

They have a very short shelf life dried, a week or so, and are best eaten as a *cucumber chip*. You'll be amazed at the concentrated cucumber flavor in a dried chip.

Supermarket cucumbers are covered with an edible wax to protect them from moisture loss.

Cucumbers are not a very good source of nutrients and their main ingredient is water. A small amount of beta-carotene is in the green peel, but if you peel them, the nutrients drop to nearly zero. A medium-size cucumber has about five calories.

Quality when dried: Poor.

Varieties best for drying: There are two types of cucumbers—pickling cucumbers and slicing cucumbers. Both can be dried.

Selection: Dry only small, fresh, firm green cucumbers that are 8 inches long or smaller.

Storage before drying: Wrap in a paper towel and store only briefly in a plastic bag in the refrigerator at 35°F to 40°F (2°C to 4°C) to maintain the highest quality.

Water content before drying: 95 percent.

Preparation: Wash and peel, if desired. The primary nutrient is in the peeling, so you'll lose nutrients if you peel them. Slice crosswise into ⅜-inch rounds. Sprinkle with seasoning salt for added flavor.

Pretreatment: None.

Drying temperature: 130°F to 140°F (54°C to 60°C) until dry.

Dryness test: Crisp and crunchy.

How to use: Keep extremely dry and use within one to two weeks. Chop dried cucumber in a blender and sprinkle dry on salads. Seasoned cucumber chips can be eaten dry with dips.

GARLIC

Garlic is a root vegetable, with the bulb growing underground. Inside of each bulb are ten to twenty individual cloves, each separate from the next and covered by a paper skin.

Garlic is a cousin to onions, leeks, chives, and shallots. Garlic plays an important role in all kinds of prepared foods.

Because fresh garlic is available all year round, the only reason to dry the individual cloves is for convenience and because you want to do it yourself. Garlic powder and garlic salt are available inexpensively at the supermarket. These are mixed with an anticaking agent and tend to keep better for longer periods than your homemade mixes.

If you're a gardener raising your own garlic, you'll want to dry the large bulbs so that your garlic will keep well through the winter. Here are some guidelines for air-drying fresh garlic and for drying the individual cloves.

Air-Drying Fresh Garlic After Harvesting

When fresh garlic is harvested, it is usually hung to air-dry. Remove most of the dirt from the roots and take care not to bruise the garlic. Leave the roots on since they will slow the drying.

Tie the bulbs together by the roots in bunches of five. Tie about twenty-five bunches to a single strong string. You want the air to be able to reach all sides of all the bulbs so they can dry evenly.

Hang strings in a dark, warm room with good air circulation, about 70°F to 75°F (21°C to 24°C). The bulbs should dry evenly and without spoilage. The outside should be quite dry, with the fresh garlic still moist. Garlic will dry in about two to three weeks at this temperature.

Storing Fresh Garlic

To keep the garlic for eating fresh, cut off the roots, leaving about ½ to 1 inch of the root, and cut off the tops. Take care to leave the skins intact. The papery wrapping protects the garlic, keeping it fresh.

Remove the dirty outer layers of the bulbs. Place the bulbs in clean mesh bags and hang in a cool room that stays about the same temperature. It should be 60°F to 65°F (15°C to 18°C) with moderate humidity and good air circulation.

If you store garlic in a cold environment, such as the refrigerator, it will sprout when it is brought to room temperature.

Drying Individual Garlic Cloves for Longer Storage

Individual cloves of garlic can also be dried to add quick seasoning to a recipe. The cloves can be stored in an airtight container for several months or in the freezer for up to a year.

Quality when dried: Excellent.

Varieties best for drying: Most varieties. The larger the bulb, the easier it is to handle.

Selection: Choose fresh, firm cloves with a good flavor. The heads should be dry with plenty of paper covering. If you can see green shoots, the garlic is beginning to sprout and is either too old and/or wasn't dried properly.

Storage before drying: Store individual garlic bulbs in a cool, dry, dark, well-ventilated place in mesh bags.

Water content before drying: 61 percent.

Preparation: Separate and peel cloves. Cut each clove in half lengthwise.

Pretreatment: None.

Drying temperature: 115°F to 130°F (46°C to 54°C) until dry. The lower temperature will keep more of the flavor.

Dryness test: Crisp.

How to use: Use dried garlic in any recipe that calls for fresh garlic. To make garlic salt, powder dried garlic in a blender. Add four parts salt to one part garlic powder and blend only a second or two. If blended longer, the salt will be too fine and will cake.

HORSERADISH

Horseradish is actually a perennial herb from the mustard family. Like the mustard seed, horseradish tissue must be broken down to release the oils.

For centuries, horseradish was only considered a folk medicine and used to cure everything from freckles to scurvy. It contains a hardy dose of vitamin C. Horseradish has only two calories per teaspoon and provides dietary fiber. It is also a natural decongestant and if you've ever breathed deep when eating it straight, you know that it can totally clear your head.

Horseradish arrived in this country with the colonists and was used to cover up the taste of less-than-fresh meat. We enjoy it today for the zest it brings to our foods. The color of horseradish varies from white to creamy beige. It is best fresh, but can also be dried.

This hardy perennial is easy to grow and takes little attention. The easiest way to keep horseradish from taking over your garden is to grow it in containers.

Freshly grated root will keep well for a couple of months in the refrigerator, longer in the freezer. Combine ¼ cup vinegar with 1 cup freshly grated horseradish, plus ½ teaspoon salt and a pinch of sugar.

Quality when dried: Good.

Selection: Fresh, firm, fully mature roots are best for drying.

Storage before drying: Wrap in a paper towel and store in a plastic bag at refrigerator temperature, 35°F to 40°F (2°C to 4°C), to maintain the highest quality.

Water content before drying: 85 percent.

Preparation: Scrub the root well with a stiff brush and then peel with a paring knife. Grate coarsely with a food processor or large grater.

As an eye irritant, horseradish starts where onions leave off. Keep a window open when you're preparing it. It's best to wear rubber gloves and take care not to touch your eyes.

Horseradish will smell extremely strong while drying. Put your dehydrator in a covered area outside of your house.

Pretreatment: None.

Drying temperature: 130°F to 140°F (54°C to 60°C) until dry.

Dryness test: Dry and brittle.

How to use: Store horseradish in airtight containers in the freezer to keep the best quality. Powder dried horseradish in a food processor or

ELEPHANT GARLIC

Elephant garlic looks like overgrown garlic, but it is more closely related to leeks. A single clove of elephant garlic can be as large as a whole bulb of ordinary garlic. Elephant garlic has a milder, almost bland flavor. It can be dried in the same manner as garlic. It is more perishable than ordinary garlic and doesn't keep as long. If you want to dry it, follow the instructions for garlic.

blender. Rehydrate with enough water to mix and use in cocktail sauce or dressings. Rehydrate grated horseradish and add ¼ cup vinegar to 1 cup horseradish. You can mix it with sour cream for a more diluted flavor. Horseradish goes well with roast beef, fish, poultry, sausages, and pork.

LEGUMES

Legumes such as shell beans, lentils, and soybeans may be partially dried on the plant. When the pod turns light brown and the seeds are mature, they should be harvested. If not harvested soon enough, the pods may break, spilling the seeds on the ground.

Place the pods in a cloth sack and hang it in a warm place for up to two weeks to finish drying. When completely dry, shake or hit the sack to break the pods and release the seeds. Remove the pods and pour off the seeds.

After packaging, pasteurize the seeds by placing them in the freezer for forty-eight hours. Store in an airtight, moisture-proof container in a cool, dark place.

MUSHROOMS

Mushrooms are actually the fruit of a colorless plant called a fungus. A fungus is a plant that has no roots or leaves, no flowers or seeds, and does not require light to grow. It grows well in the dark and reproduces by releasing billions of spores. There are about 38,000 varieties of mushrooms. Many are quite delicious; others are toxic.

A cup of raw mushrooms has about twenty calories. They contain a substantial amount of B vitamins, selenium, copper, and some other trace minerals.

It takes ten pounds of fresh mushrooms to make one pound of dried mushrooms.

Quality when dried: Good.

Varieties best for drying: Dry only cultivated or wild mushrooms that are safe to eat. Some good varieties for drying are chanterelle, porcini, porto-bello, and shiitake. Experiment to find which mushrooms you like best. Boletes that have matured past the button stage may have wormholes and should be discarded.

Selection: Dry only clean, plump, fresh mushrooms with closed caps and no visible gills under the cap. Look for mushrooms with closed *veils*, the area where the cap meets the stem. A wide-open veil indicates that the mushroom has aged and will have a shorter storage life. They should be white, cream, or tan, depending on the variety. Mushrooms darken as they age.

Storage before drying: Put them in a loosely closed paper bag or a glass dish covered with a clean kitchen towel. Do not put in the refrigerator crisper, which tends to be more humid. Store in the refrigerator at 34°F (1°C) until you dry them.

Water content before drying: 90 percent.

Preparation: Don't wash the mushrooms that you're going to dry, but clean with a soft brush or cloth and check for evidence of worms or spoilage. Cut away any questionable parts and trim the woody portion from the stem. Dry whole or slice lengthwise in half or into ½-inch-thick slices.

Because mushrooms are very aromatic when drying, you may want to put your dryer in the basement, in the garage, or on the porch. Some people are allergic to the aroma of drying mushrooms and may get a headache.

Pretreatment: None.

Drying temperature: 80°F to 90°F (27°C to 32°C) for two or three hours. Then increase the temperature to 120°F to 125°F (49°C to 52°C) until they are dry.

Dryness test: Dry and brittle.

How to use: Use about 1 ounce of dried mushrooms for each 8 to 10 ounces of fresh mushrooms called for in a recipe. Rehydrate dried mushrooms by soaking them in lightly salted or sugared water for about thirty minutes, stirring while soaking to loosen any dirt that may be present. Lift out gently with a slotted spoon and cook in your favorite recipe.

You can also grind them into a dry seasoning powder.

Additional information: More information and recipes are available from:

Email: mushroomexpert@yahoo.com

Website: www.mushroomexpert.com

OKRA

African slaves brought okra to the New World. Okra (nicknamed *gumbo*) is a tall-growing, warm-season annual vegetable from the same family as hollyhock and hibiscus. Immature pods are used in soups and stews or as a fried vegetable. When cooked in liquid, okra exudes a unique viscous juice that is responsible for its thickening power in the famous Louisiana Creole gumbo dish.

Okra is very high in soluble fiber, vitamin B_6, and folic acid. One-half cup of sliced, cooked okra only contains twenty-five calories.

Quality when dried: Fair.

Varieties best for drying: Annie Oakley, Dwarf Green Long Pod, Clemson Spineless.

Selection: When picking, use pruning shears for clean cuts that do not harm the rest of the plant. They must be picked often, at least every other day.

Dry only tender, young, fresh pods, 2 to 3 inches long. Freshness is determined by how easily the pods snap. A dull, dry appearance frequently indicates old pods. Large pods rapidly become tough and woody and should be removed and composted.

Storage before drying: Wrap in a paper towel and store in a loosely closed plastic bag in the refrigerator at 35°F to 40°F (1°C to 3°C) to maintain the highest quality. Pods will keep only for two or three days.

Water content before drying: 89 percent.

Preparation: Wash and cut off tips of stems. Slice crosswise about ½-inch thick. Discard any tough, pithy pods.

Pretreatment: Steam blanch for two to three minutes over water.

Drying temperature: 130°F to 140°F (54°C to 60°C) until dry.

Dryness test: Tough to brittle

How to use: Rehydrate okra, drain, and toss it in cornmeal seasoned with onion salt and pepper. Fry it in olive oil to a golden brown. You can also use dried okra in soups and casseroles. It is especially good in dishes with tomatoes and onions. A little vinegar or lemon juice improves the flavor. Some Southern cooks maintain that the acidity of vinegar or lemon juice in the cooking water makes cooked okra less viscous.

ONIONS

One-half cup of fresh chopped onion contains about thirty calories, is a good source of fiber, and contains a little vitamin C.

When you chop fresh onions, they sting and burn your eyes. When you cut into an onion, the cell walls are damaged and release a sulfur compound, which floats into the air. When it comes into contact with the water in your eyes, it is converted to sulfuric acid, which is why it stings your eyes. To keep from crying as you're chopping, chill the onion in the refrigerator before chopping. Chilling prevents this sulfur compound from entering the air.

Air-Drying Fresh Onions After Harvesting

Sweet varieties keep very poorly and should be enjoyed fresh soon after harvesting, because no storage method keeps them for very long.

Pull mature onions in the morning and allow the bulbs to air-dry in the garden until late afternoon. If it is very hot, bulbs may sunburn. If extremely hot, move the onions to a shaded location. At night, place them on a newspaper under a dry shelter on elevated slats or screens or tie the bulbs together by the leaves and hang.

You want the air to be able to reach all sides of all bulbs so they can dry evenly. Allow them to dry in a dark, warm room with good air circulation, 70°F to 75°F (21°C to 24°C) for two to three weeks to complete drying and curing. The bulbs should dry evenly and without spoilage. The papery wrapping protects the onion, keeping it fresh.

When completely dry, place the bulbs in clean mesh bags and hang in a cool room that stays about the same temperature. It should be 60°F to 65°F (16°C to 18°C) with moderate humidity and good air circulation.

If you store onions in a cold environment, such as the refrigerator, they will sprout when brought to room temperature. Dry onions may keep until late winter, but examine them regularly and discard any that begin to soften or rot.

Quality when dried: Excellent.

Varieties best for drying: There are many varieties of onions, although they are generally divided by color: yellow, white, or red. The white varieties have the best flavor when dried.

Selection: If growing your own, allow the plants to mature and the tops to fall over naturally. Breaking over the tops early interrupts growth, causing smaller bulbs that do not keep as well when stored. Onion bulbs should be large, fresh, and firm, heavy for their size and very pungent.

Drying Chopped Onions

During drying, the onion smell will penetrate everything in the surrounding area, so it is wise to place the dryer on a covered porch or in the garage. The dried onion pieces can be stored in an airtight container for several months or in the freezer for up to a year.

Storage before drying: Store onions in a cool, dry place with good ventilation to maintain the highest quality. Do not store them near potatoes.

Water content before drying: 89 percent

Preparation: Trim the bulb ends and remove the paper shell. Slice ¼- to ½-inch thick or chop.

Pretreatment: None.

Drying temperature: 130°F to 140°F (54°C to 60°C) until dry.

Dryness test: Feels like paper.

How to use: Dried onions readily reabsorb moisture, causing rapid deterioration during storage, so they need to be packaged with extra care. To maintain the best flavor, chop or powder dried onions only as needed. Use as you would fresh onions in any cooked dish calling for onions.

PARSLEY

See All About Herbs and Spices, page 107.

Parsley has a much higher food value than most herbs and is frequently classified as a vegetable.

When cutting parsley, always remove the outer leaves rather than the inner leaves, as growth is from the center. Dried parsley will readily reabsorb moisture from the air, so it must be packaged in airtight containers.

Quality when dried: Good.

Varieties best for drying: Italian parsley with the large, flat leaves holds its flavor better when dried. The curly variety of French parsley is the most popular for garnishing and seasoning, but it tends to diminish in flavor with drying.

Selection: Use fresh, bright green parsley.

Storage before drying: Wrap in a paper towel to absorb excess moisture. Store in a loosely closed plastic bag in the refrigerator at 35°F to 40°F (1°C to 3°C) to maintain the highest quality.

Water content before drying: 85 percent.

Preparation: Wash lightly under cold running water. Shake off excess water. Leave on stems.

Pretreatment: None.

Drying temperature: 90°F to 120°F (32°C to 49°C) until dry. You can also dry it in a warm room. See Herbs and Spices, page 99.

Dryness test: Feels like paper.

How to use: When dry, separate the leaves from the stems to make parsley flakes.

PARSNIPS

The parsnip is a member of the parsley family. Parsnips are considered a winter vegetable because they develop their fullest flavor after the roots have been exposed to near-freezing temperatures for two to four weeks in the fall and early winter. The cold changes the starch in the parsnip root into sugar, resulting in a sweet taste.

Quality when dried: Good.

Varieties best for drying: All American, Harris Model, Andover, and Lancer all dry well.

Selection: Choose fresh, smooth, small- or medium-size roots. If parsnips are yellow or tan, they're probably old. The color should be even and white to cream.

Storage before drying: Wrap in a paper towel and store in a loosely closed plastic bag in the refrigerator at 35°F to 40°F (2°C to 4°C) to maintain the highest quality.

Water content before drying: 79 percent.

Preparation: Wash, trim tops, and peel. Slice crosswise or diagonally up to ½-inch thick or cut into ½-inch dice.

Pretreatment: Steam blanch for three to five minutes or water blanch for two to three minutes.

Drying temperature: 130°F to 140°F (54°C to 60°C) until dry.

Dryness test: Very tough to brittle.

How to use: Serve rehydrated parsnips in cream sauce with or without other vegetables. Serve mashed with butter and garnished with parsley.

PEAS

Green peas are actually members of the legume family. The skins on peas slow their drying and rehydration. Home-dried peas are slightly inferior to commercially dried ones because homemakers do not have the mechanical means to pierce the skins.

One-half cup of cooked garden peas has about seventy calories, folic acid, some protein, iron, fiber, and vitamins A and C. It has about the same amount of protein as a small egg or a tablespoon of peanut butter.

Quality when dried: Fair.

Varieties best for drying: Peas are generally classified as garden peas, sugar snap peas, and snow peas. Garden pea varieties have smooth or wrinkled seeds. The wrinkled-seeded varieties are generally sweeter and dry better.

Snap peas have low-fiber pods that can be snapped and eaten along with the immature peas inside. These generally do not dry well. Snow peas are harvested as flat, tender pods before the peas are developed. These don't dry well either.

Selection: Use fresh, crisp, and medium-size pods. They should be bright green and well filled. The smaller sizes do not rehydrate well and the larger ones tend to be starchy.

Storage before drying: Process immediately after harvesting—the fresher, the better. The sugar in fresh peas begins to turn to starch even while they are refrigerated. At room temperature, as much as 50 percent of the sugar in peas is converted to starch within six hours.

Water content before drying: 78 percent.

Preparation: To shell, pinch off the ends and pull the string down on the inside of the pod. Pop the peas out.

Pretreatment: Steam blanch for three minutes.

Drying temperature: 130°F (54°C) until dry.

Dryness test: Brittle and shriveled.

How to use: Peas are good in soups and stews. Season cooked peas with allspice, basil, marjoram, thyme, or tarragon.

PEPPERS

Chilies are the most widely used spice and condiment in the world. They are members of the large and diverse nightshade family. Some peppers, such as bell peppers, are sweet. Others carry varying degrees of pungent spiciness.

Peppers are good sources of vitamins A and C. One small, raw sweet pepper, about ¾ cup, has twenty calories.

Peppers can be sweet and mild, medium, spicy hot, or so fiery hot that your mouth feels like it is on fire. There is no sure way to predict hotness, but each variety has a basic range, and the smallest varieties are generally the hottest.

Climate affects hotness. Those grown in milder climates tend to be milder than those grown in hot climates. The hotness is concentrated in the enclosed veins or ribs near the seed heart, not in the seeds as commonly believed. The seeds taste hot because they are in close contact with the veins.

Quality when dried: Good to excellent.

Varieties best for drying: There are hundreds of different varieties of peppers, all of which dry well. Sweet peppers include bell pepper, sweet banana pepper, sweet cherry pepper, and pimiento.

The mild to medium varieties include ancho, Hungarian yellow wax, and sweet banana.

Several that will make your eyes water and tongue tingle are Anaheim, cayenne, jalapeño, red chili, and serrano.

Color varies in bell peppers. Some green peppers ripen to a deep red. Other varieties ripen to a golden yellow or bright orange.

Selection: Look for firm, brightly colored, shiny pods with no signs of bruising or rotting. When peppers are mature, they break off easily from the plant, but less damage is done to the plants if the peppers are cut rather than pulled off. Hot peppers are the hottest if allowed to fully ripen.

Storage before drying: Wrap in a paper towel and store in a loosely closed plastic bag in the refrigerator at 35°F to 40°F (2°C to 4°C) to maintain the highest quality.

Water content before drying: 65 to 90 percent, depending on the variety.

Preparation: Sweet peppers such as bell or pimiento may be halved, quartered, or cut into ½-inch dice prior to drying.

If you're drying red chilies, rinse and leave them whole. String by the stems. You can slightly decrease the heat of a hot dried chili by removing the seeds and veins. Be sure to wear rubber gloves when handling hot chilies.

Pretreatment: None.

Drying temperature: 130°F (54°C) until dry.

Dryness test: Tough to brittle.

How to use: Whirl in blender or food processor for seasoning meat, poultry, or other dishes.

POPCORN

Popcorn is a very popular snack food in the United States. Americans consume about seventeen billion quarts of popped popcorn each year or an average of about fifty-four quarts per person.

One of the ancient ways to pop corn was to heat sand in a large kettle and stir kernels of popcorn in when the sand was fully heated.

Popcorn is a whole-grain, high-quality carbohydrate that is high in fiber. One cup of unbuttered popcorn has only about fifty calories.

Popcorn needs to contain 13 to 14 percent moisture in order to pop. Each kernel of popcorn contains a small drop of water stored inside a circle of soft starch. The soft starch is surrounded by the kernel's hard outer surface. As the kernel heats up, the water expands, building up pressure against the hard starch. This hard surface eventually gives way, causing the popcorn to explode. As it explodes, the soft starch inside the popcorn becomes inflated and bursts, turning the kernel inside out.

Quality when dried: Excellent.

Varieties best for drying: Popcorn is a special kind of corn. Certain varieties of popcorn can be dried at home. The best varieties are Japanese Hull-less, Crème Puff Hybrid, White Cloud, and Dynamite. Popcorn requires eighteen to twenty-four inches of water during the growing season.

Selection: Popcorn is mature when the stalk and leaves turn brown and are dry, and the kernel is hard.

Water content before drying: 73 percent.

Preparation: Leave the ears of popcorn on the stalks until the kernels are well dried. Remove dry kernels from the ears and package.

Pretreatment: None.

Drying temperature: No higher than 130°F (54°C) until dry.

Dryness test: Pop a few kernels to test.

How to use: Follow the usual procedure for popping corn.

Additional information: More information and recipes are available from:

Popcorn Board
401 N. Michigan Avenue
Chicago, IL 60611-4267
Phone: 312-644-6610
Fax: 312-321-5150
Email: gbertalmio@smithbucklin.com
Website: www.popcorn.org

SWEET POTATOES

Excellent in leathers: see Vegetable Rolls, below.

TOMATOES

See the section on Gourmet Dried Tomatoes, page 75.

VEGETABLE LEATHER ROLLS

We now see a variety of different vegetable-based dried snacks at the supermarket. While it is impossible to duplicate the sophisticated processing of commercial vegetable processors, it is quite easy to make quite delicious dried vegetable snacks at home.

This section will provide you with some guidelines for vegetables that dry well and some suggestions for enhancing the flavor of some root vegetables.

VEGETABLES THAT CAN BE MADE INTO LEATHERS

As you've probably already discovered, most vegetables are quite unappealing when dried. They tend to be tough, inedible without rehydrating, and when rehydrated, many are poor quality.

However, there are some vegetables that make quite delightful leathers. They all have a base of root vegetables such as carrots or sweet potatoes. When combined with fruits and fruit juices or concentrates, they can be dried into leathers that are nutritious and taste like the fruit instead of the vegetable.

The root vegetables need to be steamed to a tender state. They are then blended with water, juice, or fruits.

- **Sweet potatoes.** Sweet potatoes provide the best base for a variety of different combinations. The flavor of a sweet potato is mild and complements other flavors nicely. Alone, sweet potatoes make chewy leather, similar to fruit leather. Garnet or Jewel sweet potatoes, sometimes called yams, generally have more color and combine well with fruit.
- **Carrots.** Carrots naturally contain sugar and also provide an excellent base for a variety of flavor combinations.

HOW TO MAKE VEGETABLE ROLLS

Prepare Your Trays

- Line a drying tray with a solid plastic sheet that comes with your dehydrator. You can also use Mylar or food-grade 4mil plastic. Kitchen plastic wrap is quite flimsy and isn't recommended.
- Lightly coat the plastic with a nonstick vegetable spray.
- Do not use waxed paper or aluminum foil.

Wash, Steam, and Peel the Root Vegetable

- Wash and steam the root vegetable.
- Peel sweet potatoes after steaming.
- Peel carrots before steaming.

Add Additional Liquid and Puree in the Blender Until Very Smooth

- Add enough water or juice to make a puree of pouring consistency.
- Puree until it is smooth.

Add Spices or Flavorings

- Spices or flavorings will concentrate when dried, so use them sparingly.
- Experiment with different combinations. Add one spice or flavoring at a time in small amounts and taste the puree to decide if you like it. If the puree tastes good, the leather will probably taste good.
- Start with just a pinch of spice or ¼ teaspoon per quart of puree. Taste the puree before adding more.
- A small amount of fresh lemon juice is a pleasant addition to almost every combination.

Dry at the Right Temperature

- Keep a constant temperature in your dehydrator of 130°F to 140°F (54°C to 60°C) until the leather is dry.

Add a Garnish

- Garnishes add texture to vegetable leathers just as they do fruit leathers.
- Sprinkle garnishes on the vegetable leather before drying or while the leather is still quite moist so the garnish will stick.
- Try these garnishes: shredded or flaked coconut, chopped dates, or finely chopped dried fruit.

Pour the Puree onto the Drying Tray

- Pour the puree onto the prepared drying tray. Slightly tilt the tray to spread the puree evenly or spread it with a rubber spatula.
- Puree should generally be about ¼-inch thick across the entire surface of the drying tray. Leave at least a 1-inch border on flat trays to allow for spreading during drying.

How to Tell When It Is Dry

- With clean hands, touch the top of the leather in several different places. It should feel like leather and not be soft to the touch.
- When the leather is sufficiently dried, you will be able to pull it up, beginning at the edge of the tray.
- If it sticks in the center and some of the puree underneath is still moist, return it to the dehydrator for another hour or so.
- Vegetable leather dried in a dehydrator is usually done in six to eight hours.

Remove Leather from the Trays While Warm

- Remove the leather from the tray while it is still warm and roll it up. Cooled vegetable leather does not roll as easily and may crack.
- Roll into long rolls. Then cut the long rolls into shorter pieces.

How to Store Your Vegetable Leather

- Vegetable leathers have a much shorter shelf life than fruit leathers. They should be eaten in a couple of weeks.
- Store them in an airtight container in the refrigerator.
- If you're cutting the rolls into 4- or 5-inch pieces, position them upright inside of a wide-mouth one-pint canning jar. Vacuum seal if you have a home vacuum-packaging machine. If not, secure the top with a lid and screw band.
- Keep your vegetable rolls in the freezer for up to two months.

Label So You Can Remember What You Dried and Whether You Liked It

- It is helpful to label vegetable rolls clearly so you can decide what you like and don't like for next season.
- Label your containers clearly with a permanent marker or stick-on labels.
- Include the date, type of vegetable, and what was added for flavor.

VEGETABLE LEATHER RECIPES

Here are some of my favorite combinations. Puree all the ingredients in a blender until smooth. Each recipe makes one to three trays of leather, depending on the size of the trays. Dry as instructed above.

Pineapple, Raspberry, and Sweet Potato Leather

1 cup cooked, peeled sweet potato
½ cup water
1 tablespoon frozen pineapple juice concentrate
½ cup raspberry syrup
1 tablespoon fresh lemon juice

Pineapple, Raspberry, and Yam Leather

1 cup cooked, peeled Garnet or Jewel sweet
    potato (often called yam)
½ cup water
1 tablespoon frozen pineapple juice concentrate
⅜ cup raspberry syrup
1 tablespoon fresh lemon juice

Pineapple and Sweet Potato Leather

1 cup cooked, peeled sweet potato
1 cup water
2 tablespoons frozen pineapple juice concentrate
1 teaspoon fresh lemon juice

Strawberry, Raspberry, and Sweet Potato Leather

1 cup cooked, peeled sweet potato
1 cup fresh strawberries, hulled, sliced
2 tablespoons raspberry syrup
Pinch sodium bisulfite

Lime and Sweet Potato Leather

1 cup cooked, peeled sweet potato

¾ cup water

¼ cup fresh lime juice

Pineapple, Orange, and Sweet Potato Leather

¾ cup cooked, peeled sweet potato

½ cup orange juice

½ cup cooked, peeled Garnet or Jewel sweet potato (often called yam)

1 tablespoon frozen pineapple juice concentrate

Orange and Yam Leather

¾ cup orange juice

1¼ cups cooked, peeled Garnet or Jewel sweet potato (often called yam)

¼ teaspoon freshly grated orange zest

HERBS AND SPICES

Herbs and spices come from a variety of plants and parts of plants. Many herbs, such as basil, marjoram, or mint, are valued for their *leaves*, and others, such as dill and parsley, for both their *leaves* and *stems*. Cloves are *flower buds*, allspice comes from a *berry*, and nutmeg comes from the *fruit of a plant*. Poppy, caraway, and mustard are *seeds* of the plant.

Herbs are classified as any flowering plant whose stem above the ground does not become woody. This definition includes a wide variety of vegetables and some fruits. However, for those of us who grow and use herbs, they are defined as any plant valued for culinary flavor and aroma or medicinal properties.

Herbs are usually grown in temperate climates, while many spices require a tropical climate. Some fresh herbs and spices are available seasonally. Others such as parsley, basil, dill, ginger root, cilantro (fresh coriander), and tarragon are available most of the year.

Herbs and spices have little, if any, nutritive value, but their unique flavors and aromas are indispensable in creating the favorite foods of the world. Usually fresh herbs and spices have a better aroma and flavor than dried ones and are prized by food lovers and gourmet cooks. Most fresh herbs contain from 70 to 85 percent water.

Dried herbs and spices are next best and are used more often than fresh because they are readily available and convenient. They have a better flavor if they are harvested at the right time and properly dried and stored. They may lose some of their flavoring oils when dried, but drying also concentrates the flavor by removing the water. Eight ounces of fresh herbs will yield about one ounce of dried.

GROW YOUR OWN

If you have the garden space and time, you may want to plant an herb garden. Herbs grow fairly well with a minimal amount of care and under a wide range of soil conditions.

Plant outside herb gardens where they will get plenty of sunshine. Keep the area free of weeds. To avoid confusion about what is what, define an area for each herb with dividers or other plants. In milder climates, some perennial herbs such as mint or thyme can be harvested most of the year.

Herbs grow best in well-drained soils. If the soil is too wet, they will grow poorly and are subject to root rot. If you have heavy soil, add a lot of organic matter and sand to loosen the clay structure.

A number of herbs can be grown indoors on a sunny windowsill or covered porch. Herbs such as chervil, chives, marjoram, mint, oregano, rosemary, or sage will grow indoors most of the year.

For the best results, start new plants in the fall by means of rooted cuttings rather than moving an old plant indoors. Indoor plants must have plenty of sunlight and a temperature maintained well above freezing at all times. Any container is suitable for growing herbs as long as it has a drainage hole.

If you're growing herbs in containers out of doors, you can move them indoors for the winter. Gradually move them indoors a few hours at a time over the period of several days so they adjust to the differences in temperature and light. Put them in a location where they can get as much sun as possible. Water them only when the soil gets dry and give them enough water so that it drains out the bottom. The roots will rot when you give them too much water or there isn't good drainage in the bottom of the pot.

Nurseries and some produce markets have *starts*, small plants that grow more quickly than seeds.

Annual herbs are usually grown from seed and have to be planted new each year. They grow, flower, and produce seed during one season, and then die. They can be cut back quite severely during harvest. Cut just above a leaf or a pair of leaves, and leave about four to six inches of stem for later growth. If it is grown for its seed, do not harvest the leaves. Collect the seeds when the plant begins to turn brown.

Biennial herbs grow for two seasons and produce flowers and fruit the second year after planting. The tender leaves and leafstalks can be harvested the first season.

Perennial herbs grow from one season to the next and survive over the winter. Some herbs are tender perennials and do not survive severe winters unless they are overwintered indoors. Perennials are the easiest to grow indoors.

Perennials should be cut less than annuals, with only about one-third of the top growth removed at a time. Harvest time is usually in the early part of July, with a second harvest in September.

Some perennials, such as chives, rarely produce seeds. They are propagated by dividing the clumps of bulbs. Divide the clumps either in the fall or spring and subdivide them every two or three years to prevent them from overcrowding.

HOW TO DRY HERBS AND SPICES

For the best flavor, use scissors to gather leaves and stems on a sunny morning just after the dew has evaporated and before the heat of the sun has dissipated the flavoring oils. The leaves of most herbs should be still green and tender and harvested just before the plant begins to flower.

Harvest plants in the mint family when they are in full bloom for the best flavor. The new leaves at the tip of the plant are usually the most flavorful. After flowering, many herbs have a bitter taste and the leaves are not as aromatic because more energy has gone into the buds. Leaves and stems of several herbs may be harvested three or four times during the summer and others may be gathered year-round.

The flowers of some herbs are flavorful and should be harvested when they first open and while still very fresh.

Harvest fully mature seeds of plants such as mustard or caraway. Some seeds change from bright green to brown or gray as they mature.

WASH HERBS AND GET THEM READY TO DRY

Lightly rinse leaves and stems with cold water, either by submerging or holding under running water; shake off excess water. Cut off dead or discolored leaves or stems.

Tender leaf herbs, such as basil, rosemary, tarragon, and mints, must be dried quickly away from light if they are to retain their green color. They will mold if they are dried too slowly.

To dry flower petals, wash, then separate petals and trim away any tough or discolored parts. If the flowers are to be used for tea, they must be dried whole.

Seedpods, depending upon how much they have dried on the plant, may be left as is until the outer covering is sufficiently dried so that it may be easily removed. When the outer covering is fairly dry, rub the seeds between the palms of your hands, blowing to remove the *chaff* or husks. The seeds are then dried until there is no evidence of moisture when they are crushed. Do not heat seeds to be used for planting or they will not germinate.

DRY HERBS

In a Dehydrator

Dehydrator drying is the most efficient and produces the highest quality dried herbs because it takes only one to three hours and has controlled temperature and good air circulation.

You Will Need
- An electric dehydrator with a fan, heater, and adjustable thermostat that reaches a low of 90°F to 100°F (about 32°C to 38°C).
- Plastic mesh screens.

How to Do It
- Place the prepared herbs on plastic mesh screens, and then on the drying trays in a preheated dryer with the thermostat set for 90°F to 100°F (about 32°C to 38°C) and dry.
- Do not dry herbs with moist loads of fruits or vegetables. Not only will the increased humidity lengthen the drying time for the herbs but also fruits and vegetables are dried at a much higher temperature than herbs. These higher temperatures dissipate the herbs' flavoring oils.

PESKY PESTS

With some seeds, there is the possibility of insect contamination. To be sure all insects are removed, cut the stalks, dip the stalks and heads in boiling water, and drain on a paper towel before drying. Do not dip seeds that are going to be used for planting.

When They're Dry

- When the leaves are sufficiently dry, usually in two to three hours, carefully remove them from the drying trays.
  - Remove the stems and package.

In Paper Bags

Bag drying is one of the simplest ways to dry leafy herbs with long stems.

You Will Need

- Small brown paper bags
- Heavy string
- Hooks

How to Do It

- Tie the herbs in small bunches by the ends of the stems.
- Suspend them upside down in small brown paper bags, which have been labeled.
  - Tie a string firmly around the top of each bag.
- Hanging them upside down will cause the flavoring oils from the stems to concentrate in the leaves. Cut several ½-inch holes in each side of the bags to let air circulate and to speed drying.
- Hang them in the kitchen, attic, or anywhere there is a warm, even temperature and good air circulation. If you are drying large quantities of herbs and hanging a number of bags in the same place, suspend them with different lengths of string to allow good air circulation between the bags.

When They're Dry

- When the leaves are sufficiently dry, usually in two to three weeks, they will crumble easily.
- Check by opening the bag and feeling the leaves. If they are dry enough, roll the bag gently between your hands so the leaves will crumble from the stems and fall to the bottom of the bag. Leaves that are not completely dry will mold during storage.
  - Seedpods with long stems may also be dried in bags. The seeds will fall to the bottom of the bag as they dry.

In a Warm Room

Room drying on a tray works well for herbs with large leaves, such as basil, or ones with short stems. Seeds and flowers may also be tray dried.

You Will Need

- Window screen
- Cheesecloth
- Bricks or wooden blocks

How to Do It

- An old window screen works well, is inexpensive, and lets the air circulate. Wash it and cover it with a thin layer of cheesecloth.
- Place one layer of leaves, stems, flowers, or seeds on the tray and cover them with another thin layer of cheesecloth to keep off dust and insects.
- Place the tray in a clean, warm location, preferably on props, such as bricks or wooden blocks, to allow the air to circulate underneath. Turn the herbs over every day or two so they will dry evenly.

When They're Dry

- Check the trays after a week or so. When they are dry enough, the leaves will crumble from the stems.
- Keep a newspaper underneath to catch dry leaves that fall through.

Oven Drying Is the Least Effective Way to Dry Herbs

Oven drying removes more essential oils than room drying because a low, constant temperature is difficult to maintain in the oven. Most gas ovens generate enough heat with just the pilot light, but it is difficult to adjust electric ovens to keep a constant temperature below 100°F (38°C).

You Will Need
- Nylon net or window screen
- Trays
- Oven

How to Do It
- If you use your gas oven with the pilot light, cover the oven racks with a nylon net or old window screens.
- Arrange the herbs one layer deep.
- Prop the oven door open slightly to let the moisture escape.
- Convection ovens work better because air is continually circulated. Place the leaves with the stems on a cookie sheet or shallow pan and dry at 100°F (38°C) or lower, for three to four hours.

When They're Dry
- Carefully remove the leaves and stems from the rack. Place on a baking sheet or shallow pan.
- Remove the dry leaves from the stems.

Dry Small Quantities in the Microwave

Microwave ovens may be used to dry small quantities of herbs. Some ovens may work better than others, depending on the power settings.

You Will Need
- Paper towels
- Microwave oven

How to Do It
- Place four or five stems with leaves between paper towels.
- Set the microwave timer for two to three minutes and medium power.
- Check to see if the stems and leaves are sufficiently dry. If not, reset the timer for an additional thirty seconds and check again. Repeat the process if necessary.

When They're Dry
- Carefully lift out the paper towels. Place on a baking sheet or shallow pan.
- Remove the dry leaves from the stems.

Herbs Don't Dry Well in the Sun

Sun drying is not recommended for herbs because the sun causes herbs to lose too much aroma, flavor, and color.

TEST TO FIND OUT IF THEY'RE DRY

Herbs are dry when they crumble easily. Stems should be brittle and break when bent. Seeds will readily fall from the chaff, but usually need additional drying after they have been removed from the seedpods. Seeds should be brittle. If herbs and seeds are not sufficiently dry, they may mold.

PACKAGE FOR STORAGE

If you have a home vacuum-packaging system, seal dried herbs or seeds in a pint jar. Otherwise, use an airtight container with a tight-fitting lid. Check daily for condensation on the inside of the container. If any condensation appears, remove the herbs or seeds and dry them longer.

LABEL YOUR PACKAGED DRIED HERBS AND SPICES

- Herb or spice
- Date dried

SHELF LIFE

Store in a dark, cool place, preferably below 60°F (16°C), to keep the best flavor and color. Any heat, air, light, or moisture will cause dried herbs to rapidly deteriorate. The freezer is the best place, if you have the room.

Because the temperature of the kitchen is probably much warmer than your storage area, keep only small amounts ready to use and the rest in storage. Do not store herbs directly over the stove.

Whole leaf herbs and whole spices have the longest shelf life. For the fullest flavor, crush herbs and spices just before using. Crushing or grinding herbs and seeds before storage increases the loss of aroma and flavor.

With proper packaging and good storage conditions, dried herbs and spices should keep well for six months to one year.

HOW TO USE DRIED HERBS AND SPICES

How Much?

Dried herbs and spices are usually three to four times stronger than their fresh counterparts be-cause they have been concentrated. If the recipe calls for a fresh herb or spice, you can usually use one-third to one-fourth as much of the dried and expect the same result.

However, the strength of dried herbs and spices depends greatly on the conditions under which they have been stored and how old they are. Strength deteriorates with the type of herb, storage time and temperature, and the exposure to moisture or light. Some herbs, such as mint or basil, lose their flavor more rapidly than others when dried. It may take nearly an equal volume of some dried herbs to replace the amount of fresh called for in a recipe.

The safest way to use dried herbs and spices is to start with a small amount, taste, and add more if the flavor isn't quite strong enough. Their influence should be subtle, so add sparingly.

When to Add

Ground herbs and spices should be added about fifteen minutes before the end of the cooking time. Whole spices can be placed in a cheesecloth bag (for easy removal) and added at the beginning of cooking so the long simmering will extract the full flavor and aroma.

Whole or leaf herbs should be crumbled finely just before adding to a dish to release the best flavor. Seeds may be slightly roasted before using.

In order to draw out and extend the flavor of the aromatic oils in herbs, heat them with butter, margarine, or other cooking fats such as olive oil.

Cooking them too long can easily cause the loss of the delicate aroma and flavor of savory herbs. As a general rule, add herbs near the end of cooking rather than at the beginning.

How Do You Decide Which One?

Some herbs blend pleasantly with almost any food, others with only a few. A recipe should provide you with some guidelines.

Many herbs and spices may be combined for seasoning. The popular blend *fines herbes* is equal parts of chives, chervil, tarragon or rosemary, and parsley. It is used to season meats, casseroles, fish, salads, or egg dishes.

Another frequently used blend, *bouquet garni*, is made up of thyme, bay leaf, parsley, and celery leaves tied in a cheesecloth bag and used to season soup stock. Other combinations that we frequently think of as one spice or herb, such as curry powder or chili powder, are really a blend of a number of different seasonings.

Your individual taste preferences will really be the key. It's fun to experiment with different herbs and spices with different recipes. The entire flavor of a dish can be completely changed by the addition of one herb.

ALL ABOUT HERBS AND SPICES

ANISE

Anise has a very interesting flavor and you either like it or you don't. There isn't much in between. It is used in the manufacture of many commercial cough syrups and sore throat medications and to scent soaps and perfumes.

Anise seeds should ripen on the plant. If they are picked green, they will mold during storage.

When ripe, their color changes from green to grayish-brown. Cut the flower stems and hang them upside down in a brown paper bag in a warm, dry place. Seeds are collected as they fall into the bag.

Anise is grown mainly for its sweet, licorice-flavored seeds, although the small, tender leaves are used in fruit and vegetable salads, soups, stews, or sauces. Anise seed is used in baking cookies such as the German springerle, sweet breads, biscuits, and cakes. It is occasionally used in spicy meats such as sausage, and in poultry and cole slaw. Anise seed will add a distinct flavor to stewed fruits and fruit compotes.

BASIL

Basil is one of the most popular herbs in Italian- and Mediterranean-style cooking. It is delicious in all tomato dishes and improves many vegetables, green salads, vegetable soups, and meat, fish, poultry, and egg dishes.

Clip basil leaves three to four inches from the top of the plant just before the first buds appear. Cut the stem just above a leaf or a pair of leaves. The plants can have numerous cuttings later in the season.

Basil is very perishable, so handle fresh basil gently to avoid bruising.

BORAGE

Borage is a mild, rather uncommon herb with leaves and flowers, which can be used in seasoning. Salads and cooked vegetables are enhanced by a little borage, although it is used mainly as an ornamental plant.

CARAWAY

The entire caraway plant is usually dried to keep the seeds from scattering when it matures. The seeds continue to mature after the plant dies. The seeds are harvested after they turn a gray-brown color.

Caraway seeds are susceptible to aphid attacks while ripening. To destroy any hidden insects, scald ripened seeds before drying by quickly plunging them into boiling water, then ice water. Drain on a paper towel.

Caraway seeds add refreshing flavor to heavy dishes such as pork or sauerkraut. They are frequently used in Hungarian dishes, some cabbage salads, and several types of cookies, rye bread, and cheeses. Try them with green beans, beets, cabbage, carrots, cauliflower, potatoes, turnips, or zucchini. Use them sparingly until you become accustomed to their flavor.

CELERY

Although celery is known primarily as a vegetable, the leaves are frequently used for seasoning. Celery leaves can be used in main dishes, soups, stews, salads, and vegetables.

The tiny, brown celery seeds come from a different variety of wild celery called *smallage* or *lovage*. They are very strong and must be used sparingly or they will overpower accompanying flavors.

CHERVIL

Tender green chervil leaves are frequently used as a substitute for parsley, although their flavor is milder and they are a lighter shade of green. Harvest the tender leaves just before the buds break.

Chervil is popular in French cooking and can be used with other herbs in salads, sauces, soups, and fish. It should be added at the end of cooking to preserve its full flavor. Try it in cottage cheese or cream cheese for dips or sandwich spreads.

CHIVES

Chives are small, dainty, onionlike plants that grow in clumps and have a very mild onion flavor. Chives don't require a lot of attention, other than dividing when they become overcrowded. In the fall, divide some of the bulbs and plant indoors in a pot, so fresh chives are available through the winter.

Drying diminishes their already delicate flavor, but dried chives may be used when fresh are not available. Dehydrator drying is recommended. When dried, the long, tubular leaves are best used in moist dishes such as cottage cheese, soups, or vegetables to bring out their flavor.

CORIANDER OR CILANTRO

Although the terms coriander and cilantro are used interchangeably, coriander is the dried seed of the plant, and usually the fresh leaves are known as cilantro. Both the seeds and leaves have very distinctive flavors. The seeds have a warm, mild, almost citrus flavor.

Scald coriander seeds before drying to protect against insects. Uproot the entire plant, trim off the roots, scald and bag or dehydrator dry.

Coriander is extremely fragrant and will dominate other flavors if not used with restraint. It is popular in Mexican, Chinese, Indian, South American, and Mediterranean cooking. Use it prudently in fruit or vegetable dishes. The crushed seeds are flavorful in sausage, pickling spices, gingerbread, and cookies. Add coriander seed to apples, pears, or dried fruit while cooking.

CUMIN

Cumin is an annual and a member of the parsley family.

Cumin seeds have tiny bristles, hardly visible to the naked eye. The seeds should be lightly roasted before being ground to bring out the fullest flavor. Ground into a brownish-green powder, cumin has a strong, spicy-sweet aroma.

Cumin seed, whole or ground, is used in spicy dishes throughout much of the world. It is a popular ingredient in curries and chili. It should be used with restraint, because it will overpower all other flavors in a dish.

DILL

All parts of the umbrella-leaved dill plant are flavorful. Harvest the leaves just as the flowers open. Pick the seeds when they are flat and brown.

The mildly flavored leaves are a pleasant addition to many salads, potatoes, deviled eggs, green beans, cauliflower, beets, cream cheese, and fish dishes. The seeds are stronger and are mainly used in pickling. Dill pickles are a North American classic. Dill is also used in salad dressing and strong-flavored vegetable or meat dishes. Dill seed may be substituted for caraway seeds in breads such as rye.

FENNEL

Fennel has a warm, sweet, and aromatic bouquet similar to a mild anise. Although fennel is grown primarily for its licorice-flavored seed, the delicate leaves may be used in salads, vegetables, soups or stews, and seafood. The fresh leaves and tender shoots can be used during the first and following seasons.

The seeds mature in the fall of the second season. The flower heads should be harvested before the seeds fully ripen. Completely dry and then thresh out the seeds. The strong-flavored seeds are used in cookies, cakes, breads, cheese spreads, spicy meat dishes, pork roasts, or sausage.

Fennel resembles dill and should be kept at a distance from dill because it can cross-pollinate, and the resulting seed has a dulled flavor.

GARLIC

See All About Vegetables, page 85.

GINGER

Ginger is native to India and China. The fresh roots provide the best flavor. The outer skin is a light brown color. Most ginger root is imported from tropical locales and is available fresh in supermarkets or produce departments specializing in Oriental foods.

Ginger tubers should be firm and appear fresh. The small new sprouts that appear on the sides of the ginger root have a delicate flavor and may also be used. Fresh ginger freezes well and can be grated without thawing. It keeps well for several weeks in the crisper of the refrigerator. Wrap it in a paper towel and put in a loosely closed plastic bag.

Ginger can be easily rooted and grown indoors from small pieces. Set the top just below the surface of the dirt and keep the soil moist. Leave the pot in a dark place until shoots appear. Then give it plenty of light.

To dry ginger, slice it thinly or grate it. Keep it as cool as possible to retain the best flavor. If you are using dried powered ginger, ⅛ teaspoon is equivalent to 1 tablespoon grated or shredded fresh ginger root.

Powdered ginger is the buff-colored ground spice made from the dried root.

Crystallized ginger is cooked in sugar syrup, then dried and rolled in sugar.

Ginger's fresh, spicy flavor improves many chutneys and curry pastes and meat, vegetable, and dessert dishes. The tender, aromatic ginger leaves are delicious in soups. Gingerbread and gingersnaps are holiday favorites.

HORSERADISH

See All About Vegetables, page 86.

MARJORAM

Marjoram is a member of the mint family and is slightly milder and sweeter than oregano. It grows well indoors. Cut the velvety, small gray-green leaves just as the first buds begin to appear. Marjoram may be clipped two or three times during a summer.

Use marjoram in Italian dishes as well as other meat, fish, poultry, or egg dishes. It goes well with many vegetables, particularly tomatoes, onions, and mushrooms. Marjoram blends well with basil, chives, parsley, and thyme. Use sparingly until you become familiar with its flavor. It can overpower if used too generously.

MINT

The pilgrims brought mint to the United States on the *Mayflower*. There are more than forty different varieties of mint. Spearmint and peppermint leaves are deep green, long, pointed, and crinkled. Spearmint has a sweet flavor that is cooling to the mouth and is preferred for cooking because it has a milder flavor than peppermint. Peppermint has a stronger menthol taste and is used to flavor toothpaste and chewing gum.

Mint is easily cultivated in home gardens. Take care where you plant it, because it is very invasive and will quickly take over the whole garden if not contained.

The fresh leaves are considerably more flavorful than the dried. Cut the leaves just as flowering begins. Because the mint flavor is very perishable, dry quickly and store carefully.

Mild spearmint is popular in sauces and mint jelly or lamb dishes. Strong-flavored peppermint can be used in some beverages or baked goods. A variety of meat dishes improve with the addition of mint. Mint blends well with a few vegetables such as beans, eggplant, peas, and potatoes. Dried mint is sprinkled over hummus and other pulse and grain dishes. Crush the leaves just before adding to food. Add at the end of cooking for the best flavor.

MUSTARD

Mustard is one of the oldest spices and one of the most widely used. Mustard consumption today tops 400 million pounds annually.

Three main types of mustard seeds are grown:

- Black mustard, which has potent dark-brown seeds, is much more pungent than the white.

- Brown mustard, which has light to dark brown seeds, is more pungent than the white and less than the black.
- White mustard has milder yellowish seeds and milder flavor. Table mustard is made from the white seeds, blended with sugar and vinegar and colored with turmeric.

The seeds of each vary from mild to hot, depending on the variety. Mustard seeds can also be used whole in corned beef, sauerkraut, cooked cabbage, and vinegar-based salad dressings. These seeds are usually ground in combination with other seasonings. Powdered mustard is useful in barbecue sauces, baked beans, deviled eggs, and beets.

ONIONS

See All About Vegetables, page 88.

OREGANO

A member of the mint family, oregano is a stronger herb than its close cousin, marjoram, and actually smells more like thyme. Oregano grows well in poor soil and can be propagated by seed or division.

It is widely used in Italian, Greek, and Mexican foods, tomato dishes, and with some vegetables. Use prudently until you are accustomed to its strong flavor.

PARSLEY

See All About Vegetables, page 90.

Parsley has a much higher food value and is used in larger amounts than most herbs. It is frequently classified as a vegetable. Parsley is a popular seasoning for meats, fish, soups, casseroles, or vegetable dishes.

PEPPERS, SWEET AND HOT

See All About Vegetables, page 91.

ROSEMARY

Rosemary grows well indoors although it needs lots of light. It is easy to dry, and retains most of its flavor in the dried state. There are two main varieties, an upright rosemary and a creeping plant that is nice in rock gardens and hanging baskets. Both dry well.

Rosemary can be grown from seeds, but it is best to take cuttings from an existing plant or buy a *start*. It grows best in a full-sun location.

Rosemary combines well with other herbs, but has a tendency to dominate. Its needlelike leaves add unique flavor to many foods. Use rosemary in barbeque sauces and egg, meat, lamb, poultry, and some vegetable dishes, such as cauliflower, peas, beans, or zucchini.

SAGE

Sage is a member of the mint family and is very aromatic. It needs full sun to grow. Plants eventually become woody and should be renewed every three or four years.

Sage is best used fresh, but can also be dried. Because it is so strong, it can be added at the beginning of cooking and pairs nicely with other strongly flavored herbs such as rosemary, thyme, and savory.

The common gray sage has the best flavor. Golden and purple sages can be dried, but are

HERBS AND SPICES YOU CAN GROW AND DRY

HERB OR SPICE	WHEN HARVESTED	PART OF PLANT DRIED
Anise (annual)	Before blossoming	Leaves
	Fall	Seeds
Basil (annual)	Summer	Leaves
Borage (annual)	When mature	Leaves
	First blossoming	Flowers
Caraway (biennial)	Fall of second season	Seeds
Celery (biennial)	When mature	Leaves
Chervil (annual)	When mature	Leaves
Chives (perennial)	Throughout growing season	Leaves—cut 1½ to 2 inches from roots
Coriander or cilantro (annual)	Summer	Leaves and stems
	Fall	Seeds
Cumin (annual)	When mature	Seeds
Dill (annual)	First blossoming and throughout growing season	Leaves and seeds
	First blossoming	Flowers
	Fall	Seeds
Fennel (perennial)	Before blossoming	Leaves
	When mature	Seeds
Ginger (perennial)	When mature	Roots (rhizomes)
Marjoram (perennial)	When mature	Leaves
Mint (perennial)	Throughout growing season	Leaves
Mustard (annual)	When mature	Seeds
Oregano (annual)	First blossoming	Leaves
Parsley (biennial)	When mature	Leaves and stems
Rosemary (perennial)	When mature	Needlelike leaves
Sage (perennial)	Before blossoming	Leaves
Savory (annual)	When mature	Leaves
Tarragon (perennial)	Before blossoming	Leaves
Thyme (perennial)	When mature	Leaves

milder. Sage leaves are used primarily in poultry dishes such as stuffing, soups, chicken stocks, or roast poultry, but they also enhance some pork, lamb, veal, game, and fish dishes. Crush or grind the dried leaves to release their full flavor.

SAVORY

Fresh savory has a grasslike smell and a mild peppery flavor, pungent and spicy. It maintains most of its flavor when dried.

Cut the leafy tops when the plants are in bud. When dry, it should be quite crisp.

There are two seasonal varieties: summer and winter savory. The color and size vary, but the flavor is markedly similar, except the summer is usually a little sweeter than the winter savory. Savory is popular in poultry seasonings and can be used in some vegetables such as green beans or peas.

TARRAGON

Tarragon is a perennial that grows to about two feet tall. It has narrow, somewhat twisted green leaves. It will grow in full sun, but does better in semi-shade. Make new plantings every three or four years and protect it in winter in cold climates.

Dried tarragon isn't nearly as flavorful as fresh. It loses its pungency rather quickly, so take care in packaging and storage.

Tarragon has a characteristic flavor, which makes it a valuable seasoning in vinegar, sauces, salads, and fish, lamb, poultry, and veal dishes. Only fresh tarragon should be used in making tarragon vinegar.

THYME

Thyme grows best in light, well-drained soil. New plants should be started every three or four years, since the old plants become too woody to produce tender leaves.

Cut thyme leaves just as the buds appear but before they begin to blossom. French thyme has the best flavor when dried and is easily grown from seed.

Dry with the leaves attached to the stem. When it is dried, the leaves strip easily from the stem. Before adding fresh thyme to a recipe, strip the grayish-green leaves from the woody stem.

Thyme is one of the stronger herbs with a heavy aroma and spicy taste that faintly resembles cloves. Use sparingly in meat, fish, egg, and poultry dishes. It is a good seasoning for some vegetables such as green beans, beets, carrots, potatoes, and tomatoes as well as vegetable soups.

NUTS AND SEEDS

Nuts are plant seeds or fruit encased in a *shell* or *hull* or woody fiber. The nut *kernel* is the inner edible part of the nut, also called a *nutmeat*. The *husk* is the rough outer covering, which encases the shell and kernel.

Some nuts are classified as fruits or vegetables. For example, the peanut is really a member of the pea family and the almond is part of the peach family.

The kernels, or nutmeats, are extremely high in protein and fat, and contain vitamins and minerals. Nuts can be eaten fresh from the shell, roasted, or added to other foods. Their crunchy texture, nutrient content, and delicious flavor enhance appetizers, main dishes, salads, vegetables, breads, desserts, and candies.

Once harvested, nuts either in the shell or out of the shell should be dried to a relatively low moisture content to store well.

HOW TO DRY NUTS AND SEEDS

Select the Best Nuts for Drying

Select intact and reasonably well-shaped nuts with clean, bright shells. The nut with the shell should be heavy for its size. This usually indicates a fresh, meaty kernel.

Additional information and recipes about nuts can be obtained from The International Tree Nut Council, www.nuthealth.org.

Sort and Wash Them

The drying of most nuts and seeds should begin soon after harvesting, usually within twenty-four hours. Little preparation is needed for most nuts.

To sort, immerse the nuts in water, removing and discarding those that float. This also removes dirt and insects, which may have accumulated on the shells. Drain the nuts on towels.

Shelling nuts first lessens drying time, but dried, shelled nuts must be refrigerated or frozen. Nuts dried and stored in the shell will keep for several months at room temperature.

Dry Nuts in a Dehydrator or Warm Room

If your dehydrator can be adjusted to a low enough temperature, it is ideal for drying nuts because the air circulation is much better than in room drying. Unshelled nuts will dry in eight to ten hours in a dehydrator.

Spread nuts in a single layer on drying trays, letting air circulate freely on all sides. The optimum drying temperature is from 90°F to 100°F (32°C to 38°C). Temperatures above 100°F (38°C) will shorten the storage life and affect the flavor. Oil in the nuts tends to get rancid with higher temperatures.

Shelled nuts must be protected from contamination. Cover them with cheesecloth if you dry them in the sun or in a room where there might be some dust.

Small amounts of unshelled nuts can easily be dried in a furnace room, an attic, or on a radiator, as long as the temperature does not exceed 100°F (38°C) They will usually be dry in three or four days.

YIELD

The yield from different nuts will vary, depending on the amount of moisture and the weight of the shell. In general, one pound of unshelled nuts will yield the following shelled nuts:

- Almonds: 6½ ounces
- Brazil nuts: 8 ounces
- Filberts, pecans, or English walnuts: 7 ounces
- Black walnuts: 3½ ounces

Oven drying is not recommended for nuts because it is difficult to keep the temperature low enough.

Test to Find Out If They're Dry

Nuts are dry when their shells have hardened to a brittle state. Crack one. The nutmeat should be tender and not shriveled.

Nuts stored in the shell should contain roughly 7 to 8 percent moisture for the best storage stability; shelled nuts should contain about 3 to 5 percent.

Package for Storage

Nuts in the Shell

- Store them in airtight plastic, metal, or glass containers below 70°F (21°C).
- Nuts in the shell can also be vacuum packaged.
- As with other dried foods, the lower the storage temperature, the longer the storage life. Because nuts contain so much oil and fat, they quickly become rancid at higher temperatures.
- Nuts in the shell may also be stored in airtight containers in the refrigerator or freezer, although they will take a lot of space.

Shelled Nuts

- Ideally, they should be vacuum packaged in jars with a home vacuum-packaging machine like the FoodSaver to keep the best flavor.
- If you don't have a home vacuum packaging machine, package them in airtight plastic or glass containers or heavy plastic bags.
- Store them in the refrigerator or freezer if you're going to keep them for longer than a couple of months.
- When nuts are refrigerated or frozen, let the container return to room temperature before

opening. This prevents the cold nuts from drawing moisture from the air, which will cause them to mold or turn rancid more quickly.

Rancidity in Nuts

- Rancid nuts have a bitter, unpleasant oily taste.
- Sometimes they're darker in color.
- A rancid nut can ruin an otherwise perfectly prepared dish. Be sure and taste several nuts before adding them to a dish to make sure that none are rancid.
- There is no way to reverse rancidity. Throw the nuts away.
- Proper storage conditions and low temperatures are the keys for preventing rancidity.

Chopping Nuts

To chop nuts, use a good-size chef's knife on a large cutting board. There are also a variety of very clever choppers on the market that have a plunger style chopping mechanism. These are very handy for chopping most nuts, generally about ½ cup at a time.

If you want to chop them in your food processor, process only about ½ cup at a time and pulse the machine on and off just a couple of times. If you're chopping them for a cake, process them with a small amount of the flour used in the recipe.

Roasting Nuts

Roasted or toasted nuts and seeds have a fuller flavor compared to raw dried nuts or seeds. They are heated in a shallow roasting pan in a preheated 250°F to 300°F (120°C to 150°C) oven for ten to fifteen minutes and may be coated with oil, salt, or other seasonings before they are roasted.

Roasted nuts and seeds have a shorter shelf life than dried nuts and should be eaten within two or three weeks after they have been roasted.

These Nuts and Seeds Are the Best for Roasting

- Almonds
- Filberts
- Macadamia nuts
- Pumpkin seeds
- Sunflower seeds
- Walnuts

NUT BUTTERS

Nut butters are made from grinding nuts to form a paste. Before making the butters, it is best to blanch almonds and hazelnuts to remove the papery skin. See Almonds, page 114.

Nut butters can be made easily in a food processor or heavy-duty blender. A food processor tends to work better and requires less scraping to remove the nuts off the side of the container.

The flavor is a little fuller if the nuts are roasted, but they can also be made from raw nuts. Pecan butter is better if you don't roast the pecans.

Grind only a small batch at a time. Add a little bit of extra-light olive, safflower, or other vegetable oil to make the consistency smooth. If you want a crunchy butter, chop some nuts to the desired size in your food processor before you begin. Add them to the butter when it is finished.

Cashew nuts are very oily and are used in other nut butters to add extra oil and make them creamier.

Store nut butters in the refrigerator. Homemade nut butters can quickly go rancid at room temperature because they don't have the special additives that are in commercially prepared butters.

Nuts and Seeds that Make Good Nut Butters

- Almonds
- Brazil nuts
- Cashews (raw or roasted)
- Filberts (Hazelnuts)
- Macadamia nuts
- Peanuts
- Pistachios
- Sesame seeds (butter also called *tahini*)
- Sunflower seeds

❖ ALL ABOUT NUTS AND SEEDS

ALMONDS

Almonds are the oldest, most widely cultivated and extensively used nuts in the world. On the tree, almonds resemble small green peaches. They do not usually fall to the ground when mature, as do most other nuts. When the nuts mature, the hulls split open and the shells and kernels begin to dry while still on the tree. When most of the hulls in the center of the tree have split open, the nuts can be harvested by knocking them from the tree. Remove the hulls and dry the nuts.

To remove the brown almond skins, blanch 1 to 2 cups of whole almonds in boiling water for three to five minutes. Remove them with a slotted spoon and place on paper towels to cool. Slip the nuts between your thumb and middle finger to remove the skins.

The sweeter varieties such as the Nonpareil and Jordanolo are best for eating and cooking. Sweet almonds are most often eaten raw and are used in marzipan, nougat, and macaroons.

Sweet almonds are high in vitamin E and monounsaturated fat—the *good* fat responsible for lowering LDL cholesterol. The more bitter varieties are used to make almond extract.

BEECHNUTS

Beechnuts usually grow wild and are found mostly in the eastern United States. They grow inside small rough burrs about as big as cherries. Two or more of the tiny three-sided nuts are contained in each burr or husk.

The mature nuts fall from the husks to the ground. Squirrels like them, so harvest beechnuts immediately after they have fallen from the tree or the squirrels will get them before you do.

BRAZIL NUTS

Brazil nuts are grown wild, exclusively in the dense forests of South America. The fruit is similar to the coconut, 4 to 6 inches in diameter, with a pod, which contains from twelve to thirty of the nuts. The large three-sided kernels are white, oily, and flavorful and are covered by a rough, hard, dark brown shell. Because of the rough shells, commercially dried nuts are usually put through a brushing process to brighten and smooth them.

Brazil nuts are excellent alone or combined with dried fruits and other nuts.

CASHEWS

Cashews are the seeds of a soft, juicy pear-shaped fruit called a *cashew apple*. The kidney-shaped cashew nut is usually about 1 inch long and is covered by a double shell. The kernel has a delicate flavor and a firm fine texture. India and East Africa are the world's foremost producers of cashews. Some are grown on the coasts of Florida.

Cashews are excellent alone or in Asian-style main dishes. They can be used in baked goods and fruit-and-nut combinations.

FILBERTS (HAZELNUTS)

Filberts, or hazelnuts, are high in protein, fiber, iron, phosphorus, and vitamins B, C, and E. They are wonderful to eat as a snack and make a fine addition to many baked goods and candies. A 1-ounce serving of hazelnuts has about 178 calories.

About 99 percent of the hazelnuts sold in the United States come from Oregon. Turkey grows about 70 percent of the world crop. They are used extensively in the baking and confectionery industries.

These sweet, grape-size nuts usually grow in clusters of two or three with each nut covered by an open-ended husk. The husks usually open with the first frost and the mature nuts fall to the ground. They will discolor if left on the ground very long.

Commercially dried filberts are bleached by sulfuring in the shell. Because the process is strictly cosmetic and fairly complicated, it is not recommended for home use.

Filberts become spongy during drying, but regain their firm texture when dry. The filbert kernel gradually changes from white to a creamy color. When this color change is complete throughout the kernel, it is sufficiently dry.

When using filberts in cooking or baking, bring out their flavor and improve their texture by toasting them first. Place them in a shallow pan in a preheated 275°F (135°C) oven for twenty to thirty minutes, or until the skins crack. Remove from the oven and pour them into a bowl, cover, and let them sit for five minutes. Place the hazelnuts in a clean cloth towel and rub vigorously to remove the skins.

Additional Information: More information and recipes are available from:

The Oregon Hazelnut Marketing Board
21595-A Dolores Way NE
Aurora, OR 97002-9738
Phone: 503-678-6823
Fax: 503-678-6825
Email: hazelnut@oregonhazelnuts.org

The Hazelnut Council
Harborside Financial Centre, Plaza V
25th Floor, Suite 2500
Jersey City, NJ 07311
Phone: 206-270-4688
Email: info@hazelnutcouncil.org
www.hazelnutcouncil.org

HICKORY NUTS

Shagbark or shellbark hickory trees produce hickory nuts. These trees are members of the walnut family and grow principally in the central and northeastern United States.

The smooth-shelled nuts are enclosed in a green husk, which turns brown as it matures and releases the sweet-flavored nut in the shell. The nuts have an excellent flavor. The trees do not bear enough nuts to be grown commercially.

MACADAMIA NUTS

Macadamia nuts are grown in Hawaii, California, and Florida. Ninety percent of the world's macadamias are now grown in the Aloha state.

When fully ripe, the thick husks split open and the hard-shelled nuts fall to the ground. They are harvested immediately, the shells are removed, and the nuts are dried. The shells are difficult to crack and require special equipment because they are about ⅛-inch thick. This may be why they are so expensive. The eatable kernel is only about 15 percent of the whole macadamia nut.

Macadamia nut trees take a long time to bear. It takes twelve to fifteen years to reach full production.

When the macadamia is fully ripe, it still has about 20 to 25 percent moisture. It needs to have less than 2 percent to store well.

The macadamia kernel contains up to 75 percent oil and about 4 percent sugar. One cup of dry roasted macadamia nuts has a whopping 962 calories, with about 853 calories from fat!

The delicate mild-flavored nut is delicious eaten fresh or roasted, alone or in dried-fruit-and-nut combinations. To roast, place them in a shallow pan and roast in a preheated 275°F (135°C) oven for fifteen to twenty minutes.

PEANUTS

In much of the world, peanuts are called *groundnuts*. Peanuts are actually a member of the pea family and mature beneath the surface of the soil. When harvested, the entire plant, including most of the roots, is removed from the soil.

Their shell is the softest of any of the nuts. Because peanuts are legumes, they can be dried and roasted at slightly higher temperatures.

Peanuts are used in a wide range of grocery products and are a major ingredient in *mixed nuts* because they are less expensive than most other nuts.

Some people have severe allergic reactions to peanuts. When people are allergic to peanuts, even a tiny exposure can cause anaphylactic shock and may be fatal.

Spread peanuts on trays and dry at 130°F (54°C). Store them shelled or unshelled. To roast peanuts in the shell, place them in a shallow pan and roast in a preheated 300°F (150°C) oven for thirty to forty minutes. If they have been shelled, roast them for twenty to twenty-five minutes and stir frequently to prevent scorching.

Additional Information: More information and recipes are available from:

Virginia-Carolina Peanut Promotions
P.O. Box 8
103 Triangle Court
Nashville, NC 27856-0008
Phone: 252-459-9977
Fax: 252-459-7396
Email: info@aboutpeanuts.com
Website: www.aboutpeanuts.com

PECANS

Pecans are grown mostly in the southeastern and southwestern United States. They are shelled with machines and the moisture is reduced to about 4 percent.

The nuts are mature when the green husks turn brown and open. The nuts usually fall to the ground or may be knocked down with a long pole. The smooth brown shells are usually oval-shaped, but are round in a few varieties. Their dull finish is usually polished before marketing.

Pecans with higher than 6 percent moisture do not store well. They can be dried on trays or pans in a warm dry area in about two weeks.

An easy way to tell if your pecans are dry

enough to store is to shell several and bend the kernels until they break. If the kernels break with a sharp snap, they are usually dry enough to store.

Pecans will keep about 3 months stored at 70°F to 75°F (21°C to 24°C) and several years in the freezer. As long as they are kept in airtight containers, pecans can be thawed and refrozen repeatedly without loss of flavor or texture.

They are delicious in breads, cookies, candies, and many fruit dishes.

Additional information: More information and recipes are available from:

National Pecan Shellers Association
5775 Peachtree-Dunwoody Road
Building G, Suite 500
Atlanta, GA 30342
Phone: 404-252-3663
Email: info@ilovepecans.org
Website: www.ilovepecans.org

PINE NUTS (PIÑONES)

Pine nuts are the edible seeds of piñon trees in the southwestern United States. These tiny, sweet-flavored nuts, also known as *piñones*, or Indian nuts, are about the size of an orange seed. Their delicious flavor makes the tedious process of cracking them worthwhile.

Pine nuts are protein-packed, with about 31 grams of protein per 100 grams of nuts—the highest of any nut or seed. They also contain all twenty amino acids. They have been a staple food for certain tribes of Native Americans for hundreds of years. The harvesting and processing of these nuts was a tribal ritual.

They are usually sufficiently dry when they fall to the ground, but should be packaged and stored to prevent additional moisture absorption. Unshelled pine nuts can keep up to a year in the refrigerator, but deteriorate rapidly when shelled and should be refrigerated and eaten within a month.

Pine nuts are an essential component of pesto and are frequently added to meat, fish, and vegetable dishes.

PISTACHIOS

Pistachios are seeds from the fruit of the pistachio tree, which is grown primarily in California, Turkey, Italy, and Iran. The majority of pistachios are imported, but central California is a good producer. A tree can often take up to fifteen years to produce significant quantities of nuts. The kernel has a buttery sweet flavor and is naturally green, covered with a fine, thin, pale-brown skin that need not be removed before eating.

About 55 percent of the fat in pistachio nuts is monounsaturated fat, or good fat. They also contain fiber, iron, potassium, niacin, riboflavin, and zinc. One ounce of pistachios contains about 164 calories.

The shell of the pistachio is naturally a beige color. When the fruit ripens, it expands and the shells partially split open. Nonsplit shells usually contain immature kernels and should be thrown away.

To enhance splitting, the hulled nuts can be dipped into water to moisten the shell and spread out in the sun to dry. To salt them, boil in a salt solution for two minutes, then redry and store them. Unshelled pistachios will keep in the refrigerator for up to three months. In the freezer, they generally will keep up to a year.

The long, yellow-green pistachio seed is popular fresh, roasted and salted, or in candies and ice cream.

Additional information: More information and recipes are available from:

California Pistachio Commission
1318 E. Shaw Avenue, Suite 420
Fresno, CA 93710-7912
Phone: 559-221-8294
Fax: 559-221-8044
Email: info@pistachios.org
Website: www.pistachios.org

PUMPKIN SEEDS (PEPITAS)

Roasted pumpkin seeds are some of the most nutritious and flavorful seeds. As you carve that Halloween pumpkin, remove the flat, dark-green seeds and fibrous tissue with a large spoon. Carefully wash pumpkin seeds in a colander and remove the clinging fibrous pumpkin tissue.

Dry them in a dehydrator at 115°F to 120°F (46°C to 49°C) until crisp. Seeds can be oven dried at 150°F (66°C) for one to two hours. Stir them frequently to prevent scorching.

Roast dried pumpkin seeds by tossing them lightly with olive oil and salt and placing them in a preheated 250°F (121°C) oven for fifteen to thirty minutes, or until they start to turn a very light golden color. For a little variety, try adding one or more of the following: garlic powder, onion powder, cayenne pepper, Cajun seasoning, or seasoning salt. Store them in an airtight container for up to one week.

SUNFLOWER SEEDS

Sunflower seeds ripen on the flower and are usually left there to dry. The grayish-green or black seeds are encased in teardrop-shaped gray or black shells that are sometimes striped. Sunflower seeds are very high in polyunsaturated oil. One-fourth cup has more than 90 percent of your daily minimum requirement of vitamin E and 50 percent of your requirement for thiamine, with about 200 calories. They have a mild, nutty taste and a firm, but tender, texture.

If birds are enjoying the seeds, wrap cheesecloth around the flower until the seeds are dried.

The seeds may be shaken off the flower when they are mature, then dried in the sun for several days or in a dehydrator at 100°F (38°C). When dry, the seeds may be roasted in a shallow pan in a 300°F (150°C) oven for ten to fifteen minutes.

Because sunflower seeds are so high in fat, they are prone to rancidity. Keep them in the refrigerator or freezer.

Sunflower seeds are a nice complement to your favorite tuna or chicken salad recipe. They are a lovely garnish for a variety of green salads. Sprinkle on hot or cold cereals.

WALNUTS, BLACK

Black walnuts are native to the central and eastern United States. They are very flavorful, rich nuts but fewer are grown commercially than English walnuts. They grow in clusters with a thick, green husk covering the shell of each nut. Black walnuts fall from the tree as they ripen.

The dark shells have numerous coarse ridges and do not split into halves as English walnuts do. The nutmeat is very difficult to extract and you'll probably have to use a hammer. They rarely come out in halves and you'll have to pick them out with a nut pick. Wear gloves to avoid stains from the brown dye in the shells. Dry them in the shell.

One-fourth cup of black walnuts have about 190

calories, with 150 calories from fat, which is mostly polyunsaturated and monounsaturated. They have more protein than English walnuts, some vitamin E, iron, minerals, and fiber.

Their flavor is so strong that most people don't like them as a snack. They are delicious in baked goods and candies.

Black walnuts will stay fresh for up to one year in the refrigerator and up to two years when stored airtight in the freezer.

WALNUTS, ENGLISH

English walnuts, also called Persian walnuts, have a curly nutmeat with a rich, sweet flavor. The edible papery skin adds a hint of bitterness. The halves of the nut kernel can usually be removed in one piece.

Walnuts are a great source of protein and fiber. They also contain significant amounts of vitamin E, vitamin B$_6$, and thiamine. They have a high percentage of omega-3 fatty acids. One ounce of walnuts has about 180 calories.

English walnuts are the most popular of the walnut family and there are several different varieties. The trees grow best in a moderate climate and the United States is the world's foremost producer, with most of the nuts grown in California and Oregon.

The husks of mature nuts are cracked when they fall from the tree. Harvest them immediately, leaving the uncracked nuts on the ground until they are fully ripe and the husks come off easily.

The fresh nutmeat should be white. Old or rancid kernels are a dull gray. Dry walnuts until the divider between the halves breaks with a snap. If the divider is rubbery, dry further.

Because the color of the walnut's shell is not very appealing, the shells are frequently bleached commercially after the nuts are completely dry to improve their appearance. Since bleaching is only cosmetic, I wouldn't recommend it for home drying.

Sometimes a recipe will instruct you to remove the bitter walnut skin. Drop the shelled walnuts into boiling water and blanch for one minute. Drain, rinse under cold water, and rub the skin off. Bake in a preheated 300°F (150°C) oven for twenty minutes, or until crisp.

Walnuts in the shell will keep for about six months if stored in a cool, dry place. Shelled walnuts will keep at room temperature for three or four months and for up to a year in the freezer.

OTHER USES FOR YOUR DEHYDRATOR

Depending on the type and size of the dehydrator you own, you can do a variety of other things in it other than dry foods. The round dryers have the disadvantage of having less height between the trays, which would not accommodate larger items or a bowl of dough.

The box dehydrators can usually have a shelf or two removed, which makes it easier to make yogurt or raise yeast dough.

- To incubate yogurt, the temperature should be about 110°F (43°C).
- To raise yeast breads, cover the dough with a damp cloth to prevent it from drying out. Use a temperature of 80°F to 85°F (27°C to 29°C).

- Dry flowers in your dehydrator. Follow your usual flower-drying procedures and flowers that usually take three weeks to dry will be ready in a day. (See Making Dried Crafts and Flowers, page 135.)
- Place craft items in the dehydrator to shorten the drying time.
- To recrisp crackers and cookies, heat them at 160°F (71°C) for at least thirty minutes and not more than two hours.
- To *decrystallize* or reliquify raw honey, heat it at 120°F (49°C) in glass containers for twelve hours or until no sugar crystals remain. Crystals will form again after one or two months if honey is stored at room temperature. See the recipe for Creamed Honey, page 168.

MEAT JERKY

Jerky is raw meat that has been salted, sometimes smoked, and then dried. It was a staple in the diet of pioneers and is still a very popular snack. Because most of the moisture is removed, it can be stored without refrigeration.

Jerky also presents some food safety issues that we don't have to deal with in other dried foods. Certain disease-causing bacteria such as *Salmonella* and *E. coli* 0157:H7 may be present in raw meats. Drying at temperatures below 160°F (71°C) does not kill these bacteria. An internal temperature of 160°F (71°C) is required to make sure that jerky is safe to eat.

Because most of the commercial dehydrators on the market fall short of the required temperature, I recommend that you use your oven as well as your dehydrator when making jerky. A good-quality thermometer will indicate whether or not your dehydrator can reach safe temperature levels.

I recommend that you heat all prepared jerky *before drying* in a preheated 175°F (80°C) oven for thirty minutes prior to placing in the dehydrator. This will ensure that it is safe from bacteria, especially E. coli. Another option is to heat it *after* drying in a preheated 275°F (135°C) oven for fifteen minutes.

KEEPING JERKY SAFE

The USDA Meat and Poultry Hotline's current recommendation for making jerky safely is to heat meat to 160°F (71°C) before drying it. This step assures that any bacteria present will be destroyed by *wet heat*. Some of the Nesco/American Harvest dehydrator models achieve this temperature consistently.

When the meat is then transferred to a dehydrator, a constant temperature of 130°F to 140°F (54°C to 60°C) must be maintained during drying because:

Nesco/American Harvest dehydrators have been the leader in the home drying industry for almost three decades. They're convenient to use, dry evenly, are well designed, sanitary and easy to clean, and expandable.

One of the best features on the FD-75PR Nesco/American Harvest Professional is that it has the ability to dry foods at 160°F (71°C). This means that you would not have to cook meats or fish in the oven prior to drying them in the dehydrator. You can be assured of the safety of meats and fish because the dryer gets hot enough to kill disease-causing bacteria.

It is expandable to twelve trays. There is a drip tray on the bottom to catch drips from juicy fruits or marinated meats. A convenient handle makes it easy to take off the top. This is an unusual dehydrator because the heating element, fan, and thermostat are in the top instead of the bottom. It still dries quite evenly due to the patented Converga-Flow design. The double wall construction allows for air vents in each tray, so air is forced evenly from the outside to the center through each tray. This design means that you can dry successfully on all of the trays without rotating.

- The process must be fast enough to dry the meat before it spoils.
- The drying process must remove enough water so that microorganisms are unable to grow.

USDA research has also shown that jerky made with sodium nitrite curing mix had greater destruction of bacteria than jerky made without it. Jerky made with the mix and heated before dehydrating had the highest destruction rate of bacteria.

CAUTION: NO SUN DRYING

Do not sun dry jerky or dry in dehydrators that are not thermostatically controlled. The risks of food poisoning and spoilage are too great.

WHICH MEATS TO USE

Use fresh or frozen lean meat for jerky. The leaner the meat, the better the quality of the dried jerky. About four pounds of lean, boneless meat will make one pound of jerky.

Beef

- Flank, round, and sirloin tip cuts are more economical than less expensive cuts, which contain more bone and fat.
- Rump cuts may be used, but they have more gristle.
- Highly marbled cuts, which are great for steaks, are not the best choices for jerky because they have more fat and will become rancid more quickly.

Game Meats

- Deer, elk, antelope, and other game meats all make good jerky.

SMOKING AND DRYING YOUR JERKY IN A COMMERCIAL SMOKER

If you have a commercial smoker, smoke the jerky *before* drying for added flavor because the smoke penetrates raw meat better than dried.

- Follow instructions for preparing jerky, including heating in the oven before drying to reduce risk of any bacterial contamination. (See page 123.)
- After removing from the oven, dry in the smoker for four to eight hours at 140°F to 160°F (60°C to 71°C) or until dry.
- If you want a smoked flavor without going through the smoking process, there are two types of smoke-flavored seasonings available. These seasonings are flavor enhancers and do not have any preservative qualities.
- **Liquid smoke** is made by a wood distilling process and gives a very strong smoke flavor. Use it sparingly, mixed with water and other seasonings.
- **Hickory-flavored smoked salt** is also available for seasoning meat and fish. Adjust the salt in the recipe accordingly.

- Any cut can be used, but the flank, loin, and round cuts are best.
- Great care should be taken when processing game meats since there are many opportunities for contamination.
- Game meats can be heavily contaminated with fecal bacteria, depending on the hunter's skill, wound location, and sanitation during dressing the animal. While fresh beef is usually rapidly chilled, deer carcasses are typically held at ambient temperatures, allowing greater bacteria multiplication.
- Whenever possible, get your game on ice as soon as you can to reduce contamination and take care when dressing it.
- As a precaution against parasites, freeze game meats for at least sixty days at 0°F (−18°C) before drying.

Lamb

- Lamb makes less desirable jerky because it contains more fat than beef.
- To make lamb jerky, use the leg or shoulder cuts.
- Cutting the meat from the bone is easier if it has been partially frozen.

Pork

- Fresh pork should not be used for jerky because drying temperatures are not high enough to kill harmful bacteria or the trichinella parasite, which causes trichinosis, a disease that can be fatal.
- Ham jerky may be made from fully cooked ham and should be used within one week.

Poultry

- Raw poultry is usually not made into jerky because the flavor and texture is much better cooked.

- There is also a danger of salmonella food poisoning, which is very common in poultry.

- Fully cooked, smoked turkey breasts can be sliced and dried into an acceptable jerky, although it has a very short shelf life.

PREPARE MEATS TO DRY

Slice meat into long strips ¼-inch thick. Uniform slices will shorten the drying time, so use a meat slicer or have your butcher slice it for you. Partially freezing it first makes cutting easier. Cut *across* the grain for increased tenderness. Remove any excess fat.

Layer the strips of meat in single layers in a shallow glass or stainless-steel pan. Liberally sprinkle both sides with a salt and seasoning mixture, or use a commercial curing preparation, making sure that each piece is exposed to the cure.

Marinate in the refrigerator for six to twelve hours. Stir occasionally to be sure that each piece is covered with the salt and seasoning mixture. Keep the meat tightly covered, particularly if liquid smoke is used, because the smell will penetrate everything in the refrigerator.

SALT AND SEASON YOUR MEATS

Brine cures use a salt and water mixture for soaking meat until the salt has been absorbed. Brines may also contain seasonings and other curing ingredients.

Dry cures use a mixture of salt and seasonings, which are applied directly to the surface of the meat.

The amount of salt used varies with the type of meat, how it is going to be dried, taste preference, and how long the meat will be stored.

Any type of fine-quality sodium chloride salt intended for food use may be used. Pure pickling salt is a good choice because it does not contain iodine, although it is slightly coarser than table salt. Do not use *rock salt* because it does not dissolve easily and contains impurities.

Salt acts as a preservative in meats, directly inhibiting bacterial growth and also drying the meat, which slows bacterial growth. Most bacteria require substantial amounts of moisture to live and grow.

Sugar is frequently added to reduce the harshness of the salt.

Spices and flavorings (including smoking or smoke flavorings) are added to give jerky its characteristic taste.

Sodium nitrite is a salt that enhances the shelf life of cured meats, including jerky. Sodium nitrite is a compound that has long been used in the curing and preservation of meat. In the presence of heat, sodium nitrite combines with muscle pigment to give the characteristic color and flavor to cured meat. In addition to giving color and flavor, sodium nitrite slows spoilage and the growth of harmful bacteria, particularly the food poisoning toxins that causes botulism. It also retards oxidation, which gives cured meats an undesirable flavor.

Sodium nitrite is recognized as a safe additive

CAUTION: CHECK THE TEMPERATURE

When in doubt about the temperature of your dehydrator, measure the temperature with a good thermometer. Measure the top rack and the bottom rack so that you are assured of the safety when drying meats and fish. Some dryers run hotter than the thermostat will show, and others run cooler. A temperature of 160°F (71°C) is required for at least thirty minutes.

USE THESE SAFE FOOD HANDLING AND PREPARATION METHODS WHEN MAKING JERKY

- Always wash hands thoroughly with soap and hot water before and after working with meat products.
- Use clean utensils and equipment. Using the plastic mesh screens that come with the Nesco/American Harvest dehydrator allows for easier cleanup of the trays afterward. After making jerky, wash trays and plastic mesh screens in the dishwasher.
- Always sanitize cutting boards, utensils, and counters with hot, soapy water before and after any contact with raw meat or meat juices. To make a sanitizing solution, use 1 teaspoon of household chlorine bleach per quart of water.
- Keep meat refrigerated at 35°F to 40°F (2°C to 4°C) prior to making into jerky.
- When using ground beef, make sure that it is freshly ground and from a clean meat shop. Do not hold ground beef more than one day in the refrigerator. Nesco/American Harvest offers a clever jerky gun with three attachments for making jerky strips and jerky sticks from ground beef.
- Use whole red meats within three days of purchasing.
- Defrost frozen meat in the refrigerator, not on the kitchen counter.
- Partially freeze meats so they are easier to slice evenly. Generally ¼ inch is the best thickness to achieve the food safety recommendations.
- Marinate meat in the refrigerator. Marinades are used to tenderize and flavor the jerky before dehydrating. Discard any used marinades. Do not reuse.
- Use a meat thermometer to test the temperature of jerky in the oven or dehydrator to make sure that it has reached 160°F (71°C).
- Dry meats in a food dehydrator or smoker that allows you to maintain a temperature of 130°F to 140°F (54°C to 60°C) throughout the drying process.

by the U.S. Food and Drug Administration (FDA). People generally consume more nitrates from their vegetable intake than from the cured meat products they consume. Spinach, beets, radishes, celery, and cabbages contain quite high concentrations of nitrates. No evidence currently exists that implicates nitrite as a carcinogen.

In dried meats, nitrite greatly delays the development of *Clostridium botulinum*, the causative agent of the toxin botulism. It also brightens the color, retards rancidity and off odors, and preserves the flavor of the spices that are added to jerky.

If you choose to use a cure containing sodium nitrite, I recommend that you use one of the com-

mercial jerky seasoning mixes available from Nesco/American Harvest. Jerky seasoning mixes are available in a variety of flavors. Each spice and cure packet is sized for one pound of meat or ground beef. This is one of the best-tasting spice mixes and you know the exact quantity to add for the weight of meat that you're drying.

HEAT JERKY IN THE OVEN *BEFORE* DRYING

Preheat the oven to 175°F (80°C). Place one layer of the prepared meat strips in a shallow pan or cookie sheet.

Heat marinated jerky *before drying* in a preheated 175°F (80°C) oven for thirty minutes prior to placing in the dehydrator. This will ensure that it is safe from bacteria, especially E. coli. Use a meat thermometer to make sure that the internal temperature of the meat strips is 160°F (71°C).

OR HEAT IT IN THE OVEN *AFTER* DRYING

Another option is to heat it *after* drying. Arrange strips in a single layer in a shallow pan or baking sheet. Heat the jerky for fifteen minutes in a preheated 275°F (135°C) oven. *When the meat is dry, higher temperatures are required to assure that all bacteria are killed.*

FINISH DRYING IN YOUR DEHYDRATOR OR SMOKER

Remove the meat strips from the oven and place them on drying trays. Dry them at 140°F to 160°F (60°C to 71°C), until dry, in a dehydrator or smoker. Occasionally remove the jerky from the dehydrator and blot it with paper towels as it dries to remove beads of oil.

CAUTION: SALT RESTRICTIONS

If you are on a sodium-restricted diet, consuming large quantities of heavily salted foods, such as jerky, may have health risks. If you have high blood pressure, kidney disease, or water retention during pregnancy, it is wise to limit your jerky consumption.

FINISH DRYING IN YOUR OVEN

Place the strips of meat on drying trays. If you left them on the solid baking sheets, they don't dry as well because the air can't circulate completely around the meat. Place a piece of aluminum foil or a baking sheet underneath the drying tray to catch the drippings. Dry in a preheated 275°F (135°C) oven until dry.

TEST TO FIND OUT IF THE JERKY IS DRY

Remove a piece from the dehydrator or oven and allow it to cool. When it is cool, it should crack when bent, but not break. There should be no moist spots.

Allow the jerky to cool and cut into two- to four-inch pieces with kitchen scissors before storing.

PACKAGE FOR STORAGE

Jerky containing salt and cured without a sodium nitrite mixture may be stored at room temperature for one to two months. If the air humidity is low, the container should have a loose-fitting lid or one with a couple of holes punched in it. Good air circulation keeps the flavor fresher.

If the humidity of the air is more than 30 percent, store jerky in an airtight container. Jerky may be refrigerated or frozen in an airtight container to increase the shelf life and maintain the flavor.

If a commercial curing preparation containing sodium nitrite was used, store the jerky according to the package directions.

Storage life is affected by the curing preparation and the temperature of the storage area.

HOW TO USE JERKY

Take jerky along on outdoor activities or anywhere you need a high-protein, lightweight snack. You can assemble an interesting appetizer platter with a variety of jerky and cheese. Spread jerky with cream cheese and top with a sliced green or red pepper garnish.

DRIED COOKED MEATS

Dried cooked meat is easy to make and is lightweight. It is used mainly by backpackers and campers where the weight of canned meats is a disadvantage or refrigeration is not available. It is much less expensive than buying commercially prepared freeze-dried meats. The storage life of dried cooked meats is less than two weeks. I do not recommend preserving meats this way for general home use.

SELECT THE LEANEST CUT AND COOK THOROUGHLY

Use any type of fresh lean meat or poultry. It should be cooked thoroughly. If it is cooked in a broth, remove it from the broth and chill it. Remove any fat that forms. If you are going to dry roast the meat before drying, use a rack so the fat will drip off during cooking.

The shelf life of dried cooked pork is much shorter than that of dried cooked beef. This is because the fat in pork oxidizes and becomes rancid more quickly.

PREPARE IT TO DRY

Trim excess fat from the cooked meat. Cut the meat into ½-inch cubes for the best rehydrated quality.

HOW TO DRY COOKED MEATS

Hold all cooked meats at refrigerator temperatures prior to drying. Allowing meats to stand at room temperature or mishandling with dirty utensils or hands can result in bacterial growth prior to drying, and the bacteria will not be killed with normal drying temperatures.

Place the cubed meat in a dryer or oven at 140°F (60°C) for five or more hours until completely dehydrated and crisp.

TEST TO FIND OUT IF IT'S DRY

The meat should be hard and crisp with no evidence of moisture.

STORE IT FOR A SHORT TIME

Dried cooked meat may be kept at room temperature up to two weeks. For better quality when rehydrated, store dried cooked meat in an airtight container in the refrigerator before use.

HOW TO USE COOKED DRIED MEATS

Soak the dried meat chunks in boiling water or broth for thirty minutes to one hour, or until plump. Simmer it for fifteen to twenty minutes and use it in soups, stews, or casseroles.

FISH JERKY

Any lean fish may be smoked or made into jerky. Varieties high in fat, such as salmon or smelt, can be smoked, but fatty smoked fish has a shorter shelf life. Be sure that your fish is the highest quality. Smoking or jerking will not improve the quality.

KEEP IT COOL

Clean fish as soon as possible after taking them from the water to remove blood, slime, and harmful bacteria. Deterioration begins almost as soon as the fish leaves the water. Warm temperatures hasten deterioration. Small fish are more perishable than large ones and whole fish are more susceptible to spoilage than dressed fish.

To minimize the chance of spoilage, clean the fish and put it on ice or refrigerate it as soon as possible after it is caught. Cure and smoke the fish as soon as you can for safety and the best-tasting smoked fish.

Thaw any frozen fish in cool water or in the refrigerator. Do not refreeze fish.

PREPARE THE FISH FOR BRINING

Cut pieces of uniform size so that they will have more uniform salt absorption without the risk of oversalting. Start the brining process as soon as possible after cleaning.

Different species of fish require different preparation. Remove the backbone of salmon and split. Bottom fish, such as sole, cod, and flounder, should be filleted. Remove the heads and gut smaller fish, such as herring and smelt, before brining.

Open the cleaned fish into one piece by cutting along the back. In larger fish, cut out the front half of the backbone. Thoroughly wash the fish inside and out.

BRINE THE FISH

Brining or curing fish means soaking fish in a solution of salt, water, and spices. Brining is important for two reasons—it helps firm and preserve the fish by removing moisture, and it adds flavor. Even though salt acts as a preservative for smoked fish and fish jerky, it still must be refrigerated, cooked, and stored properly to remain safe to eat.

Brining gives a more uniform salting than dry salting. See one of the recipes starting on page 156. About thirty minutes will properly salt a gutted herring. Large or oily fish may take one to two hours. A thirty-pound salmon will take a good two hours to absorb sufficient salt. Nonfat fish and skinned fish will take less time.

- Completely dissolve salt and sugar in the water before brining the fish. *You may vary the spices, but use the exact amount of salt and water.*
- Soak fish for one hour in a brine solution of one part of salt to seven parts of cold water by volume. One cup of salt and seven cups of water will cure two to three pounds of fish.
- Soak fish in the seasoned brine in the refrigerator at 40°F (4°C). Use ice in plastic bags to keep the brine cold if you don't have refrigeration.
- Use a serving plate to hold floating fish under the brine. Stir the fish occasionally, particularly if the container is full.
- Remove and discard surface film from the brine as it accumulates.
- When you have brined for the recommended time, remove and thoroughly rinse the fish.

How Long to Brine

The time required to cure fish in salt will vary according to the following factors:

- **Taste preference:** The longer the cure, the heavier the salt content will be in the cured fish.
- **Size:** Larger fish or thicker pieces require longer curing.
- **Fat content:** The higher the fat content, the longer it should be cured.
- **Fresh or frozen:** Thawed frozen fish absorb salt faster than fresh fish. The fresher the fish, the slower the rate of salt absorption and the longer the curing time.

Tips for Properly Brining/Curing Fish

- Immediately clean and ice the fish.
- Use the recommended amount of salt.
- Use the correct proportions of brine or cure to the weight of the fish.
- Refrigerate the fish at 40°F (4°C) during brining.
- Brine the same size fish or fish pieces in one batch.
- Brine the same types of fish together.
- Stir occasionally so that all pieces are covered with the brine or dry cure.

HOW TO SMOKE FISH

Smoking fish at home is a delicious, simple, economical way to preserve a large catch. It also can be dangerous if you don't follow food safety instructions to the letter. Certain bacteria that can cause food poisoning can and will grow in smoked fish under the right conditions. Carefully follow the precautions for preparing, smoking, drying, and storage. Smoked fish must be refrigerated or frozen if it is to be stored.

Prepare a brine cure from one of the recipes on pages 156 to 157. Soak for the recommended time.

Thoroughly rinse the fish in fresh water. Allow it

to air-dry, about thirty minutes to one hour, to prevent surface spoilage during drying. The smoke will not deposit evenly on the surface of the fish if there are wet spots.

Smoke and Cook the Fish

Smoke alone isn't a sufficient preservative. You also have to use salt and have adequate temperature. You can begin smoking at 140°F to 160°F (60°C to 71°C). The fish usually reaches that temperature within an hour. Fish that are high in fat will always have an oily feel and may never *feel dry*.

A typical smoker should bring the fish to higher than 160°F (71°C) internal temperature within six to eight hours. Don't allow this process to take longer than eight hours to reach 160°F (71°C). Once at 160°F (71°C), make sure that the fish stays at this temperature for at least thirty minutes. If your smoker cannot provide an air temperature of 200°F to 225°F (93°C to 107°C), you'll have to cook the fish in your kitchen oven.

Use a standard meat thermometer to check the internal temperature of the largest piece. You may want to check several pieces, because some smokers have *cool* spots. You may use a long-stemmed dial thermometer inserted through a hole in the smoker to make monitoring easier. This allows you to keep the door closed.

CAUTION: MAKE SURE YOUR FISH IS SAFE TO EAT!

Heat the fish to an internal temperature of at least 160°F (71°C) for at least thirty minutes at some time during smoking. This is the only way you can protect smoked fish from developing *botulism*.

Use only hardwood for burning in your smoker. Maple, oak, alder, hickory, birch, and fruitwoods all do well for smoking. Do not use fir, spruce, pine, or cedar because they tend to leave an unpleasant taste on the fish.

Package for Storage

Place smoked fish in the refrigerator covered with paper toweling until it is cool enough to package in an airtight container. Smoked fish is very perishable and should not be left at room temperature for any period of time. Package in an airtight container and refrigerate smoked fish at 35°F (2°C) for up to two weeks. For longer storage, package in airtight containers and freeze for up to two months.

HOW TO JERK FISH

Fish jerky is a lightly salted dried fish, usually smoke flavored, with very little moisture, 15 to 20 percent. This low moisture is sufficient to inhibit the growth of harmful bacteria.

SMALL METAL SMOKERS

If you purchase a small metal smoker from a hardware or sporting goods store, be aware that it may have difficulty heating the fish to an internal temperature of 160°F (71°C). If this is the case, transfer the fish to the oven and heat it at 175°F (80°C) for at least thirty minutes sometime during the smoking process. It is better to do it at the beginning rather than at the end to make sure all bacteria is killed.

Also, make sure that your smoker can maintain a minimum temperature of 140°F (60°C) to keep your meat or fish safe while smoking.

Prepare Fish for Jerky

Cut the fish in ¼- to ⅜-inch thick strips. Soak the strips for thirty minutes in a cold (40°F [4°C]) brine, consisting of ½ cup salt to 1 quart water. Rinse the fish strips in fresh cold water and place them on a clean, flat surface.

Prepare a dry-cure seasoning mixture from the recipes on pages 157 to 158.

Liberally sprinkle both sides of each fish strip with the dry-cure seasoning mixture, using about 1 tablespoon salt mixture per 2 pounds of fish. Place the seasoned strips in an airtight glass or stainless-steel container. Refrigerate for four to eight hours so that the fish will absorb the salt and seasonings.

How to Cook and Dry Fish Jerky

Place the fish strips in a shallow pan or baking sheet. Heat marinated fish strips in a preheated 175°F (80°C) oven for thirty minutes prior to placing in the dehydrator. Use a meat thermometer to make sure that the internal temperature of the fish strips is 160°F (71°C). This will ensure that it is safe from bacteria, especially E. coli.

Another option is to heat it *after* drying. Arrange fish strips in a single layer in a shallow pan or baking sheet. Heat for fifteen minutes in a preheated 275°F (135°C) oven. *When the fish jerky is dry, higher temperatures are required to assure that all bacteria are killed.*

If you own a Nesco/American Harvest dehydrator, check the model to ensure that it has the ability to dry foods at 160°F (71°C). This means that you would not have to cook meats or fish in the oven prior to drying them in the dehydrator. You can be assured of the food safety because the dryer goes to a hot enough temperature to kill disease-causing bacteria.

Dry It in a Dehydrator

If heating in the oven prior to drying, remove from the oven and place strips of fish on drying trays. Dry at 140°F to 160°F (60°C to 71°C) until dry. Occasionally remove the fish from the dehydrator and blot it with paper towels as it dries to remove beads of oil.

Dry It in a Smoker

Smoke the fish strips for three to four hours at 140°F to 160°F (60°C to 71°C) or until dry.

Dry It in the Oven

Place fish strips on drying trays. If left on the solid baking sheets, they don't dry as well because the air can't circulate completely around the fish. Place a piece of aluminum foil or a baking sheet underneath the drying tray to catch the drippings. Dry in a preheated 160°F to 175°F (71°C to 80°C) oven.

Dryness Test

Feel and squeeze the fish to check for moisture. Fish that have a lot of fat will not appear or taste as dry as fish with a low-fat content. High-fat fish may show signs of oily moisture that won't evaporate. Fish jerky should feel firm, dry, and tough, but it should not crumble. There should be no moist spots.

Package for Storage

Store fish jerky in an airtight container in the refrigerator. Use fish jerky within two weeks. It will keep two months if frozen.

MAKING DRIED CRAFTS AND FLOWERS

DRIED FLOWERS

It's easy to preserve flower garden favorites by drying. Summer flowers and foliage are readily available and inexpensive to preserve, compared to many other hobbies.

Materials needed:

- Fresh flowers
- 20- to 24-gauge wire
- Desiccant such as silica gel or sand
- Containers to hold flowers for drying
- Flower foam to hold flowers till you're ready to arrange them
  - Acrylic spray
  - Decorative containers for arrangements

Select Perfect Flowers for Drying

The shape, color, and texture of flowers don't improve with drying, so choose the best. Collect more than you think you'll need, because some won't turn out the way you want. Use only flowers and plants that are free of insect and disease damage. When picked, immediately place them in a container of water to keep them from wilting. You can also dry leaves, stems, seedpods, cones, grains, grasses, and berries to add to your flower arrangements.

Wire the Stems

To allow you to create a suitable stem when the flower is dry, insert wire into the flower before drying.

Cross wire flowers that have a hard base or center, such as roses, by pushing the wire through the base of the flower at right angles to the stem. Bring the ends of the wire together at the center of the flower base and bend them together to form a short stem.

Hook wire flowers with soft centers, such as daisies, marigolds, and zinnias. To hook wire a flower, push a wire through the center of the stem or the bottom of the flower. Push it out the top of the flower and bend a small hook in the end of the wire. Pull the hook back into the flower, hooking the center, making sure that it is well hidden in the center.

Air-Dry

Warm air is the oldest and simplest method of drying flowers and works well on many flowers. *When you are air-drying flowers, cut them just before they are fully open.*

When plants are air-dried, they are very stiff and some flowers shrink. Blue and yellow flowers keep their colors when air-dried, but pink flowers fade.

To air-dry, remove foliage from the stems. Tie the stems together with a rubber band and hang them upside down in a dark, warm, dry room. It usually takes two to three weeks. A dark attic, closet, or furnace room generally is warm enough. The colors stay brighter in the dark. If stems become very brittle after drying, cut them off and attach a stub wire.

Flowers That Can Be Air-Dried

- Baby's breath
- Bachelor's button
- Bells of Ireland
- Cockscomb
- Edelweiss
- Larkspur
- Scarlet sage
- Strawflower
- Yarrow

Use a Dehydrator

Drying flowers flat on dehydrator trays is a simple way to preserve many flowers, foliage, flowering grasses, seedheads, cones, and nonflowering plants. Simply place on drying trays and dry at 130°F to 150°F (54°C to 66°C) until they're crisp and papery.

Use a Dessicant

Drying flowers with *desiccants* is the most commonly used method and produces some of the best results. A desiccant is a substance that absorbs moisture. It speeds drying, especially when used in a dehydrator. Flowers with petals, leaves, ferns, fungi, and some varieties of mosses are best preserved with a desiccant to keep their shape and color during drying. The vibrant colors and delicate structure of flowers with petals are better preserved using a desiccant.

Using a desiccant in combination with your dehydrator allows flowers to dry in a day or two instead of two to three weeks.

There are several brands of flower desiccants available from craft stores.

- **Silica gel** is the best to use and absorbs up to 40 percent of its weight in moisture. It is a granular substance that is quite expensive, but can be reused indefinitely. Simply heat it in a shallow pan in a 250°F (121°C) oven to remove the moisture. It is blue when dry and light pink when it has absorbed water. Keep silica gel in airtight containers until you're ready to use it.

- **Sand** can be used. Buy builders' sand or play sand and wash it thoroughly in a bucket with a little dishwashing detergent. Stir and pour off the water, rinsing until there are no soap bubbles left in the water. Dry it in a 250°F (121°C) oven. When dry, weigh fifteen pounds and again place it in a 250°F (121°C) oven until it is evenly heated. Remove and place the sand in a large bowl. Using a large spoon, stir in 3 tablespoons melted paraffin wax. When cool, add 1 tablespoon bicarbonate of soda and 1 tablespoon fine silica gel, and stir well. The wax smooths the sharp edges of the sand, but reduces its absorbency. The soda raises the pH, which helps to preserve the color. The gel increases its absorbency.

Select and Wire Your Flowers

Use perfect fresh flowers. Yellows and blues maintain their color better than reds or whites. Remove the stems from the flowers and insert a short 20- to 24-gauge stub wire. You'll add a longer stem later when using it in an arrangement.

Dry in a Dehydrator

Most flowers are too large to dry in one of the round stackable dryers. If you're drying small flowers, and your container is very shallow, you can dry in a round dryer. The rectangular dehydrators work well when you remove one or more trays.

- Place 1 inch of desiccant in the bottom of containers that are no higher than 4 inches.
- Place *flat-faced flowers* facing downward, with the petals resting easily on the desiccant.
- Place *rounded double flowers* such as roses and daffodils with their heads facing upward.
- Lay *trumpet or bell-shaped* flowers on their sides.
- Gently sprinkle the desiccant along the perimeter of the container, away from the flower, building up a continuous mound of about an inch.

ORRIS ROOT POWDER

Orris root powder is made from the root of a variety of iris. It has a sweet, fragrant, almost cosmeticlike smell. It is used as a fixative when making pomander balls or potpourri to keep the fragrance. Buy it online or from a craft or spice store.

Lightly tap on the container and the desiccant will move to the flower, keeping the shape of the petals. Continue adding more desiccant and tapping on the container, until the flower is completely covered. Then add an inch of desiccant to the top.

- Do not cover the container.
- Set the thermostat to 145°F (63°C) and plug in the dryer.
- Most flowers will be totally dry in twenty-four hours or less.

Dry in a Warm Room

Choose a warm room with good air circulation.

- Follow the steps for drying in a dehydrator, except cover your containers.
- It will usually take two to three weeks for the flowers to be completely dry.

Test to Find Out If They're Dry

To test for dryness, gently scrape back the desiccant and remove one flower. Hold the flower to your ear and give it a gentle tap. If it is dry, it will sound crisp and papery. If flowers are removed too soon, their petals will droop. If dried too long, the petals are brittle and break easily.

When you are certain that all the flowers are dry, remove the remaining flowers by carefully pouring off the desiccant into a bowl, letting it fall slowly through your fingers. Catch each flower and carefully remove it by its stem. Stand preserved flowers in a block of flower foam until you're ready to arrange them.

If you're not arranging them right away, store them in airtight tins. In humid climates, protect loose-petal flowers with a light application of acrylic spray to prevent them from absorbing moisture from the air.

Arrange and Display Your Flowers

Insert a longer wire for the stem and wrap with florist tape. Arrange in an attractive container.

Pomander Balls

Pomander balls are a lovely way to scent your home for the holidays and are thoughtful gifts. It's easy to make pomander balls in your food dryer or a warm room. These old-fashioned aromatic delights dry quickly and easily when placed in a dehydrator. If you're going to *room* dry them, put them in a furnace room or other room of your house that stays fairly warm.

MATERIALS NEEDED FOR ONE POMANDER:
Apple, lemon, lime, or orange
2 ounces whole cloves
Rolling Mixture (below)
Ribbon, lace, and netting

With a permanent marker, divide the fruit into quarters, marking vertical rows or designs where your ribbon will go. Allow about ⅜ inch for a ribbon.

Using a metal skewer or ice pick, punch holes evenly all over the skin of the fruit except where the ribbon will be. Push a whole clove into each hole. The skin of the fruit should be completely covered with the cloves.

In a small glass bowl, mix the rolling mixture. Roll the ball in the rolling mixture, thoroughly coating it. Let it stand in the mixture for a week, turning the pomander every day. Place the pomander on a solid sheet on a dryer tray and dry it at 95°F to 105°F (35°C to 41°C) until it is shrunken and lightweight, or continue to air-dry it for another week or two.

When it is dried, decorate it with ribbons, lace, or netting. In the area without cloves, wrap a ribbon around the middle of the pomander ball vertically and tie it with a double knot at the top. Wrap a second piece of ribbon in the second area and tie with a double knot. Top it with a bow and a loop for a hanger.

Rolling Mixture

COMBINE THE FOLLOWING IN A SMALL BOWL FOR THE ROLLING MIXTURE:
½ cup ground cinnamon
¼ cup ground cloves
1 tablespoon ground allspice
1 tablespoon ground nutmeg
¼ cup powdered orris root
1 teaspoon glitter

Dried Apple Wreath

Apple wreaths are an attractive and interesting change from traditional wreaths.

MATERIALS NEEDED:
8 or more apples (depending on the size of the wreath)
Sodium bisulfite (available from winemaking supply stores)
Apple peeler/corer/slicer
Thin wire
Plastic/foam wreath form
Hot glue gun

Glue sticks

Brush

Mod Podge sealer (available in craft supply stores)

Ribbon bow

Baby's breath

Cinnamon sticks

Cardboard

Grapevines

Straw

Slice and dry the apples. Slice unpeeled apples into ⅛- to ¼-inch uniform slices into a solution of 1 tablespoon sodium bisulfite to 1 gallon of water. A commercial apple slicer works best. Do not core or peel the apples, since the core forms an attractive star shape when it's dried. The dried peeling adds a touch of color.

Soak apples for ten minutes in the sodium bisulfite solution, drain, and place on dryer trays to dry. Dry at 140°F (60°C) until they are leathery with no pockets of moisture.

Arrange the apples on the wreath form. Anchoring the wire on the front of the wreath form, feed the wire through the wreath form to the back to make a wire loop for hanging. Place the wreath form on a large piece of cardboard to protect your table from hot glue spills.

With the glue gun, squeeze hot glue along the outside edge about as wide as the apples. Do just a few inches at a time because the glue sets up very quickly. Place the apple slices on the hot glue. Continue around the wreath. Then place a second layer of apples, overlapping the slices for a fuller look.

Seal and add a decorative touch. When the apples are all glued in place, seal by brushing Mod Podge on both sides of the wreath, one side at a time. Add a ribbon bow, baby's breath, and cinna-

mon sticks for decoration. Depending on your personal preference, you can add touches of grapevines or straw.

Potpourri

Home-dried potpourri and sachets are fun and easy to do in your dehydrator.

Take advantage of your flower garden in the summer by dehydrating petals for potpourri. Combine petals with store-bought spices, fixatives, and essential oils to make inexpensive, elegant gifts.

MATERIALS NEEDED:

Flowers for drying

2 to 3 tablespoons orris root powder per 4 cups of petals

Dehydrator

Plastic mesh screens

Airtight container for storing dried potpourri

Bowl for mixing

Decorative bowls

Pick flowers. Pick flowers when they are about three-quarters open. They lose fragrance when they are fully open. Gather about four times the amount you believe you'll need, since they shrink as they dry. Gather them in the early morning just after the dew has evaporated for the best scent.

Prepare the flowers for drying. Remove petals from flower heads and pull herb leaves from their stems. Spread in a single layer on a plastic mesh screen and place in the dehydrator.

Dry. Set the temperature to 90°F to 100°F (32°C to 38°C). Dry until brittle dry, which may take from two to twelve hours, depending upon the plants, the amount, the model of dehydrator that you are using, and the relative humidity.

Store until ready to use. Store different flowers and herbs separately in covered jars until you're ready to mix. Keep them in a cool place, out of sunlight. In airtight jars, they'll hold their scent until opened and ready to offer your favorite herbal scents to any room.

Mix. Experiment with different combinations, mixing small quantities and recording the results until you come up with a blend that you like. The orris root powder is used to preserve the scent of the potpourri.

To make your potpourri, measure the dried materials and orris root powder into a large bowl and stir until well mixed. Store in airtight containers until ready to use.

Display. Place in a clear, decorative bowl and set out as a decoration and to give your room an amazing aroma.

Salt Dough Ornaments

Salt dough ornaments can be a wonderful family project. Children can also use this dough for play dough, but it doesn't keep for another playtime. Once mixed, this dough has a satiny texture and begs to be shaped.

MATERIALS NEEDED:
1½ cups hot tap water
1 cup salt
4 cups all-purpose flour
Beads
Glitter
Small cloth appliqués
Ornament hangers, craft wire loops, small hairpins or paper clips for hanging
Acrylic paint
Artist's brushes
Spray acrylic varnish or polyurethane varnish

HELPFUL TOOLS:
Cookie cutters
Wooden picks
Garlic press
Cheese grater
Popsicle sticks
Knife
Rolling pins, regular and small
Aluminum foil
Emery board

Mix the dough. In a medium bowl, stir the hot water and salt together to dissolve the salt. Gradually add enough flour so that the dough pulls away from the sides of the bowl. Turn out onto a lightly floured board and knead until the dough becomes smooth and manageable. Add a little more flour as needed. Cover with a plastic bag and let it rest for an hour before shaping.

Shape the ornaments. Shape each ornament on aluminum foil. Don't do an assembly line. If the surface of an ornament dries out, it becomes difficult to work with.

Cover any dough not in use with plastic to keep it from drying out. Dough should be used within eight hours.

Beginners and children may want to use cookie cutters to make basic shapes. A garlic press is great for making hair. Wooden picks are helpful in making small details. Small appliqués add a nice touch—a heart on a teddy bear or a star on a Christmas tree. Beads or glitter can be added.

If you're adding a small molded piece (arms, legs, hats) to a three-dimensional ornament, always put a dab of water in the spot where the piece is going to be added. If it is a fragile attachment, put a paper clip in between for extra strength. If you're making a large ornament, reinforce the body with wire. Dough has no strength and requires support for larger ornaments.

Add the hanger. When your ornament is complete and all the details are in place, insert the hanger at the top of the ornament.

Give it a final check. Check to make sure that all the details are just as you want them. If there are loose pieces or undesirable marks in the dough, they will be there in the final ornament.

Bake and finish drying. Place the aluminum foil holding each ornament on a baking sheet and bake in a preheated 250°F (121°C) oven for two hours. Transfer the aluminum foil to your dehydrator and continue drying at 115°F to 120°F (46°C to 49°C) until totally dry. You can usually tell if it's dry by pressing on the underside in the center of the ornament. If it has any give, it's not dry. When the top is completely dry, you can flip the ornament over and dry the underside.

Smooth any rough edges. When the ornament is completely dry, smooth any rough edges with an emery board.

Paint. Paint the ornaments with acrylic paint. Acrylic paints are available in jars and tubes. They mix easily and dry quickly. If you are adding different colored layers over one another, use a coat of sealer between them to prevent them from running or smearing.

If you're giving an ornament as a Christmas gift, it's a nice touch to write your name or initials and the year on the back.

Return the ornaments to the dehydrator and dry on the highest temperature setting until the paint is dry.

Seal each ornament. It is very important to seal salt dough ornaments to prevent moisture from reentering and causing disintegration. There are several varnishes that can be used, but they should be transparent and nonpenetrating so that the surface of your dough art is strengthened with a hard, protective coating. Acrylic spray and polyurethane varnish are both good choices.

Place the ornaments in a well-ventilated area, preferably outdoors, before applying the varnish. When the paint is totally dry, spray one side with acrylic or polyurethane varnish. When totally dry, turn over and spray the other side. Allow the ornaments to dry thoroughly before handling.

Repeat the varnishing process until a minimum of four complete coats has been applied to both sides of the ornament. Allow the ornament to dry completely in between coats. Use your dehydrator to speed the process.

Bread and Glue Ornaments

This recipe is a no-bake mixture that is particularly adaptable to making small, delicate ornaments. The pliable mixture can be rolled very thin and formed into fragile ornaments. It is easier to handle than salt dough and can be used for more intricate ornaments.

The white acrylic paint or shoe polish gives the

dough whiteness. Glycerin softens the dough and prevents it from cracking and bubbling.

MATERIALS NEEDED:

3 slices white bread, crusts removed

3 tablespoons white glue

1 teaspoon white acrylic paint or white shoe polish

1 teaspoon glycerin (available at drugstores)

Tools (see Salt Dough Ornaments, page 140)

Mix the dough. Tear the bread into small pieces. Add remaining ingredients and stir together. Knead until the mixture no longer sticks to your fingers and has a smooth texture, about fifteen minutes. A few drops of glycerin on your fingers keep the dough from sticking as you knead it.

Shape the dough. Remove small bits of the dough at a time and shape. Keep any unused dough in a plastic bag. If dough tends to dry out, add a little more glue and reknead.

For thin layers, roll dough between two pieces of waxed paper. To smooth the appearance of the ornament, brush lightly with equal parts glue and water.

Shape pieces of dough on pieces of aluminum foil and follow the directions for Salt Dough Ornaments (page 140).

Dry the ornaments. Dry shaped dough in your dehydrator at the highest temperature setting. This recipe does not need to be baked in the oven. If air-dried, objects may take twenty-four hours or more. In the dehydrator, they are usually dry in six to twelve hours.

Paint and seal. Paint and seal as directed in the recipe for Salt Dough Ornaments, page 140.

RECIPES

It's easy to include dried fruits and fruit snacks in lunch boxes and for afternoon snacks. Dried foods also can bring new flavor and variety to everyday meals. When you have some extra dried fruits that you've hidden from your family, there are lots of ways to incorporate them into your meals.

Here are some tempting recipes to include your home-dried foods into everyday meals. These are our family's favorites . . . and will probably be yours!

TIPS FOR RECONSTITUTING DRIED FRUITS AND VEGETABLES

- Dried vegetables take longer to rehydrate than dried fruits because they have less residual moisture.
- Correct blanching results in better rehydration for vegetables. Over-blanched vegetables are mushy when reconstituted.

- The smaller the piece of dried fruit or vegetable, the shorter the time it takes to reconstitute. Foods that have been shredded, grated, or powdered take the shortest time. Large pieces take the longest time.
- Dried foods will take longer to reconstitute in hard water than in soft water. Minerals give water its taste, so hard water will add a little different flavor than soft water.
- Heating water to boiling before adding dried foods shortens the reconstituting time. Be sure to remove the pan from the heat while foods absorb the water.
- Fully rehydrate vegetables before cooking them or they will cook in their shriveled condition and be tough.
- Save any leftover liquid from rehydrating to use in the recipe. If a recipe calls for milk, use evaporated or powdered milk with the drained liquid as part of the required water.

- Add salt, sugar, and seasonings *after* the food has been fully rehydrated or at the end of cooking.

- When rehydrating fruits, fruit juice gives a fuller flavor than water, but it takes a little longer.

- Only partially rehydrating fruit gives a little nicer texture in a cooked recipe. Fruits won't be mushy.

- Most dried fruits and vegetables measure about half as much dried as they do fresh. Finely chopped or powdered, their dried volume is about one-fourth of their volume when fresh.

APPETIZERS AND SNACKS

Fruit Pillows
Makes 40 appetizers

This creamy and crunchy filling makes this appetizer out of the ordinary. The filling can be made ahead and refrigerated.

40 large slices of dried apricots, dates, figs, peaches, pears, or prunes

FILLING
½ cup (4 ounces) cream cheese, at room temperature
¼ cup small curd cottage cheese
2 tablespoons sour cream
2 tablespoons honey
1 teaspoon vanilla extract
2 tablespoons toasted sesame seeds

¼ cup wheat germ
⅓ cup sunflower seeds
2 tablespoons finely chopped almonds, lightly toasted (page 113)

½ cup sweetened shredded coconut (optional)
Raisins or whole unblanched almonds

If the dried fruit has hardened, steam over boiling water for 1 to 2 minutes to soften. Remove and place on waxed paper.

Make the filling: Beat the cream cheese and cottage cheese in a medium bowl until fluffy. Stir in the remaining filling ingredients until combined.

Spoon 1 heaping teaspoon of the filling into the pit cavity of each piece of dried fruit.

Gently dip the filled side of the fruit in the coconut, if desired. Garnish with a raisin.

Fruit-Cheese Hors d'Oeuvres
Makes 20 appetizers

These hors d'oeuvres are easy to make and a delight to eat!

20 halves of dried apricots, dates, figs, peaches, pears, or prunes

FILLING
2 tablespoons low-fat cream cheese, at room temperature
2 tablespoons low-fat sour cream
⅛ teaspoon sweet paprika
½ cup lightly packed finely shredded Cheddar cheese
¼ cup finely shredded raw carrots

⅓ cup finely chopped almonds, lightly toasted
   (page 113)

If the dried fruit has hardened, steam over boiling water for 1 to 2 minutes to soften. Remove and place on waxed paper.

Make the filling: Beat the cream cheese until fluffy in a medium bowl. Stir in the sour cream, paprika, Cheddar cheese, and carrots, mixing well. Spoon 1 teaspoon filling into pit cavity of each piece of dried fruit.

Gently dip filled fruit in the almonds.

Devilish Eggs
Makes 12 halves

Dried tomatoes give traditional deviled eggs that special flavor. The fresher the eggs, the more difficult hard-cooked eggs are to peel.

   6 eggs
   2 tablespoons low-fat mayonnaise
   4 tablespoons low-fat sour cream
   1 tablespoon white wine vinegar
   ½ teaspoon light Worcestershire sauce
   1 teaspoon stone-ground Dijon mustard
   1 tablespoon finely chopped chives
   1 tablespoon dried tomato bits, plus additional for
      garnish
   Sweet paprika

Cover the eggs with water and bring to a boil. Reduce heat to lowest setting, cover, and simmer for 10 minutes. Plunge immediately into ice water to cool. If eggs are very fresh, use very sharp knife to cut into halves. Gently lift egg half out with spoon. If eggs are more than a week old, they can be peeled first and then cut into halves.

Remove yolks and set whites aside. Mix yolks with mayonnaise, sour cream, vinegar, Worcestershire sauce, and mustard. Stir in chives and tomato bits. Spoon the mixture back into the white halves. Sprinkle a few tomato bits on top for color and sprinkle with paprika.

Artichokes with Zesty Mayonnaise
Makes 4 servings

I love artichokes. This garlic-tomato mayonnaise is my favorite dip. Reduced-fat mayonnaise helps cut the calories.

   4 large artichokes
   2 tablespoons extra-light olive oil
   2 cloves garlic, crushed
   ¼ cup fresh lemon juice

   ZESTY MAYONNAISE
   1⅓ cups low-fat mayonnaise
   2 cloves garlic, crushed
   ¼ cup fresh lemon juice
   3 tablespoons dried tomato bits

Wash the artichokes, letting running water spray in between the leaves. Shake to remove excess moisture.

Holding each artichoke by the stem, cut the thorny tip off each leaf with kitchen scissors. Lay the artichoke flat and cut off the top. Pull off any darkened lower leaves. Cut off the stem.

Place a steaming rack in the bottom of a large

pot. Add enough water to reach the steaming rack. Place the artichokes on the steaming rack.

Mix the olive oil, garlic, and lemon juice in a small bowl. Drizzle the mixture over the tops of the artichokes. Bring the water to a boil. Cover and boil gently until the leaves near the center pull out easily, 30 to 40 minutes. Carefully lift out artichokes with a slotted spoon and drain. Place in a serving dish.

Make the mayonnaise: Combine the mayonnaise, garlic, lemon juice, and tomato bits in a small bowl. Stir until well mixed.

medium bowl. Stir in the coconut, almonds, lemon peel, and cinnamon.

In a small saucepan, slightly warm the honey, orange juice, and lemon juice. Stir to mix well. Slowly pour honey mixture over the fruit mixture, stirring until the ingredients stick together evenly. Form into small balls, about ¾ inch in diameter. Place on fruit roll sheets from your dehydrator.

Dry the balls at 120°F (49°C) until no longer sticky to touch, up to 6 hours on a dry day. If desired, roll the balls in powdered sugar.

Golden Crunch Balls
Makes 48 balls

These slightly tart balls provide lots of energy. Put them in lunch boxes or take them on a hike.

½ cup dried apricots
½ cup dried apples
½ cup dried peaches
½ cup finely grated unsweetened coconut
¼ cup slivered almonds
1 teaspoon grated lemon peel
½ teaspoon ground cinnamon
3 tablespoons honey
3 tablespoons orange juice
1 tablespoon fresh lemon juice
Powdered sugar (optional)

Grind the dried fruits in a food processor or blender, ½ cup at a time, until pieces are the size of rock salt. Pulsing the blender tends to keep them from getting stuck. Combine fruits together in a

Nutty Fruit Balls
Makes 36 balls

These high-energy fruit snacks are perfect for hiking or lunch boxes. Substitute walnuts, pecans, or hazelnuts for the almonds and you'll have a different flavor.

¼ cup dried apricots
½ cup dried cherries or figs
1 cup dried dates
½ cup dried prunes
¼ cup raisins
⅓ cup angel flake coconut
⅓ cup sunflower seeds
1 cup slivered almonds, finely chopped
3 tablespoons fresh lemon juice
2 to 3 tablespoons white corn syrup

Finely chop dried fruits in a food processor or blender, ½ cup at a time, until the pieces are the size of rock salt. Pulsing the blender helps them keep from getting stuck. Combine the fruits together in a medium bowl. Stir in the coconut, sunflower seeds, and almonds.

Mix the lemon juice with corn syrup in a small bowl. Add to the dried fruit mixture and mix well. Shape the mixture into 1-inch balls. Place on fruit roll sheets in your dehydrator.

Dry the balls at 130°F (54°C) until firm to the touch, about 6 hours on a dry day. Wrap individually in plastic wrap and store in an airtight container in a cool place. Use within 2 to 3 weeks.

Golden Gorp
Makes about 4 cups

Gorp is a funny name for a mixture of high-energy foods, such as nuts and dried fruits. It originally meant "good old raisins and peanuts," but now other ingredients are used. This combination is good any time, anywhere for some quick energy. I am on the go a lot, so I like to keep a bag in the car. This mix is one of my favorites.

½ cup dried apples
½ cup dried apricots
¼ cup dried peaches
½ cup dried pears
½ cup dried pineapple
½ cup dried mango
¼ cup sweetened flaked coconut
½ cup golden raisins
½ cup cashews or whole almonds

Cut the apples, apricots, peaches, pears, pineapple, and mango into ½-inch pieces.

Combine all ingredients in a medium bowl. Package in airtight plastic bags and store in a cool, dry place. Use within 3 to 4 weeks.

Trekky Trail Mix
Makes about 4½ cups

M&M's candies add a little color and chocolate to this mix.

½ cup dried apricots
½ cup dried peaches
½ cup dried pineapple
½ cup dried cherries
½ cup raisins
¾ cup M&M's plain chocolate candies
¼ cup sunflower seeds
½ cup golden raisins
½ cup dry-roasted peanuts

Cut the apricots, peaches, and pineapple into ½-inch pieces.

Combine all ingredients in a medium bowl. Package the trail mix in airtight plastic bags and store in a cool, dry place. Use within 3 to 4 weeks.

Tangy Sunflower Seeds
Makes 2 cups

Soy sauce adds a little extra salt. You can buy flavored sunflower seeds, but it is fun to make your own.

2 tablespoons vegetable oil
1 tablespoon soy sauce
¼ teaspoon sweet paprika
½ teaspoon celery salt
Dash cayenne pepper
2 cups raw shelled sunflower seeds

Preheat the oven to 300°F (150°C). In a medium bowl, mix the oil, soy sauce, paprika, celery salt, and cayenne pepper. Add the sunflower seeds and stir until the seeds are evenly coated. Spread the seeds in a shallow baking pan. Bake for 20 minutes, stirring frequently. Cool on paper towels. Store in an airtight jar and use within 2 weeks.

SOUPS AND SIDE DISHES

Scandinavian Fruit Soup
Makes 6 to 8 servings

Serve this fruit soup hot or cold with sour cream, whipped cream, or vanilla yogurt. Fresh fruit and juices combine with dried ones to make this interesting dessert or breakfast fruit dish.

3 cups water
2 cups 1- to 1½-inch pieces mixed dried fruit such as apples, apricots, cherries, figs, peaches, pineapple, prunes, and raisins
2 slices fresh lemon
1 slice fresh orange
1 cinnamon stick
3 whole cloves
1 cup orange juice
1 cup fresh or canned pineapple chunks, drained
½ cup honey
1 tablespoon fresh lemon juice
1⁄16 teaspoon salt
2 tablespoons tapioca
Sour cream, whipped cream, or vanilla yogurt

In a medium saucepan, combine 2 cups of the water, dried fruit, lemon and orange slices, cinnamon stick, and cloves. Bring to a boil and remove from the heat. Cover and let stand for 30 minutes.

While the fruit is soaking, combine the remaining 1 cup water and the remaining ingredients, except the sour cream. Let stand for at least 15 minutes. Drain the fruit. Remove and discard cinnamon stick, cloves, and lemon and orange slices. Add the pineapple mixture to the drained fruit in the saucepan. Bring to a boil and simmer until thickened, 15 minutes.

Serve hot or chilled. Ladle into bowls and top with sour cream.

Pasta and Bean Soup with Dried Tomatoes
Makes 4 to 6 servings

This bean soup is dressed up with some dried tomatoes and veggies. It goes together quickly and is perfect for one of those nights when I've worked late and have little energy for cooking.

⅓ pound fettuccine

2 tablespoons extra-light olive oil

1 onion, chopped

3 ribs celery, chopped

4 cloves garlic, minced

2 (15-ounce) cans white beans, drained and rinsed, or 2 cups cooked navy beans

3 cups chicken broth

3 cups water

1 teaspoon dried rosemary

3 carrots, in small dice

2 tablespoons minced parsley

¼ cup finely chopped dried tomatoes

Salt and black pepper to taste

Cook the pasta in salted boiling water according to package directions, adding 1 tablespoon of the olive oil to the water. Slightly undercook. Drain. Rinse in cold water and set aside.

Heat the remaining 1 tablespoon oil in a skillet over medium heat. Add the onion, celery, and garlic and sauté until lightly brown. Add the beans, chicken broth, water, and rosemary to a pot. Bring to a boil. Add the carrots and sautéed vegetables. Bring to a simmer, cover, and simmer gently for 10 minutes. Puree about half of the soup in a food processor. Return to the pot. Stir in the parsley, dried tomatoes, salt, and pepper. Add the fettuccine and heat until hot.

Beefy Hobo Stew
Makes 6 to 8 servings

This meal-in-one-bowl stew is hearty and easy to make. Serve it with a salad and crusty French bread. The dried tomatoes add a little zing without adding too much tomato flavor.

2 cups mixed dried vegetables such as green beans, carrots, corn, and peas or 4 cups fresh

4 to 5 tablespoons extra-light olive oil

¼ cup unbleached all-purpose flour

½ teaspoon salt

¼ teaspoon black pepper

½ teaspoon dried thyme

½ teaspoon dried marjoram

2 tablespoons parsley flakes

2 to 3 pounds lean stew beef, cut into 1-inch cubes

1 quart water plus ½ cup

4 cups canned beef broth, or 4 beef bouillon cubes and 4 cups water

2 cups 1-inch potato cubes

2 medium onions, quartered

½ cup cold water

If using dried vegetables, cover them with boiling water and allow to rehydrate up to 2 hours, depending on the type of vegetable and size of the pieces.

Heat the oil in a large, heavy kettle. Combine the flour, salt, pepper, thyme, marjoram, and parsley flakes in a brown paper bag. Shake the beef cubes in the bag to coat with the flour mixture. Keep leftover flour mixture to thicken the stew later.

Brown the beef cubes, in batches, in the hot oil. Add the 1 quart water and broth. Bring to a boil, reduce heat, and simmer until the meat is tender, about 30 minutes. Add the potatoes, onions, and reconstituted or fresh vegetables to the beef mixture. Simmer until the vegetables are tender, 15 to 20 minutes.

Dissolve the reserved flour mixture in the ½ cup water and slowly add to the stew, and cook, stirring constantly, until the stew thickens.

Cream of Vegetable Soup
Makes 6 to 8 servings

To make cream of vegetable soup, mix and match the vegetables that you have on hand. This soup can be made with a mix of dried, frozen, and fresh or all fresh vegetables. The potatoes provide the base and you can make it low-fat by substituting milk for the cream, although I think it tastes a little better with the cream. I also add fresh broccoli to this recipe for a delightful cream of broccoli soup. Finely cut the broccoli and add it right at the end so that it isn't mushy.

> ½ cup dried mixed vegetables or vegetable flakes (beans, celery, corn, peas), or 1 cup chopped fresh vegetables
> ¼ cup dried carrots, or ½ cup sliced, peeled carrots
> 6 bacon slices, diced
> 1 cup chopped onion
> 6 cups cubed, peeled potatoes
> Water
> 1 teaspoon salt
> 2 cups milk
> 2 cups light cream
> ¼ teaspoon black pepper
> 1 cup sliced celery

> ¼ cup dried tomato bits
> 2 tablespoons finely chopped fresh parsley
> Shredded Cheddar cheese

If using dried mixed vegetables and carrots, cover them with boiling water and allow to rehydrate for up to 1 hour, depending on the type of vegetable and size of the pieces.

Fry the bacon in a large skillet until crisp. Drain the bacon, reserve, and discard the fat. Add the onion and lightly brown. In a large pot, combine the onion, potatoes, carrots, rehydrated vegetables (or fresh vegetables), and salt. Measure enough water from the rehydrated vegetables to make 3 cups. Add the water to the vegetables.

Cover and simmer until the vegetables are tender. Remove half of the potato mixture and place in the blender with the milk and cream. Puree the mixture until smooth. Return the pureed mixture to the pot. Heat the soup till it is almost boiling. Add the celery, dried tomato bits, pepper, and parsley and stir. (The celery and tomato bits add some crunch.) Ladle into bowls and garnish with cheese and pieces of bacon.

Country Chicken-Vegetable Soup
Makes 6 to 8 servings

This chicken soup is really a one-dish meal. It's great on a cold evening with hot corn bread and a tossed salad. Homemade chicken soup is definitely one of my comfort foods.

> 2 cups boiling water
> 2 cups mixed dried vegetables such as green beans, carrots, corn, and peas, or 3 cups fresh vegetables

2 tablespoons extra-light olive oil

1 cup chopped onion

½ cup chopped celery

1 (3- to 4-pound) chicken, cut up

3 (14.5-ounce) cans chicken broth

½ cup chopped carrot

1 bay leaf

2 tablespoons parsley flakes

½ teaspoon poultry seasoning

2 (14.5-ounce) cans tomatoes, undrained

½ teaspoon sweet paprika

½ teaspoon salt

⅛ teaspoon black pepper

2 cups cooked noodles (optional)

Rehydrate dried vegetables by pouring 2 cups of boiling water over the vegetables. Let them stand for up to 1 hour, depending on the type of vegetable and size of pieces.

Heat the olive oil in a skillet over medium heat. Add the onion and celery and sauté until tender. Remove. In the same skillet, brown the chicken pieces, in batches.

In a large kettle, combine the chicken, chicken broth, sautéed onion and celery, carrot, bay leaf, parsley flakes, poultry seasoning, and tomatoes. Simmer until the chicken is tender, 45 minutes to 1 hour. Skim the foam from the top and discard. Remove the chicken from the pot to cool. Strain the broth through a large-mesh sieve and discard the spices and vegetables. Remove the bones from the chicken.

Place the chicken pieces in the kettle with the broth, undrained dried vegetables (or fresh vegetables), paprika, salt, and pepper. Simmer for 15 minutes. Add cooked noodles to the soup, if desired. Serve piping hot.

Fiesta Corn
Makes 2½ cups

I like to make this with frozen corn. Since frozen corn is already blanched and off the cob, it's easy to add the peppers, onions, and spices.

4 cups blanched fresh corn kernels (see page 84), or 4 cups frozen whole-kernel corn

1 cup finely chopped onion

1 cup finely chopped red or green bell pepper or a mix of both

1 teaspoon cornstarch

½ teaspoon seasoned salt

¼ teaspoon salt

⅛ teaspoon black pepper

Toss the corn, onion, and bell pepper in a medium bowl. Mix the cornstarch, seasoned salt, salt, and black pepper in a small bowl. Sprinkle over the corn mixture and stir until seasonings are evenly distributed. Spread on drying trays on a plastic mesh screen. Dry at 140°F (60°C) until crispy, about 6 hours on a dry day.

Fruited Rice
Makes 8 to 10 servings

Rice is just rice unless it's dressed up. Chunky fruit pieces add a sweet touch to this side dish for chicken or fish.

- 4 quarts cold water
- 2 tablespoons salt
- 3 cups basmati rice, rinsed with cold water until water runs clear
- ½ cup golden raisins
- ½ cup dried apricots
- 8 tablespoons (½ stick) unsalted butter
- ½ teaspoon ground cardamom
- ½ teaspoon black pepper
- ¾ cup coarsely chopped pistachios

Bring the water to a rolling boil in a large saucepan and add the salt. Add the rice to the boiling water and bring to a boil again. Cook the rice for 5 minutes after the water again comes to a boil. Drain in a sieve. Clean the pan.

Toss the fruit together in a medium bowl. Melt 6 tablespoons of the butter in the bottom of the pan. Add the cardamom and pepper and stir. Layer the rice and dried fruit in the bottom of the pan, beginning and ending with the rice.

Cook over low heat for 20 to 25 minutes. A light crust will form on the bottom. Remove from heat and let the rice stand for 15 minutes, still covered.

Lightly sauté the pistachios in the remaining 2 tablespoons of butter. Spoon the rice into a large bowl. Break apart the crust and stir into the rice. Sprinkle with the pistachios.

MEATS, FISH, AND CHICKEN

Apple-Glazed Stuffed Pork Chops
Makes 6 servings

These juicy pork chops have a spicy apple stuffing and a tangy fruit glaze.

APPLE-LEMON GLAZE
- 1 tablespoon cornstarch
- 1 tablespoon sugar
- ¼ teaspoon ground nutmeg
- 1 cup apple cider or apple juice
- 1 teaspoon fresh lemon juice

STUFFING
- ½ cup chopped dried apples, or ¾ cup chopped, peeled, fresh apples
- 2 tablespoons raisins
- ¾ cup apple cider or apple juice
- 1½ teaspoons fresh lemon juice
- 1 tablespoon extra-light olive oil
- 2 tablespoons dried onion flakes, or 4 tablespoons chopped fresh onion
- ¼ cup chopped celery
- 2 cups bread crumbs
- ¼ teaspoon salt
- ¾ teaspoon poultry seasoning
- 1 tablespoon parsley flakes
- 1 egg, beaten
- Salt and black pepper

PORK CHOPS

6 (1-inch thick) pork chops
1 tablespoon extra-light olive oil

Make the glaze: Combine the cornstarch, sugar, and nutmeg in a small saucepan. Stir in apple cider and lemon juice. Cook over medium heat, stirring, until the glaze thickens and boils. Remove from heat.

Preheat the oven to 350°F (180°C).

Make the stuffing: In a small bowl, combine the dried apples, raisins, apple cider, and lemon juice. Let stand to soften. Heat the olive oil in a skillet over medium heat. Add the onion flakes and celery and lightly brown. Stir in the apple-raisin mixture. Add the bread crumbs, salt, poultry seasoning, and parsley flakes. Stir in the egg and mix well.

Cut a large pocket in the side of each pork chop. Lightly season the chops inside and out with salt and pepper to taste. Spoon the apple mixture loosely into the pockets. Heat 1 tablespoon of olive oil in a large skillet over medium-high heat. Add the pork chops and brown chops on both sides. Place the pork chops in a 13 × 9-inch baking pan.

Pour the glaze over the chops in the baking pan. Cover with foil and bake for 30 minutes. Uncover and baste with the glaze. Leave uncovered and bake for 15 to 20 minutes.

Great Jerky
Makes ¼ pound jerky

Flank steak or round makes the best jerky. Sometimes I buy an eye of round and have the butcher slice it for me.

¾ teaspoon salt
¼ teaspoon cracked pepper
1 tablespoon brown sugar
1 clove garlic, crushed
2 tablespoons soy sauce
1 tablespoon Worcestershire sauce
1 pound lean meat, sliced ³⁄₁₆- to ¾-inch thick

Combine all of the ingredients, except the meat, in a small bowl. Stir to mix well. Place the meat slices in a single layer in a shallow glass or stainless-steel container. Spread with the salt mixture. Cover tightly and marinate for 6 to 8 hours in the refrigerator. Stir occasionally. Follow directions on pages 123 to 129 for smoking, drying, and storing jerky.

Teriyaki Jerky
Makes ¼ pound jerky

The soy sauce adds some extra salt.

½ teaspoon salt
¼ teaspoon cracked pepper
½ teaspoon ground ginger
2 tablespoons brown sugar
1 clove garlic, crushed
¼ cup soy sauce
1 pound lean meat, sliced ³⁄₁₆- to ¾-inch thick

Combine all of the ingredients, except the meat, in a small bowl. Stir to mix well. Place the meat slices in single layer in a shallow glass or stainless-steel container. Spoon the soy sauce mixture over the meat. Cover tightly. Marinate for 6 to 8 hours in the refrigerator, stirring occasionally. Follow directions on pages 123 to 129 for smoking, drying, and storing jerky.

Sweet and Sour Jerky
Makes ¼ pound jerky

This jerky has a pleasant sweet and sour flavor.

- 1 teaspoon salt
- ¼ teaspoon cracked black pepper
- ½ teaspoon onion powder
- 3 tablespoons light brown sugar
- 1 clove garlic, crushed
- 1 tablespoon soy sauce
- ¼ cup red wine vinegar
- ¼ cup pineapple juice
- 1 pound lean meat, sliced ³⁄₁₆- to ¾-inch thick

Combine all of the ingredients, except the meat, in a small bowl. Stir to mix well. Place the meat slices in a single layer in a shallow glass or stainless-steel container. Spoon the mixture over the meat. Cover tightly. Marinate for 6 to 8 hours in the refrigerator, stirring occasionally. Follow directions on pages 123 to 129 for smoking, drying, and storing jerky.

Curried Jerky
Makes ¼ pound jerky

If you like curry, you'll enjoy this jerky. It's a nice change from the usual jerky flavors.

- 1 teaspoon salt
- ¼ teaspoon cracked black pepper
- ⅛ teaspoon ground cinnamon
- ¹⁄₁₆ teaspoon ground cloves
- ⅛ teaspoon ground cumin
- 1½ teaspoons curry powder
- ½ teaspoon garlic powder
- 1 teaspoon ground ginger
- 1 pound lean meat, sliced ³⁄₁₆- to ¾-inch thick

Combine all of the ingredients, except the meat, in a small bowl. Stir to mix well. Place the meat slices in a single layer in a shallow glass or stainless-steel container. Sprinkle the mixture over the meat. Cover tightly. Marinate for 6 to 8 hours in the refrigerator, stirring occasionally. Follow directions on pages 123 to 129 for smoking, drying, and storing jerky.

Frontier Jerky
Makes ¼ pound jerky

This jerky has a smoky flavor from the liquid smoke without the hassle of smoking.

- 1 teaspoon salt
- ¼ teaspoon cracked black pepper
- ½ teaspoon garlic powder
- ½ teaspoon onion powder
- 2 tablespoons Worcestershire sauce
- 2 tablespoons liquid smoke
- 1 pound lean meat, sliced ³⁄₁₆- to ¾-inch thick

Combine all of the ingredients, except the meat, in a small bowl. Stir to mix well. Place the meat slices in a single layer in a shallow glass or stainless-steel container. Spoon the mixture over the meat. Cover tightly. Marinate for 6 to 8 hours in the refrigerator, stirring occasionally. Follow directions on pages 123 to 129 for smoking, drying, and storing jerky.

Western Barbecue Jerky
Makes ¼ pound jerky

This jerky is a tasty reminder of the Old West.

1 teaspoon salt
¼ teaspoon cracked black pepper
⅛ teaspoon cayenne pepper
1 teaspoon garlic powder
1 teaspoon onion powder
1 teaspoon dry mustard
3 tablespoons light brown sugar
⅓ cup red wine vinegar
⅓ cup ketchup
1 pound lean meat, sliced ³⁄₁₆- to ¾-inch thick

Combine all of the ingredients, except the meat, in a small bowl. Stir to mix well. Place the meat slices in a single layer in a shallow glass or stainless-steel container. Spoon the mixture over the meat. Cover tightly. Marinate for 6 to 8 hours in the refrigerator, stirring occasionally. Follow directions on pages 123 to 129 for smoking, drying, and storing jerky.

Hot and Tangy Jerky
Makes ¼ pound jerky

This jerky is fairly spicy. If you want to cool it down a bit, decrease the cayenne pepper.

1 teaspoon salt
¼ teaspoon cracked black pepper
¼ teaspoon cayenne pepper
1 teaspoon onion powder
½ teaspoon sweet paprika
2 cloves garlic, crushed
2 tablespoons A.1. Steak Sauce
3 tablespoons Worcestershire sauce
1 pound lean meat, sliced ³⁄₁₆- to ¾-inch thick

Combine all of the ingredients, except the meat, in a small bowl. Stir to mix well. Place the meat slices in a single layer in a shallow glass or stainless-steel container. Spoon the mixture over the meat. Cover tightly. Marinate for 6 to 8 hours in the refrigerator, stirring occasionally. Follow directions on pages 123 to 129 for smoking, drying, and storing jerky.

Teriyaki Fish Brine
Makes enough brine for 3 to 5 pounds of fish

Soy sauce and ginger add a pungent flavor to this brine. The salt in this recipe is slightly decreased because the soy sauce adds salt.

- ¾ cup salt
- 2 cups firmly packed light brown sugar
- 2 cloves garlic, crushed
- 1 tablespoon ground ginger
- 1 teaspoon black pepper
- 2 cups soy sauce
- 7 cups water

Combine all of the ingredients in a 4- to 5-quart glass, stoneware, or stainless-steel container. Stir until sugar and salt are dissolved. Follow directions for Brine the Fish (page 132).

Gourmet Fish Brine
Makes enough brine for 3 to 5 pounds of fish

Just a hint of tarragon adds a different flavor.

- 1 cup salt
- 2 cups sugar
- ½ cup fresh lemon juice
- 3 cloves garlic, crushed
- 1 teaspoon black pepper
- 2 teaspoons dried tarragon, crushed
- 2 tablespoons parsley flakes, crushed
- 2 cups dry white wine
- 7 cups water

Combine all ingredients in a 4- to 5-quart glass, stoneware, or stainless-steel container. Stir until sugar and salt are dissolved. Follow directions for Brine the Fish (page 132).

Spiced Fish Brine
Makes enough brine for 3 to 5 pounds of fish

Molasses and garlic add a full, rich flavor.

- 1 cup salt
- 1½ cups firmly packed light brown sugar
- ⅓ cup molasses
- ½ cup lemon juice
- 2 garlic cloves, crushed
- 1 medium onion, cut into rings
- 1 tablespoon black pepper
- 7 cups water

Combine all of the ingredients in a 4- to 5-quart glass, stoneware, or stainless-steel container. Stir until sugar and salt are dissolved. Follow directions for Brine the Fish (page 132).

Hot and Spicy Fish Brine
Makes enough brine for 3 to 5 pounds of fish

Cayenne pepper is the secret ingredient. If it's too hot, decrease the amount of cayenne.

- 1 cup salt
- 2 cups firmly packed light brown sugar
- 1 tablespoon onion powder
- 2 cloves garlic, crushed

1 tablespoon sweet paprika

1 teaspoon black pepper

½ teaspoon cayenne pepper

7 cups water

Combine all of the ingredients in a 4- to 5-quart glass, stoneware, or stainless-steel container. Stir until sugar and salt are dissolved. Follow directions for Brine the Fish (page 132).

Pickled Dry Cure for Fish Jerky
Makes ¼ pound fish jerky

The pickling spice adds a pickle flavor.

1 tablespoon salt

1 teaspoon ground allspice

1 tablespoon mixed pickling spices

2 bay leaves, crushed

2 medium onions, cut into rings

2 tablespoons apple cider vinegar

2 pounds fish, sliced 3/16- to 3/4-inch thick

Combine all of the ingredients, except the fish, in a small bowl. Stir to mix well. Place the fish slices in a single layer in a shallow glass or stainless-steel container. Sprinkle the mixture equally over each piece of fish. Cover tightly. Marinate for 6 to 8 hours in the refrigerator, stirring occasionally. Remove the onion rings before drying the fish. Follow directions on pages 131 to 134 for smoking, drying, and storing fish jerky.

Lemon Dry Cure for Fish Jerky
Makes ¼ pound fish jerky

Freshly squeezed lemon juice is one of the secrets to the delightful taste of this jerky.

4 teaspoons salt

2 teaspoons onion powder

2 tablespoons parsley flakes, crushed

¼ cup fresh lemon juice

2 pounds fish, sliced 3/16- to 3/4-inch thick

Combine all of the ingredients, except the fish, in a small bowl. Stir to mix well. Place the fish slices in a single layer in a shallow glass or stainless-steel container. Sprinkle the mixture equally over each piece of fish. Cover tightly. Marinate for 6 to 8 hours in the refrigerator, stirring occasionally. Follow directions on pages 131 to 134 for smoking, drying, and storing fish jerky.

Spicy Dry Cure for Fish Jerky
Makes ¼ pound fish jerky

If it's too hot for you, decrease the Tabasco sauce. If you smoke this jerky in a smoker, leave out the liquid smoke.

  1 tablespoon salt
  1 teaspoon onion powder
  1 teaspoon garlic powder
  2 tablespoons liquid smoke
  2 tablespoons soy sauce
  3 drops Tabasco sauce
  2 pounds fish, sliced ³⁄₁₆- to ¾-inch thick

Combine all of the ingredients, except the fish, in a small bowl. Stir to mix well. Place the fish slices in a single layer in a shallow glass or stainless-steel container. Sprinkle the mixture equally over each piece of fish. Cover tightly. Marinate for 6 to 8 hours in the refrigerator, stirring occasionally. Follow directions on pages 131 to 134 for smoking, drying, and storing fish jerky.

Herbed Dry Cure for Fish Jerky
Makes ¼ pound fish jerky

Subtly blended herbs and wine give this cure its warm flavor.

  1 tablespoon salt
  ½ teaspoon celery salt
  2 tablespoons parsley flakes, crushed, or 4
     tablespoons chopped fresh

  ½ bay leaf, crushed
  ½ teaspoon cracked black pepper
  ⅛ teaspoon dried thyme
  1 medium onion, cut in rings
  2 tablespoons dry white wine
  2 pounds fish, sliced ³⁄₁₆- to ¾-inch thick

Combine all of the ingredients, except the fish, in a small bowl. Stir to mix well. Place the fish slices in a single layer in a shallow glass or stainless-steel container. Sprinkle the mixture equally over each piece of fish. Cover tightly. Marinate for 6 to 8 hours in the refrigerator, stirring occasionally. Remove the onion rings before drying the fish. Follow directions on pages 131 to 134 for smoking, drying, and storing fish jerky.

Grilled Salmon with Pesto
Makes 6 servings

You can bake this in the oven, but it's better over the grill. Use the pesto recipe given in Pesto Pasta with Dried Tomatoes (page 160). It's delightful.

  1½ pounds salmon fillet with the skin
  Salt and freshly ground pepper to taste
  ½ cup pesto (page 160)

Pat the salmon dry between paper towels and sprinkle with salt and pepper. Place the salmon skin-side down on a flat pan. Spread the pesto evenly over top of the salmon. Pat the pesto in place, making sure that the layer of pesto is even and completely covers the top of the salmon. Grill over medium heat about 15 minutes, covered.

Or preheat the oven to 425°F (220°C). Place on

a flat baking sheet and bake for 12 to 15 minutes, depending on the thickness of the fillet, or until cooked through.

Creamy Baked Halibut
Makes 6 servings

Low-fat mayonnaise cuts the calories without altering the flavor. Dried tomatoes give it a zing.

  1½ cups low-fat mayonnaise
  1½ cups finely grated Parmesan cheese
  1 teaspoon garlic salt
  ½ teaspoon black pepper
  2 tablespoons fresh lemon juice
  ¼ cup dried tomato bits
  2 large onions, sliced ¼-inch thick
  2 pounds fresh halibut fillets

Preheat the oven to 350°F (180°C). Spray a 13 × 9-inch casserole with nonstick cooking spray.

Combine the mayonnaise, Parmesan cheese, garlic salt, pepper, lemon juice, and tomato bits in a small bowl. Spread half of the onions in the casserole. Lay the halibut fillets over the onions. Cover the halibut with the remaining onions. Spread the Parmesan mixture over the onions and halibut. Cover with foil.

Bake for 30 minutes. Remove the foil and bake for 7 to 10 minutes, or until the top is slightly browned.

Stuffed Chicken Breasts
Makes 6 servings

This dish is easy to make, but is elegant enough for company.

STUFFING
1 tablespoon extra-light olive oil
½ medium red onion, chopped
½ large red bell pepper, finely chopped
1 (10-ounce) package frozen chopped spinach, thawed and drained
½ teaspoon dried rosemary, or 1 tablespoon chopped fresh rosemary
½ teaspoon salt
½ teaspoon black pepper
½ cup shredded mozzarella cheese
¼ cup finely chopped dried tomatoes

6 boneless, skinless chicken breast halves (about 3 pounds)

RUB
1 tablespoon extra-light olive oil
1 teaspoon dried rosemary, or 2 tablespoons chopped fresh rosemary
½ teaspoon salt
¼ teaspoon black pepper

Make the stuffing: Heat the olive oil in a large skillet over medium heat. Add the onion and bell pepper and sauté for 5 minutes. Add the spinach, rosemary, salt, and black pepper. Cook for 3 minutes. Remove from the heat and cool. Stir in the cheese and dried tomatoes.

Cut a horizontal pocket in the side of each

chicken breast. Fill the pocket with 3 to 4 table-spoons of the spinach stuffing. Secure the pocket closed with 2 wooden picks.

Make the rub: Combine all the rub ingredients in a small bowl. Rub on both sides of each chicken breast.

Preheat a grill. Place chicken on grill rack and grill on both sides until an instant-read thermome-ter inserted in the chicken registers 170°F (77°C), 10 to 12 minutes per side.

Veggie Lasagna
Makes 8 servings

Dried tomato bits adds a rich tomato flavor in this easy-to-make vegetable lasagna. It also freezes well.

 2 teaspoons extra-light olive oil

 1 large zucchini, cubed

 1 red bell pepper, diced

 1 medium onion, diced

 2 cloves garlic, crushed

 8 ounces fresh mushrooms, sliced

 3 tablespoons chopped fresh basil

 2 fresh plum tomatoes, chopped

 ½ cup dried tomato bits

 1 (10-ounce) package frozen chopped spinach, thawed and squeezed dry

 2 cups low-fat cottage cheese or ricotta cheese

 1⅓ cups shredded low-fat mozzarella cheese

 ¼ cup grated Parmesan cheese

 ¼ teaspoon salt

 ¼ teaspoon black pepper

 4 cups prepared spaghetti sauce

 16 no-boil lasagna noodles

Preheat the oven to 350°F (180°C).

Heat the olive oil in a large skillet over medium-high heat. Add the zucchini, bell pepper, onion, garlic, and mushrooms and sauté until barely ten-der. Add basil and set aside.

Combine the plum tomatoes, dried tomatoes, spinach, cottage cheese, 1 cup of the mozzarella cheese, Parmesan cheese, salt, and black pepper in a bowl.

Spread ¾ cup of the spaghetti sauce evenly over the bottom of a 13 × 9-inch baking pan. Layer 4 noodles on top of the sauce. Top with 1 cup of the vegetables with juices and 1 cup of the spinach-cheese mixture. Cover with 4 more noodles and ¾ cup of the sauce. Repeat layers twice. Top with remaining noodles and sauce.

Cover tightly with foil and bake for 45 min-utes. Uncover, sprinkle with remaining ⅓ cup mozzarella cheese, and bake for 15 minutes longer. Let stand for at least 15 minutes before serving.

Pesto Pasta with Dried Tomatoes
Makes 4 to 6 servings

This pasta is one of our summertime favorites. A green salad and garlic bread make it a perfect meal. Go ahead and use your hands to mix the pesto and pasta together. You can also add grilled chicken strips to this for more protein, or buy some cooked shrimp, take the tails off, and toss them into the pasta and serve it hot.

 1 pound spinach pasta, whole wheat pasta, or pasta of your choice

1 teaspoon salt

1 tablespoon extra-light olive oil

PESTO

2 cloves garlic, peeled

2 cups lightly packed fresh basil leaves

½ cup extra-light olive oil

¼ cup slivered almonds

1 cup finely grated Parmesan cheese

2 tablespoons chopped dried tomatoes

Cook the pasta according to package directions, adding salt and olive oil to the water. Do not overcook. When slightly tender, rinse in cold water and set aside. The pasta should just be just barely cooked, not soft. Drain.

To make the pesto: Finely chop the garlic in a blender or food processor. Add the basil and olive oil, and pulse until the basil leaves are finely chopped. Add the almonds and pulse 1 to 3 seconds to chop the almonds. Add the cheese and pulse to combine.

In a large bowl, toss the pasta, pesto, and dried tomatoes. Serve at room temperature or heat in the microwave on low power until hot.

❖
SALADS AND
SALAD DRESSINGS

Alyson's Exotic Chicken Salad
Makes 8 to 12 servings

This chicken salad is one of my daughter's favorites. Double the recipe and it's perfect to serve at a shower luncheon.

8 boneless, skinless chicken breast halves (about 4 pounds)

1 (8-ounce) can sliced water chestnuts, drained and rinsed

1 cup finely chopped celery

1 cup slivered almonds, toasted (page 113)

1 pound Thompson seedless grapes, halved

½ cup dried cranberries, dried cherries, or golden raisins

DRESSING

1 cup low-fat mayonnaise

½ teaspoon curry powder

1 tablespoon soy sauce

1 tablespoon lemon juice

½ teaspoon salt

¼ teaspoon black pepper

Romaine lettuce hearts

Poach or grill the chicken: To poach, place chicken in a large pan with 1½ cups water. Cover and simmer until tender, 45 minutes to 1 hour. To grill, lightly brush with olive oil and cook on grill until cooked through, about 25 minutes. Cool chicken and cut into ½-inch cubes.

Cut the water chestnuts into ½-inch pieces. In a large bowl, place the chestnuts, celery, almonds, grapes, and dried fruit.

Make the dressing: Combine all the dressing ingredients in a medium bowl. Pour the dressing over the fruit and chicken and toss to combine. Serve on hearts of romaine.

Romaine Ribbons with Blue Cheese
Makes 4 to 6 servings

You can buy roasted garlic, but it's easy to make. We eat a green salad almost every night, so I'm always trying to figure out creative ways to make a more interesting salad so we don't get bored. Cutting the romaine in thin ribbons changes the entire look of this salad.

1 head romaine lettuce
¼ cup diagonally sliced green onions, including greens
½ cup diced celery
Roasted Garlic Dressing (right)
¼ cup crumbled blue cheese
¼ cup chopped walnuts, toasted (page 113)

Wash the lettuce and place single layer in paper towels to absorb moisture. Store the lettuce in the refrigerator for 2 to 3 hours before preparing the salad. Stack the leaves and cut in ½-inch ribbons crosswise. Put in a large bowl. Cut the green onions and celery and place in the bowl with the lettuce. Toss with ¼ cup of the dressing and taste. Add more, a little at a time, depending on your preference.

Place the dressed salad on salad plates and garnish with a sprinkle of blue cheese and walnuts.

Roasted Garlic Dressing
Makes ¾ cup

Make this the day before so you have time to roast the garlic and allow the flavors to blend.

1 head garlic
4 tablespoons extra-light olive oil
2 tablespoons unseasoned rice vinegar
2 tablespoons apple cider vinegar
1 tablespoon honey
1 teaspoon Dijon mustard
¼ teaspoon freshly ground pepper
¼ teaspoon salt
2 tablespoons dried tomato bits

To roast the garlic, preheat the oven to 350°F (180°C). Slice the top from the garlic to expose the tips of the cloves. Place the garlic, cut side up, in a small ovenproof dish. Drizzle 1 tablespoon of the olive oil over the top of the garlic. Cover the dish tightly with foil. Bake for about 45 minutes, or until cloves are soft.

Squeeze the roasted garlic out of each clove into a mini food processor. Add any leftover oil from the garlic roasting. Add the vinegars, honey, mustard, pepper, salt, and remaining olive oil. Pulse briefly to combine. Add the tomato bits and pulse briefly just to combine. Serve immediately or cover and refrigerate for up to 3 days.

Hearts of Romaine with Dried Tomatoes
Makes 6 to 8 servings

This arranged salad is elegant for guests, and yet it's a cinch to prepare.

3 heads romaine lettuce

DRESSING
⅓ cup plus 1 tablespoon red wine vinegar
¼ cup water
¼ cup dried tomato bits
2 teaspoons dried basil, or 1 tablespoon chopped fresh
½ teaspoon sugar
½ teaspoon salt
2 large cloves garlic, crushed
Cracked black pepper to taste
1 cup extra-light olive oil

6 ounces blue cheese, crumbled

Wash lettuce, drain, and place in paper towels to absorb moisture. Store the lettuce in the refrigerator for 2 to 3 hours before preparing the salad.

Make the dressing: Combine all dressing ingredients, except olive oil and blue cheese, in a food processor or blender. Pulse to mix. Add oil and pulse for 1 to 2 seconds.

Remove the outer lettuce leaves and save for later use. With a sharp knife, slice leaves in half horizontally and arrange on chilled salad plates.

Drizzle 2 to 3 tablespoons of the dressing over the lettuce and sprinkle with blue cheese.

Peppery Pasta Salad
Makes 6 to 8 servings

Make this a couple of hours before serving so that the flavors have a chance to blend. Vary the vegetables, based on what you have on hand.

1 pound small pasta shells or twists

DRESSING
½ teaspoon salt
¼ cup red wine vinegar
1 teaspoon Dijon mustard
2 cloves garlic, finely minced
1 tablespoon Worcestershire sauce
½ cup oil (reserved from Marinated Dried Tomatoes in Olive Oil, page 167)
¼ teaspoon freshly ground black pepper

1 cup chopped celery
½ cup chopped red onion
½ cup chopped green bell pepper
½ cup diced zucchini
8 ounces Monterey Jack cheese, cut in ½-inch cubes
½ cup Marinated Dried Tomatoes in Olive Oil (page 167)

Cook the pasta according to package directions until tender but firm. Rinse in a colander with cool water and drain. Transfer to a large bowl.

Make the dressing: Add the ingredients for the dressing to a small bowl. Whisk until combined.

Add the dressing to the pasta and toss to coat. Add the remaining ingredients and toss. Cover and chill for 2 hours.

Creamy Apricot Dressing
Makes about 2 cups

Fruit salad becomes an elegant dessert topped with this creamy dressing. Serve over fruit salad, chilled pudding, or ice cream.

- ¾ cup pineapple juice
- 1 teaspoon fresh lemon juice
- ½ cup coarsely chopped dried apricots
- 1 cup whipping cream or frozen nondairy whipped topping
- 3 tablespoons sugar
- ½ teaspoon vanilla extract

Pour the pineapple juice and lemon juice over the dried apricots in a blender. Let stand for 30 minutes to soften. Blend until smooth. Chill. Whip cream in a chilled medium bowl until soft peaks form. Beat in the sugar and vanilla. (If using whipped topping, omit the sugar and vanilla.) Fold the apricot mixture into the whipped cream.

Couscous Salad
Makes 6 servings

Dried fruits add some pizzazz to this simple accompaniment. My favorites are dried cherries and cranberries.

- 2 cups water
- 1 tablespoon butter
- 1 (10-ounce) box plain couscous
- ¾ cup dried cherries, apples, pears, or cranberries
- 4 bacon slices, cooked crisp and crumbled
- 2 green onions, sliced
- 1 cup chopped fresh spinach
- ½ cup chopped fresh red bell pepper
- ¼ cup slivered almonds, toasted (page 113)
- Sesame-Sherry Dressing (below)

Cook the couscous: In medium saucepan, bring the water and butter to a boil. Stir in the couscous. Cover, remove from the heat, and let stand 5 minutes. Fluff with a fork and refrigerate.

Add the dried fruit, bacon, green onions, spinach, bell pepper, and almonds to chilled couscous and toss to combine.

Pour the dressing over the salad and toss to mix well. Cover and refrigerate until well chilled, at least 1 hour.

Sesame-Sherry Dressing
Makes about 1 cup

Try this dressing with romaine lettuce, sliced red onions, and grilled chicken breasts.

- ⅓ cup extra-light olive oil
- ⅓ cup unseasoned rice vinegar
- 2 tablespoons soy sauce
- 2 tablespoons dry sherry
- 2 tablespoons sugar
- 2 teaspoons sesame oil
- ¼ teaspoon ground ginger
- 1 clove garlic, crushed

Whisk all the ingredients in a medium bowl until combined. Serve immediately or store in the refrigerator in an airtight container for up to 3 days.

Spinach, Pear, and Walnut Salad
Makes 8 servings

Raspberry vinaigrette gives this tangy salad its tang! If you're out of dried pears, you can substitute fresh ones. Bosc pears are very firm and hold up well in this salad. You can also use pecans instead of walnuts. Whenever I serve this salad, my guests ask for the recipe.

1 (10-ounce) package washed and ready-to-eat fresh spinach
½ cup coarsely chopped walnuts or pecans
¾ cup chopped dried pears, or 1 cup 1-inch pieces fresh pears, sprinkled with Fruit-Fresh fruit protector
¼ cup thinly sliced red onion
⅓ cup crumbled blue cheese
Raspberry Vinaigrette (below)

Combine all ingredients in a large bowl and toss to combine. Serve immediately.

Raspberry Vinaigrette
Makes ¾ cup

The raspberry vinegar and garlic combine to make a dramatic flavor. This dressing is also good on hearts of romaine.

2 cloves garlic, peeled
¼ cup raspberry vinegar
¼ cup extra-light olive oil
¼ cup vegetable oil
¼ teaspoon sugar
¼ teaspoon salt
¼ teaspoon freshly ground black pepper
1 teaspoon fresh lime juice

Chop the garlic in a mini food processor. Add the remaining ingredients and pulse for 5 seconds. Serve immediately or store in the refrigerator in an airtight container for up to 3 days.

Spinach Strawberry Salad
Makes 8 servings

Fresh strawberries combine with dried fruit and fresh oranges in this delightful salad.

1 pint strawberries
3 oranges
1 (10-ounce) package washed and ready-to-eat fresh spinach
⅓ cup slivered almonds, toasted (page 113)
½ cup dried cranberries or cherries
Sesame-Poppy Seed Vinaigrette (page 166)

Wash, completely drain, and slice the strawberries into a large bowl. Peel the oranges, removing all white pith. Slide a very sharp knife along sides of dividing membranes and remove the orange segments. (Squeeze the juice and set aside for other use.)

Add the orange segments and the remaining ingredients and toss to combine.

Sesame–Poppy Seed Vinaigrette
Makes ¾ cup

This sesame vinaigrette is also nice on romaine lettuce.

½ cup extra-light olive oil

¼ cup red wine vinegar

¼ cup sugar

2 tablespoons toasted sesame seeds

1 tablespoon poppy seeds

1½ teaspoons Worcestershire sauce

½ teaspoon onion salt

Combine all ingredients in a medium bowl. Serve immediately or store in the refrigerator in an airtight container for up to 3 days.

Mixed Greens with Dried Cherries
Makes 8 servings

The rich, slightly sweet flavor of balsamic vinegar brings out the sweetness of dried fruits in this salad. I love feta cheese and it always gives salad a special flair. Use just enough vinaigrette to dress the salad without overpowering the delicate flavor of the lettuce.

8 cups mixed baby lettuce

½ cup crumbled feta cheese

¼ cup diagonally sliced green onions, including greens

½ cup diced celery

⅔ cup dried Bing cherries, cut in half, or dried strawberries or cranberries

Balsamic Vinaigrette (below)

Wash lettuce and place in paper towels a layer at a time to absorb moisture. Store the lettuce in the refrigerator for 2 to 3 hours before preparing the salad. Transfer lettuce to a large bowl. Add the cheese, green onions, celery, and dried cherries.

Toss gently with ¼ cup of the vinaigrette. Taste and add more if needed. Serve immediately.

Balsamic Vinaigrette
Makes ½ cup

You can taste the difference in good- and poor-quality balsamic vinegar. The extra price is frequently worth the improved taste, plus you need less of the better quality ones.

⅓ cup extra-light olive oil

2 tablespoons balsamic vinegar

1 tablespoon stone-ground mustard

1 teaspoon honey

1 clove garlic, crushed

¼ teaspoon salt

¼ teaspoon freshly ground pepper

Combine all ingredients in a medium bowl. Whisk until combined. Serve immediately or store in the refrigerator in an airtight container for up to 3 days.

Broccoli and Apple Salad
Makes 8 servings

Crisp bacon pieces should be added to this salad right before you serve it.

½ pound bacon slices
2 medium broccoli heads
1 small red onion, diced
¾ cup dried cranberries, dried cherries, or raisins
1 tart apple, such as Granny Smith or Gravenstein, cut into ¾-inch pieces
½ cup coarsely chopped cashews
Light Creamy Dressing (below)

Fry the bacon until crisp and drain on paper towels. Wash the broccoli, cut off the leaves, and trim each end. Slice the broccoli stem diagonally into ¼-inch pieces. Cut each diagonal slice into ½-inch slices. Cut off flowerets. Mix broccoli and the other ingredients in a large bowl and toss with dressing just before serving. Top with bacon pieces and toss to combine.

Light Creamy Dressing
Makes ¾ cup

Good on vegetables salads—toss the dressing with the salad just before serving.

½ cup low-fat mayonnaise
¼ cup red wine vinegar
¼ cup extra-light olive oil

1 teaspoon sugar
1 teaspoon onion powder

Combine all ingredients in a small bowl and whisk until sugar dissolves. Use immediately or cover and refrigerate up to 2 days.

Marinated Dried Tomatoes in Olive Oil
Makes 2 pints

Dried tomatoes have an intense tomato flavor with a wonderful chewy texture. They are delectable additions to all kinds of dishes. You can store them in oil in the refrigerator for up to one month, but they never last that long around our house.

2½ cups extra-light olive oil
4 cloves garlic, crushed
2 tablespoons dried rosemary, or 1 tablespoon fresh rosemary
1 small dried red chili
2 cups dried Roma tomatoes
1 tablespoon dried leaf parsley, or 2 tablespoons chopped fresh
1 tablespoon dried leaf oregano, or 2 tablespoons chopped fresh

Heat ½ cup of the olive oil in a medium saucepan over medium heat until hot. Remove from heat and add the garlic, rosemary, and chili. Remove from heat and let stand for 1 hour.

Soak the dried tomatoes in boiling water to cover in a medium bowl until softened, about 30 minutes. Drain the tomatoes and pat dry with paper towels.

Pack the tomatoes, parsley, and oregano into sterilized 1-pint jars. Pour in the flavored oil through a strainer, discarding the seasonings. Add additional olive oil to cover the tomatoes. Close the jars with canning lids and keep refrigerated for up to one month.

Savory Salad Sprinkles
Makes about 1 cup

Salad sprinkles are expensive to buy, but they are easy to make at home for just a few pennies. This combination adds zip to salads. Sprinkle over crisp greens, potato salad, or pasta salad.

½ cup grated Parmesan cheese
2 tablespoons sesame seeds
2 tablespoons carrot flakes
2 tablespoons onion flakes
2 tablespoons parsley flakes
1 tablespoon dried tomato bits
½ teaspoon garlic salt
½ teaspoon sweet paprika
½ teaspoon freshly ground black pepper

Combine all the ingredients in a small bowl. Mix until evenly distributed. Put in an airtight container or vacuum seal. Label and store in the refrigerator. Use within 1 month.

Seasoned Salt
Makes 1 cup

This homemade seasoned salt does wonders for eggs, cheese, fish, and meat dishes.

1 teaspoon tomato powder
1 teaspoon green bell pepper powder
1 teaspoon onion powder, or 1 tablespoon onion flakes
1½ teaspoons garlic powder
2 teaspoons sweet paprika
1 teaspoon dry mustard
1 teaspoon dried oregano
¾ teaspoon dried thyme
1 teaspoon celery salt
½ cup iodized salt

Add all the ingredients, except the iodized salt, to a food processor or blender. Pulse until fine. Add the salt. Pulse for 1 or 2 seconds to mix. If mixture is too fine, it will have more of a tendency to cake during storage. Store in a shaker container that has an airtight lid.

SPREADS AND DIPS

Creamed Honey
Makes about 9 cups

Creamed honey is easy to make and costs a fraction of what you would pay at the supermarket. When creamed, it stays uncrystallized for up to a year. It's great on toast or sandwiches. Different brands of creamed honey are available at the supermarket and they all work quite well as a starter for making your own.

8 cups honey
10 ounces prepared creamed honey

Remove the crystals from the honey by placing it in your dehydrator at 120°F (49°C) for 12 hours or until no crystals remain in the honey. It is best if you warm it in a glass container. Plastic tends to flavor the honey. You can also decrystallize it over warm water. Take care to not overheat or get any water into the honey. Allow the honey to cool.

Combine the creamed honey and the decrystallized honey in a large bowl. Beat with an electric mixer until thoroughly blended, 10 to 15 minutes. Place in appropriate-size jars for use. Wipe the rims. Cover with tight-fitting lids. Allow the honey to stand at room temperature for 2 weeks before using. It is then ready to use and may be stored at room temperature.

Peanut Butter and Fruit Spread
Makes 1½ cups

This gooey spread is a nutritious after-school snack. Serve on apple wedges, crackers, or bread.

1 cup smooth or crunchy peanut butter
2 tablespoons butter, at room temperature
⅓ cup finely chopped dried fruit
1 tablespoon fresh lemon juice
2 tablespoons honey (optional)

Make the spread by combining all the ingredients in a small bowl until smooth and well mixed.

Cream Cheese Spread
Makes 1½ cups

This cream cheese and fruit-nut spread is a nice change from peanut butter for lunches and after-school snacks.

1 (8-ounce) package cream cheese, at room temperature
1 to 2 tablespoons milk
¼ cup finely chopped nuts (almonds, filberts, pecans, sunflower seeds, or walnuts)
⅓ cup finely chopped dried fruit (apples, apricots, cherries, dates, figs, peaches, pears, pineapple, prunes, raisins, or strawberries)

Beat the cream cheese and milk in a small bowl to a spreading consistency. Stir in the nuts and dried fruit. Spread on crackers, bread, or fresh fruit.

Pesto Cream Cheese
Makes 10 to 12 servings

Cream cheese topped with this pesto and dried tomatoes always gets oohs and aahs from my guests. Serve it with toasted baguette rounds, bagel chips, crackers, or vegetable sticks.

PESTO
2 cloves fresh garlic, peeled
2 cups lightly packed fresh basil leaves
¼ cup extra-light olive oil
¼ cup slivered almonds
½ cup finely grated Parmesan cheese

1 (8-ounce) package low-fat or regular cream
   cheese, at room temperature
2 tablespoons very finely chopped dried tomatoes
¼ cup finely grated Parmesan cheese

To make the pesto: Finely chop the garlic in a blender or food processor. Add the basil and olive oil, and pulse until the basil leaves are finely chopped. Add the almonds and pulse 1 to 3 seconds to chop the almonds. Add the Parmesan cheese and pulse to combine. Set aside.

Place plastic wrap on the bottom and up the sides of a 10- to 12-ounce shallow plastic storage container with a lid, allowing it to hang over the edge. Using a table knife, press the cream cheese into the bottom of the container, making sure all the air bubbles are out.

Using a small spoon, press the pesto mixture onto the top of the cream cheese. Top with the dried tomatoes. Sprinkle the Parmesan cheese on top of the tomatoes.

Cover and refrigerate for at least 2 to 4 hours. When ready to serve, gently lift the cheese out of the container by the edges of the plastic. Peel the plastic off the bottom and carefully set it on a serving dish.

Creamy Smoked Fish Dip
Makes 2¼ cups

Crumbled smoked fish is quite nice in a dip. Serve this with crisp crackers, potato chips, or raw vegetables.

1 cup low-fat or regular sour cream
¼ cup low-fat or regular mayonnaise
2 tablespoons fresh lemon juice
1 clove garlic, crushed
¼ teaspoon black pepper
1 tablespoon dried parsley flakes, or 1 teaspoon
   chopped fresh parsley
¾ to 1 cup crumbled smoked fish

In a medium bowl, stir together sour cream, mayonnaise, lemon juice, garlic, pepper, and parsley until blended. Stir in the crumbled fish. Cover and refrigerate for flavors to blend.

Hummus
Makes 2½ cups

Hummus is one of those interesting foods with which not everyone is familiar. I like it with pita triangles and an assortment of fresh vegetables. Tahini is a paste made out of sesame seeds. You can find it in health food stores, gourmet shops, and many grocery stores. I like it with the dried tomatoes.

2 cups canned garbanzo beans, drained and rinsed

⅓ cup tahini

2 garlic cloves, halved

¼ cup fresh lemon juice

2 tablespoons extra-light olive oil

½ teaspoon salt

⅛ teaspoon sweet paprika

2 tablespoons dried tomato bits

Blend the garbanzo beans, tahini, garlic, lemon juice, olive oil, salt, and paprika in a blender until smooth. Add the tomato bits and blend just to combine. Transfer to a serving bowl.

Mango Salsa
Makes about 2 cups

Serve this salsa with your favorite low-fat chips or fresh vegetable sticks. Do not use store-bought dried mangoes in this recipe. They are about 60 percent sugar, and too sweet for my taste.

1½ cups dried mango chunks, or 2 cups fresh diced
   mangoes

1 cup orange juice

1 medium red onion, diced

1 cucumber, peeled, seeded, and diced

1 jalapeño chili, seeded and minced

1 clove garlic, minced

¼ cup chopped fresh cilantro

1 teaspoon ancho chili powder

Juice of 2 large limes

2 tablespoons extra-light olive oil

Salt and black pepper to taste

Cover the dried mangoes with the orange juice and allow to soak for 30 minutes to 1 hour to soften. If you are using fresh mangoes, omit the orange juice.

Drain any remaining juice from the mangoes. Combine the mangoes and remaining ingredients in a small bowl and refrigerate until ready to use.

Tomato Pesto
Makes 2½ cups

Tomato pesto is delicious on bread or as the topping on a cream cheese dip. It's good on pasta and focaccia. Bake the focaccia first and then spread the pesto on each piece as you eat it.

1 cup drained dried tomatoes from Marinated
   Dried Tomatoes in Olive Oil (page 167), with
   1 cup of the oil

½ cup pine nuts

3 cloves garlic, crushed

½ teaspoon salt

¼ teaspoon freshly ground black pepper

2 tablespoons chopped fresh basil

⅔ cup grated Parmesan cheese

In a food processor with the metal blade, process the tomatoes until finely diced. Add the oil from the tomatoes, pine nuts, garlic, salt, pepper, and basil and pulse until combined but not pureed. Add the Parmesan cheese and process for 30 seconds. This pesto may be stored in an airtight container in the refrigerator up to 1 week.

Crab Dip with Dried Tomato Bits
Makes 1½ cups

If you like crab, you'll love this dip. The dried tomato bits give it extra flavor. This is nice with toasted baguettes, sourdough rounds, bagel chips, or vegetable sticks.

¼ cup low-fat or fat-free sour cream
1 tablespoon milk
8 ounces low-fat or regular cream cheese, at room temperature
1 tablespoon fresh lemon juice
3 tablespoons chopped chives or green onion tops
1 clove garlic, crushed
3 tablespoons dried tomato bits
½ pound crabmeat, shredded

Mix the sour cream, milk, and cream cheese in a medium bowl until smooth. Add the lemon juice, chives, garlic, and tomato bits and stir to combine. Gently fold in the crabmeat. Cover and refrigerate until ready to serve.

❖
BREADS AND PASTRIES

Mango Banana Bread
Makes 3 small loaves or 1 large loaf

A family favorite, this banana bread is "mmmmm, good." Serve it warm or cool. You can also substitute chopped dried apricots, bananas, cherries, cranberries, dates, or pears for the mango.

¾ cup butter, at room temperature
1½ cups granulated sugar
2 eggs
1 teaspoon vanilla extract
1 teaspoon grated fresh orange peel
2 cups unbleached all-purpose flour
1 cup chopped pecans
½ cup dried mango, chopped in small pieces
1 teaspoon baking soda
½ teaspoon salt
1½ cups mashed ripe bananas (4 to 6)
½ cup buttermilk
¼ cup turbinado sugar

Preheat the oven to 350°F (180°C). Generously grease and flour 3 (5 × 3½-inch) loaf pans or 1 (9 × 5-inch) loaf pan. Line the bottoms with parchment paper or waxed paper.

Beat the butter with the granulated sugar in a large bowl until creamy. Add the eggs, vanilla, and orange peel and beat well.

Set aside ¼ cup of the flour in a small bowl. Mix the pecans and mango with the reserved flour. Sift together the remaining flour, baking soda, and salt. Add the flour mixture to the creamed mixture alternately with the bananas and buttermilk. Stir in the mango mixture. Mix well with a fork.

Pour into prepared loaf pans. Sprinkle the tops with the turbinado sugar.

Bake for 45 minutes for small loaves and for 1 hour for the large loaf, or until a wooden pick inserted in the center comes out clean. Cool for 10 minutes on a rack in the pans. Remove from the pans and cool on a wire rack.

Orange-Date Bread
Makes 1 large loaf or 3 small loaves

Fruited breads are popular for brunch or to tuck into a lunch box. This bread keeps well for 2 to 3 days.

1 cup butter, at room temperature

½ cup firmly packed light brown sugar

½ cup granulated sugar

1 egg

2¼ cups unbleached all-purpose flour

1 cup chopped dates

½ cup coarsely chopped pecans

1 tablespoon grated orange peel

1 teaspoon baking powder

1 teaspoon baking soda

¾ teaspoon salt

1 cup strained fresh orange juice

Preheat the oven to 350°F (180°C). Grease and flour a 9 × 5-inch loaf pan or 3 (5 × 3½-inch) loaf pans. Line the bottom with parchment paper or waxed paper. Set aside.

Cream the butter with the brown sugar and granulated sugar in a large bowl. Add the egg and beat well.

Set aside ¼ cup of the flour in a small bowl. Mix the dates, pecans, and orange peel with the reserved flour. Sift together the remaining flour, baking powder, baking soda, and salt. Add the flour mixture to the creamed mixture alternately with the orange juice. Stir in the date mixture. Mix well with a fork.

Pour into prepared pan. Bake for 40 to 50 minutes for the large loaf or for 30 to 35 minutes for the small loaves, or until a wooden pick inserted in the center comes out clean.

Cool for 5 minutes in the pan. Remove from the pan and cool completely on a cooling rack.

Herbed Buttermilk Biscuits
Makes 12 (2-inch) biscuits

These fluffy biscuits are lovely to serve on a cold winter's night with a hot soup. For a different taste, try tarragon or chives instead of dill.

2 cups unbleached all-purpose flour

2 teaspoons baking powder

¾ teaspoon salt

½ teaspoon baking soda

2 teaspoons dried dill, or 2 tablespoons chopped fresh dill

2 teaspoons dried parsley, or 2 tablespoons chopped fresh parsley

2 tablespoons shortening

3 tablespoons unsalted butter, chilled, cut into small chunks

¾ cup plus 2 tablespoons buttermilk

2 tablespoons butter, melted

Preheat the oven to 400°F (205°C).

Mix the biscuits: Whisk together the flour, baking powder, salt, baking soda, dill, and parsley in a large bowl. Add the shortening and butter to the dry ingredients. Cut in with a pastry blender or two knives until the mixture resembles coarse cornmeal.

Add the buttermilk and toss lightly with a fork until just combined. Turn it out onto a lightly floured cutting board.

Gently pat the dough and fold it back over itself

about half a dozen times, just until smooth. Roll to an even ¾-inch thick. Cover the dough lightly with plastic wrap and refrigerate for about 20 minutes.

Remove from the refrigerator and cut the dough with a biscuit cutter, getting as many rounds as possible. Shape the remaining dough into a ball and roll, cutting the rest of the biscuits. Place on a parchment-lined baking sheet. Brush the tops lightly with melted butter. Bake until raised and golden brown.

Apple-Apricot Pastry Squares
Makes 16 servings

This delicate pastry is better than good for breakfast or for dessert. Serve it with a wedge of Gouda cheese.

DOUGH

2½ cups unbleached all-purpose flour

1 teaspoon salt

1 cup plus 2 tablespoons unsalted butter, chilled

1 egg yolk plus enough milk to make ⅔ cup total

1 cup Honey Bunches of Oats, raisin bran, or cornflakes cereal

FILLING

8 cups sliced rehydrated or fresh apples

⅔ cup sugar

½ teaspoon ground ginger

½ teaspoon ground cinnamon

½ cup dried apricots, dates, or pears, chopped into small pieces

TOPPING

1 egg white, stiffly beaten

GLAZE

1 cup sifted powdered sugar

½ teaspoon vanilla extract

1 to 2 teaspoons water

Preheat oven to 400°F (205°C).

Make the dough: Stir flour and salt together in a large bowl. Cut in the butter with a pastry blender until crumbly. Beat egg yolk lightly with fork in a 1-cup measuring cup. Add enough milk to egg yolk to make ⅔ cup. Stir milk mixture into flour mixture. Mix with a fork to blend, stirring lightly until mixture holds together and clings to the side of the bowl.

Divide the dough into two parts. Roll half of the dough into a rectangle large enough to line a 16 × 11-inch jelly-roll pan. Place the dough in the pan, pressing lightly to form the bottom crust. Sprinkle with the cereal.

Make the filling: Combine the apples, sugar, ginger, and cinnamon in a large bowl. Stir to mix. Add the dried fruit and stir. Spread the apple mixture over the bottom crust. Roll out the remaining half of the pastry dough and place on the top. Fold the edges of the top dough over the bottom dough and pinch to seal.

Make the topping: Beat the egg white in a small bowl until stiff peaks form. Brush the egg white over the top crust with a pastry brush.

Bake for about 50 minutes to 1 hour, or until golden brown.

Make the glaze: Combine the powdered sugar, vanilla, and water in a small bowl. Drizzle the glaze delicately over the top of the pastry while it is still warm. Cool on a rack. Cut into squares.

English Orange-Pear Scones
Makes 8 scones

Scones are perfect for Saturday morning breakfast. Vary them occasionally by substituting dried currants, cranberries, cherries, or blueberries for the pears.

1 cup unbleached all-purpose flour

¾ cup pastry flour

2 teaspoons baking powder

½ teaspoon salt

1 tablespoon sugar

½ cup (1 stick) unsalted butter, chilled

½ cup chopped dried pears

Grated zest of 1 medium orange

¾ cup buttermilk

3 tablespoons turbinado or coarse sugar

Preheat the oven to 400°F (205°C).

Whisk the flours, baking powder, salt, and sugar in a medium bowl. Cut the butter into ⅓-inch cubes and add to the flour mixture, stirring to coat the butter. Use a pastry blender to cut the butter to the size of large peas.

Stir in the pears and orange zest. Gradually add ⅔ cup of the buttermilk and mix until the dough pulls away from the side of the bowl. Overmixing results in a heavier scone.

Shape the dough into a ball and pat into a 7-inch circle. Cut the dough into quarters and then again into eighths. Line a baking sheet with parchment paper and set the scones on the parchment. Brush the tops with the remaining buttermilk.

Sprinkle each scone with turbinado sugar and bake for 15 to 20 minutes, or until well browned.

Cinnamon Streusel Coffee Cake
Makes 10 to 12 servings

This coffee cake is baked in a tube pan so that the streusel topping makes a crunchy top. The coffee cake is moist and delicious with a surprise fruit filling.

STREUSEL TOPPING

¾ cup unbleached all-purpose flour

½ cup granulated sugar

¾ cup firmly packed light brown sugar

2 tablespoons ground cinnamon

2 tablespoons unsalted butter, cut into cubes

1 cup chopped pecans

CAKE BATTER

4 large eggs

1½ cups sour cream

1 tablespoon vanilla extract

2¼ cups unbleached all-purpose flour

1¼ cups sugar

1 tablespoon baking powder

¾ teaspoon baking soda

¾ teaspoon salt

¾ cup (1½ sticks) unsalted butter, cut into ½-inch cubes

1 cup chopped dried apples, apricots, or dates

Preheat the oven to 350°F (180°C). Grease a 10-inch tube pan (without a removable bottom) with butter. If you use a Bundt pan, the top won't be crisp. Set aside.

Make the topping: Combine the flour, sugars, and cinnamon in a medium bowl. Measure 2 cups of the mixture into another bowl. In the bowl containing the remaining mixture, cut in the butter with a pastry blender. Stir in the pecans. Set both bowls aside.

Make the batter: Combine the eggs, 1 cup of sour cream, and the vanilla and whisk until combined.

Combine the flour, sugar, baking powder, baking soda, and salt in a large bowl. Mix on low speed for 30 seconds to blend. Add the butter and remaining ½ cup sour cream. Mix on low speed until the dry ingredients are moistened, but not well mixed. Increase the speed and mix until the batter comes together. Scrape the sides of the bowl with a rubber spatula. Gradually add the egg mixture in thirds, mixing for 20 seconds after each addition. Beat until the batter is light and fluffy, about 1 minute.

Pour about 2 cups of the batter into the bottom of the prepared pan. Sprinkle evenly with the dried apples. Sprinkle about ¾ cup of the topping without the butter and nuts over the apples. Repeat with another 2 cups of the batter and remaining topping without the butter and nuts. Spread remaining batter on top and sprinkle with the topping with the butter and nuts.

Bake for 50 to 60 minutes, or until a wooden pick inserted into the center comes out clean. Cool the cake in the pan on a wire rack for 30 minutes. Invert the cake onto a rimmed baking pan and remove the tube pan. Place the wire rack on the top of the cake and reinvert the cake so that the nut topping is on top. Cool.

Isaac's Cinnamon Buns
Makes 24 buns

My son's favorite, these cinnamon buns have always been our family's traditional Christmas morning bread. Isaac has been known to eat six or seven at one time. Occasionally, there may be a few to give away to the neighbors.

DOUGH

2 packages active dry yeast (about 4½ teaspoons)

1 cup warm water (110°F or 45°C)

⅔ cup plus 1 teaspoon granulated sugar

1 cup milk, warmed

⅔ cup butter (1⅓ sticks)

2 teaspoons salt

2 eggs, slightly beaten

7 to 8 cups unbleached all-purpose flour

FILLING

1½ cups sugar

3 tablespoons ground cinnamon

1 cup chopped pecans

1 cup raisins, dried cherries (cut in half), or dried cranberries

½ cup butter (1 stick), melted

GLAZE

⅔ cup butter, at room temperature

4 cups powdered sugar

2 teaspoons vanilla extract

4 to 8 tablespoons hot water

In a small bowl, combine yeast, warm water, and 1 teaspoon sugar and stir. Set aside.

Mix the milk, the ⅔ cup sugar, butter, salt, and

eggs until blended. Stir in the yeast mixture. Add half of the flour and beat until smooth. Stir in the remaining flour until the dough forms a ball and pulls away from the side of the bowl. Turn out onto a well-floured board and knead until the dough is smooth and elastic, 5 to 10 minutes. Place in a well-buttered bowl, turning to coat the top. Cover and let the dough rise in a warm place until doubled in bulk, 1 to 1½ hours. Punch down and shape into a large ball. Let the dough rest for 10 minutes.

Make the filling: Mix the sugar and cinnamon together in a medium bowl. Stir in the pecans and dried fruit.

Shape the dough: Butter the bottom of a 13 × 9-inch baking pan and an 8-inch-square baking pan. Roll out the dough into a 20 × 15-inch rectangle on a floured surface. Spread the melted butter over the top of the dough. Sprinkle the fruit mixture evenly over the dough. Roll up jelly-roll fashion and pinch the edges together to seal. Cut into 24 slices. Place in the pans, cut-sides down. Cover and let rise in a warm place until doubled in bulk, about 45 minutes.

Preheat the oven to 350°F (180°C). Bake for 20 to 25 minutes, or until golden brown. Let cool.

Make the glaze: Beat the butter and powdered sugar together in a medium bowl. Add the vanilla and enough hot water to make it the consistency of heavy frosting. Spread a light glaze on each bun.

Serious Bran Muffins
Makes 20 to 24 muffins

Adding more fiber to your diet is easy with this tasty muffin. Bran is usually available in the bulk foods section of your supermarket. Use either wheat bran or oat bran or a combination. Each will have a slightly different flavor.

3 cups wheat or oat bran
1 cup boiling water
½ cup butter
2 cups buttermilk
2 eggs, beaten
1½ cups sugar
2½ cups unbleached all-purpose flour
2½ teaspoons soda
½ teaspoon salt
1 cup dried apples, dates, apricots, or raisins, chopped
¼ cup turbinado sugar

Preheat the oven to 400°F (205°C). Spray 24 muffin cups with nonstick cooking spray. In a medium bowl, pour boiling water over 1 cup of the bran. Add the butter to the bran mixture and stir until melted.

In another medium bowl, stir together the buttermilk, eggs, sugar, and the remaining 2 cups bran. Combine with the bran/boiling water mixture.

In a large bowl, mix the flour, baking soda, and salt. Stir until well mixed. Gradually stir in the buttermilk mixture. Mixture should be lumpy. Stir in the dried fruit. Do not overmix.

Fill each muffin cup two-thirds full. Sprinkle the tops with turbinado sugar. Bake for 20 to 25 minutes. Remove from the pan and place on racks to cool.

❖══════════════════════════════════════❖

Divine Danish Pastry
Makes 40 pastries

This pastry is a lot of work, and worth every moment the minute you taste it.

PASTRY DOUGH

1½ cups unsalted butter, at room temperature

4 cups unbleached all-purpose flour

2 packages active dry yeast (about 5 teaspoons)

½ cup warm water (110°F [43°C])

¾ cup milk

⅓ cup sugar

1 teaspoon salt

½ teaspoon ground cardamom

1 egg, beaten

Almond Crunch Filling (page 180), Golden Apricot Filling (opposite), Prune-Orange Filling (opposite), or Old-Fashioned Date Filling (opposite)

SUGAR GLAZE:

2 cups powdered sugar

3 to 4 tablespoons milk

½ teaspoon vanilla extract

½ teaspoon almond extract

⅔ cup sliced almonds

Draw a 16 × 8-inch rectangle on a piece of waxed paper. Sprinkle a few drops of water on the counter and place the waxed paper on top of it.

Make the dough: In a small bowl, beat the but-ter and ¼ cup of the flour until fluffy. Spread on the waxed paper to the outline of the rectangle. Transfer the butter mixture on the waxed paper to a flat baking sheet and refrigerate.

In a large bowl, sprinkle the yeast over the warm water. Stir to dissolve.

Heat the milk to lukewarm. Add the sugar, salt, and cardamom and stir to dissolve the sugar. Stir the milk mixture into the yeast mixture.

Add the egg and 2 cups of the flour and beat until smooth. Stir in the remaining flour with a wooden spoon until the dough pulls away from the side of the bowl. On a floured surface, lightly knead the dough for 1 minute. Place in an ungreased bowl. Cover with a clean towel and refrigerate for 30 minutes.

Turn the dough out onto a lightly floured surface and roll out to a 16-inch square. Invert the waxed paper with the chilled butter mixture over half the dough. Remove the waxed paper. Gently fold the other half of the dough over the butter, pinching the edges to seal. With a rolling pin, lightly pound the dough to a 16 × 12-inch rectangle. If the butter breaks through the dough, brush lightly with flour. Fold one-third of the dough into the center, and then fold in the remaining one-third, making three layers. Pinch the edges together. Wrap the dough in foil or waxed paper and refrigerate for 1 hour.

Repeat the rolling and folding. Seal the edges. Chill for 30 minutes. Repeat the rolling, folding, sealing, and chilling once or twice more. Wrap the dough in foil and refrigerate for 3 hours or overnight.

Line baking sheets with parchment paper. Cut the dough in half. Roll out half of dough to a 20-inch square. Cut into 4 (5-inch-wide) strips. Cut each strip into 4 squares, making 16 (5-inch) squares. Place 1 tablespoon filling in the center of each square. Fold together 2 opposite corners; seal edges. Place the pastries on prepared baking sheets.

Repeat with the other half of dough. Let rise in a warm place for 45 minutes.

Preheat the oven to 375°F (190°C). Bake the pastries for 15 to 20 minutes, or until browned. Cool slightly on a cooling rack.

Make the glaze: Combine all the ingredients in a small bowl. Drizzle the glaze over the warm pastry. Garnish with the almonds.

Golden Apricot Filling
Makes 1¾ cups

Tangy apricots and lemon gives this filling its zest. It's great in filled cookies and works as a dessert topping for ice cream or cake.

½ cup water
1 cup orange or pineapple juice
1½ cups dried apricots, chopped
¾ cup sugar
1 tablespoon fresh lemon juice

In a small saucepan, combine the water and juice. Add the apricots. Cook over medium heat until thickened, 20 to 25 minutes, stirring frequently. Stir in the sugar and lemon juice.

Prune-Orange Filling
Makes 2 cups

Cookies have an extra bit of fiber with this filling. Use it in any fruit-filled cookie recipe or for Fruit Wontons (page 182).

½ cup water
2 cups prunes, chopped
½ cup orange juice
½ cup sugar
1 teaspoon finely grated orange peel
2 tablespoons lemon juice

In a medium saucepan, combine the water, prunes, orange juice, and sugar. Cook over low heat until thickened, 30 to 35 minutes, stirring occasionally. Stir in the orange peel and lemon juice. Cool.

Old-Fashioned Date Filling
Makes 1¾ cups

Dates are hard to beat in filled cookies. This recipe also works well with figs. Try this filling in Isaac's Cinnamon Buns (page 176).

½ cup water
1½ cups dates, chopped
½ cup sugar
1 teaspoon finely grated lemon peel
1 teaspoon fresh lemon juice

In a medium saucepan, combine the water, dates, and sugar. Cook over low heat until thickened, 20 to 25 minutes, stirring frequently. Stir in the lemon peel and juice. Cool.

Almond Crunch Filling
Makes 2 cups

Use this filling in filled drop cookies and for Danish pastry. It has a delicate almond flavor and the zwieback crumbs give it a good texture.

1 cup (8 ounces) almond paste
½ cup butter, melted
1 egg
½ teaspoon almond extract
¾ cup zwieback crumbs (8 pieces)
¼ cup finely chopped almonds

In a medium bowl, combine the almond paste, butter, egg, and almond extract. Beat until smooth. Stir in the zwieback crumbs and almonds.

Focaccia with Dried Tomatoes
Makes 2 loaves

For a head start, make the yeast dough a day ahead and let it rise in the refrigerator overnight. It isn't really that hard to make once you've made it a time or two. I decide what kind of toppings to use based on what I have in the refrigerator. I nearly always use dried tomatoes on this since they just give it a more piquant flavor. Be sure and layer them underneath other vegetables and cheese so they don't burn. If you have a pizza stone, use it and the crust will be crisper. Leftovers are also good warmed up

the next day. This recipe generally makes two focaccias if I use my 12-inch pizza stone.

SPONGE
1 teaspoon dry yeast
¾ cup warm water (110°F [43°C])
¾ cup unbleached all-purpose flour

DOUGH
1 teaspoon dry yeast
1 cup warm water (110°F [43°C])
¼ cup extra-light olive oil
1½ teaspoons salt
3½ to 3¾ cups unbleached all-purpose flour
2 tablespoons extra-light olive oil, plus extra for bowl and brushing
1 teaspoon rosemary (optional)

Topping suggestions (see below): use one or more

Make the sponge: Sprinkle the yeast over the water in a large bowl. Stir in yeast and let stand for 10 minutes. Stir in the flour. Cover with plastic wrap. Let stand in a warm place until very bubbly, about 45 minutes.

Make the dough: Sprinkle the yeast over the water in a small bowl. Stir in yeast and let stand for about 10 minutes. Add the yeast mixture and the olive oil to the sponge. Stir in the salt. Add 1 cup of the flour and beat with an electric mixer on low speed until the dough is elastic, 3 to 5 minutes. Stir in the rosemary, if desired. Add the remaining flour a little at a time until the mixture pulls away from the side of the bowl.

To knead with a dough hook: Beat until the dough cleans the side of the bowl, about 5 minutes. If dough is sticky, add a little more flour, 1 tablespoon at a time. Take care not to add too much flour.

HOW TO DRY FOODS

To knead by hand: Scrape dough onto a lightly floured board. Add only enough flour to keep the dough from sticking to your hands. Knead until smooth and elastic, 5 to 10 minutes. Place dough in a bowl oiled with 1 tablespoon olive oil and turn so that the oil covers the top.

Cover the bowl tightly with plastic wrap and let rise in a warm place until doubled in bulk, 45 minutes to 1 hour. Or let it rise in the refrigerator until the next day. Punch down dough and turn out onto lightly floured board. Divide dough in half.

If you have a pizza stone and pizza peel, lightly sprinkle the peel with semolina flour or cornmeal. Roll the dough the size of the stone. Roll the dough over the rolling pin and unroll on the pizza peel. Press and stretch the dough to fit the peel.

If using a pan, lightly oil 2 (12-inch) round pans. Roll dough with rolling pin to the size of the pan. Roll the dough over the rolling pin and unroll in the pan. Press and stretch the dough to fit the pan.

Let the dough rise on the peel or in the pan in a warm place until doubled, about 45 minutes. Using a pastry brush, brush the surface with 1 tablespoon olive oil. With oiled fingers, gently press dimples all over the surface of the dough. Push dough gently to fit the pan.

Top with one or more of the toppings (below).

Remove the top rack from the oven. If using the pizza stone, place it on the center rack in the center of the oven. Preheat the oven to 375°F (190°C). Carefully slide the dough from the peel onto the pizza stone. If using a pan, place it in the center of the oven. (You can also place the pan directly on the stone.) Spray the oven underneath the pizza stone or pan with water using a spray bottle.

Bake the focaccia for 10 minutes, then spray twice more with water. Bake 10 to 15 minutes, or until the dough is well browned on the edges and bottom. If the topping is brown before the bread is done, lightly cover the top with foil for the last 10 to 15 minutes.

Transfer the focaccia to a cutting board and cut into serving pieces while hot. To reheat, bake, lightly covered with foil, in a 350°F (180°C) oven for 10 to 15 minutes, or until warm to the touch.

Suggested Toppings

TOMATO PESTO

1 cup drained marinated dried tomatoes
    (Marinated Dried Tomatoes in Olive Oil, page 167)
½ cup pine nuts
2 tablespoons chopped fresh basil
3 cloves garlic, crushed
½ teaspoon salt
¼ teaspoon freshly ground black pepper

Process all ingredients in a food processor or blender until finely chopped.

ALMOND PESTO

2 cups lightly packed fresh basil leaves
¼ cup extra-light olive oil
2 cloves garlic, crushed
¼ cup slivered almonds
½ cup finely grated Parmesan cheese

Process all ingredients in a food processor or blender until finely chopped.

- Green or black olives, or a combination, cut in half and pressed into the dough.
- Sprinkle on dried tomatoes, either with or without olive oil. If you use dry-packed dried

tomatoes (not marinated), be sure they are under another ingredient such as cheese or fresh vegetables so they won't burn.

- Sauté onion rings over medium heat in 2 tablespoons olive oil until light golden brown.

- Use 1 cup of any of the following vegetables: zucchini or green or red bell peppers sautéed in 2 tablespoons olive oil until light golden brown.

- 1 (6½-ounce) jar thinly sliced artichoke hearts, drained.

- 2 cups grated mozzarella cheese.

- 1 cup finely grated Parmesan cheese.

DESSERTS, CAKES, AND PIES

Fruit Wontons
Makes 20 to 25

This is a simple dessert that appears fancy! It is good with any of the recipes for fruit filling.

½ cup any fruit filling (pages 179 to 180)
20 to 25 wonton skins or wrappers
Vegetable oil for frying
Powdered sugar

Prepare the fruit filling. Place about 1 teaspoon of fruit filling in the center of each wonton skin. Moisten the edges of the skin with water. Fold 2 opposite corners together to make a triangle. Seal by pressing the edges firmly together with your fingers. Pull the right and left corners of the folded triangle down and below the folded edge so they

slightly overlap. Moisten the overlapping corners and press firmly together.

Heat 2 inches of oil in a mini fryer or wok to 375°F (190°C).

Fry filled wontons until crisp and golden, about 1 minute. It is not necessary to turn the wontons if you are cooking enough at the same time to keep the oil bubbling over the wonton edges.

Drain on paper towels. Lightly sift powdered sugar over wontons. Serve warm.

Best Baked Apples
Makes 6 servings

These baked apples are filled with a scrumptious filling. The unusual cutting and filling make them a special company dessert. If you have an apple corer, it will pull the core out of the apple. You can use a very thin sharp knife, but it won't work quite as well. Core all the way through to the base of the apple.

6 large baking apples
Fruit-Fresh produce protector, an ascorbic acid
    mixture, or lemon juice

FILLING
½ cup finely chopped dates
½ cup finely chopped prunes
¼ cup firmly packed light brown sugar
1 teaspoon ground cinnamon
2 tablespoons chopped pecans
2 tablespoons butter, melted
2 teaspoons fresh lemon juice

⅓ cup water
½ cup light corn syrup
Whipped cream or vanilla ice cream

Preheat the oven to 350°F (180°C). Wash the apples, remove the cores, and peel the upper third of each apple to prevent the skin from splitting while baking and to give a decorative touch. With a large knife, cut across each apple 4 times, through the peeled top to the peel, making 8 even sections. Sprinkle the tops of the cut apples with Fruit-Fresh, an ascorbic acid mixture, or lemon juice, to prevent them from turning brown.

Make the filling: Mix the dates, prunes, brown sugar, cinnamon, nuts, butter, and lemon juice in a small bowl. Evenly distribute the date mixture in the centers of the apples. Pour the water into a baking pan that will hold the apples. Place the apples in the pan. Pour the corn syrup over the apples.

Bake for 50 to 60 minutes, or until apples are tender, basting occasionally with the hot liquid from the bottom of the pan. Place the apples in individual serving dishes. Pour the cooking juices from the bottom of the baking pan into a small saucepan. Boil over medium heat to the consistency of light syrup. Pour over the apples. Serve warm with whipped cream.

2 tablespoons fresh lemon juice

⅓ cup raisins

⅓ cup unbleached all-purpose flour

2 tablespoons wheat germ

¾ cup firmly packed light brown sugar

1 teaspoon ground cinnamon

⅓ cup butter, chilled

½ cup rolled oats (not quick cooking)

Vanilla ice cream or whipped cream

Rehydrate the dried apples: pour enough water over the dried apples in a large bowl to cover. Let stand for 20 to 30 minutes. Drain. If using fresh fruit, toss with lemon juice to prevent darkening.

Preheat the oven to 375°F (190°C). Generously butter an 8-inch-square baking pan. Place the dried fruit in the prepared pan. Sprinkle the lemon juice and raisins over the fruit.

Blend the flour, wheat germ, brown sugar, cinnamon, and butter until crumbly. Toss with the rolled oats.

Sprinkle the flour mixture evenly over the fruit in the pan. Bake for 25 to 30 minutes, or until golden brown. Serve warm with vanilla ice cream.

Dried Fruit Crisp
Makes 6 to 8 servings

This is quick to make and one of my favorites when I'm in a hurry. Use fresh or dried apples or peaches.

Boiling water or apple juice

3 cups dried apples or peaches, or 5 cups fresh apples or peaches, peeled and sliced

Mom's Apple Pudding Cake
Makes 6 to 8 servings

This old-fashioned, very moist cake is an elegant dessert when garnished with a little vanilla ice cream or whipped cream. You can use fresh or dried apples. The dried apples give it a chewier texture. If I'm using fresh apples, I peel them with my apple peeler/corer/slicer and then put them through the grater on my food processor. It's quick. Cut dried apple rings with scissors, or break into pieces, depending on how crisp they are.

CAKE

1 cup hot apple juice or water

1½ cups shredded dried apples, or 2 cups fresh shredded peeled apple

¼ cup butter

1 cup sugar

1 egg

1 teaspoon vanilla extract

1 cup unbleached all-purpose flour

1 teaspoon baking soda

½ teaspoon salt

1 teaspoon ground cinnamon

¼ teaspoon ground allspice or nutmeg

½ cup chopped dates or prunes

½ cup chopped walnuts or pecans

Whipped cream or vanilla ice cream

If using dried apples, pour the apple juice over the apples in a medium bowl. When using fresh apples, omit the apple juice.

Preheat the oven to 350°F (180°C). Grease and flour an 8-inch-square baking pan.

Beat the butter and sugar in a large bowl until creamy. Add the egg and vanilla, and beat well. Drain the dried apples and add to the butter mixture. In a medium bowl, combine the flour, baking soda, salt, spices, dates, and nuts. Stir to mix well. Gradually add to the butter mixture, beating well. Pour into the prepared pan.

Bake the cake for 40 to 50 minutes, or until a wooden pick inserted in the center comes out clean. Serve with vanilla ice cream or whipped cream.

Pear Cheesecake
Makes 10 servings

This cheesecake is a cross between a cheesecake and pear cobbler.

CRUST

1 cup unbleached all-purpose flour

¾ cup quick-cooking oats

½ cup firmly packed light brown sugar

1 teaspoon ground cinnamon

½ cup (1 stick) butter, chilled

FILLING

8 ounces reduced-fat cream cheese, softened

½ cup sugar

1 egg

1 teaspoon vanilla extract

TOPPING

1 cup coarsely chopped dried pears

¼ cup pecans, chopped

Preheat the oven to 350°F (180°C). Grease a 9-inch pie pan and set aside.

Make the crust: Combine the flour, oats, brown sugar, and cinnamon in a medium bowl. Cut in the butter with a pastry blender until the mixture resembles coarse crumbs. Press two-thirds of the mixture into the bottom of the prepared pan. Bake for 10 minutes.

Make the filling: Beat the cream cheese with the sugar, egg, and vanilla until blended. Spread over the baked crust.

Top with the dried pears, pecans, and remaining oat mixture. Bake for 30 minutes. Refrigerate for at least 2 hours before cutting.

Pumpkin·Apricot Bundt Cake
Makes 16 servings

This Bundt cake is a cinch to make because it uses a basic yellow cake mix as a starter. Serve it at a shower or make it for company.

CAKE

1 (18¼-ounce) package yellow cake mix

1 (3.4-ounce) package instant butterscotch pudding mix

4 eggs

¼ cup water

¼ cup vegetable oil

1 cup canned pumpkin

2 teaspoons pumpkin pie spice

½ cup dried apricots, chopped into small pieces

WHIPPED CREAM GARNISH

2 cups heavy whipping cream

¼ cup granulated sugar

½ teaspoon vanilla extract

Preheat the oven to 350°F (180°C). Grease and flour a 10-inch fluted Bundt pan. Set aside.

Make the cake: Combine the cake ingredients in a mixing bowl. Beat for 30 seconds with an electric mixer on low speed. Increase speed to medium speed and beat for 4 minutes. Pour into the prepared pan.

Bake for 45 to 55 minutes, or until a toothpick inserted near the center comes out clean. Cool in the pan for 15 minutes. Turn out cake onto a wire rack and cool completely.

Chill the beaters and bowl before whipping the cream. Whip cream until soft peaks form. Add the sugar and vanilla and continue beating until stiff peaks form. Place a dollop of cream on top of each slice of cake before serving.

Grandma's Golden Fruitcake
Makes 2 large loaves

This fruitcake uses golden dried fruits and is made without as much sugar as most fruitcakes. If you don't have any dried fruits, dry some using canned apricots or peaches. They will have a glacéed flavor because the fruit syrup makes them sweeter.

3 eggs, separated

1 cup butter, at room temperature

1 cup sugar

2 cups unbleached all-purpose flour

½ teaspoon salt

½ teaspoon baking soda

2 cups ½-inch pieces dried apricots, mangoes, or peaches, or a combination

½ cup whole red candied cherries

½ cup dried pineapple

1 cup golden raisins

1 cup slivered almonds, chopped macadamia nuts, or chopped pecans

1 teaspoon grated lemon peel

Preheat the oven to 300°F (150°C). Generously grease and flour 2 (8 × 4-inch) loaf pans. Line bottoms with parchment paper or waxed paper.

Beat the egg whites in a medium bowl until soft peaks form. Beat the butter and sugar in a medium bowl until fluffy. Beat in the egg yolks, one at a time, beating after each addition. Fold in the egg whites and mix well. In a separate bowl, combine

1½ cups of the flour, the salt, and the soda. Stir into the butter mixture.

In a medium bowl, combine the remaining ½ cup flour, apricots, cherries, pineapple, raisins, nuts, and lemon peel. Stir to coat with flour. Add to the batter and blend well.

Spoon the batter into the prepared loaf pans. Bake for about 1¼ hours, or until a wooden pick inserted in the center comes out clean. Cool for 10 to 20 minutes in the pan. Remove from the pan and cool on a rack.

Scrumptious Carrot Cake
Makes 8 to 10 servings

Of all the cakes in the world, this carrot cake is my husband's favorite. I shred the carrots in the food processor. Be sure to peel them first.

- 1½ to 2 cups dried shredded carrots, or 3 cups fresh shredded carrots
- 2 cups unbleached all-purpose flour
- 1 cup granulated sugar
- 1 cup firmly packed light brown sugar
- 2 teaspoons baking powder
- 2 teaspoons baking soda
- 1 teaspoon salt
- 2 teaspoons ground cinnamon
- ½ teaspoon ground nutmeg
- 4 eggs
- 1½ cups vegetable oil
- 2 cups chopped walnuts
- Lemon Cream-Cheese Frosting (right)

To rehydrate the dried carrots, cover them with boiling water and let stand for 20 minutes. Drain.

Preheat the oven to 350°F (180°C). Generously grease and flour 2 (9-inch) round cake pans or a 13 × 9-inch baking pan. Set aside.

In a large bowl, combine the flour, sugars, baking powder, baking soda, salt, cinnamon, and nutmeg. In a small bowl, whisk the eggs and oil together. Add to the flour mixture. Stir 300 strokes or mix with an electric mixer on low speed until blended. Fold in the carrots and 1 cup of the walnuts.

Pour the batter into the prepared baking pans. Bake for 25 to 30 minutes, or until a wooden pick inserted in the center comes out clean. Cool in the pans on a wire rack for 10 minutes. Turn out onto the rack and cool completely. When cool, frost with Lemon Cream-Cheese Frosting. Sprinkle the remaining 1 cup walnuts over the top.

Lemon Cream-Cheese Frosting
Makes enough frosting for a 9-inch layer cake

This cream cheese frosting is also good on Isaac's Cinnamon Buns (page 176) and the Pumpkin-Apricot Bundt Cake (page 185).

- ½ cup (1 stick) butter, at room temperature
- 1 (8-ounce) package cream cheese, at room temperature
- 1 (1-pound) box powdered sugar
- 2 teaspoons vanilla extract
- 1 teaspoon grated lemon peel

With an electric mixer on low speed, beat the butter and cream cheese in a medium bowl until fluffy. Gradually beat in the powdered sugar. Beat in the vanilla and lemon peel.

Schnitz Pie

Makes 6 to 8 servings

Schnitz Pie was handed down from the Pennsylvania Dutch settlers. It's a traditional apple pie made from dried apples and is especially nice to use when fresh apples are expensive and out of season. In season, you can use fresh apples. The apple juice gives a little richer apple flavor than rehydrating the dried apples in water.

Hot apple juice or boiling water
4 cups dried apple slices, or 5½ cups fresh sliced, peeled apples
¼ cup fresh lemon juice
Flaky Pie Crust (page 188)
¼ cup flour
1 cup sugar
1½ teaspoons ground cinnamon
½ teaspoon ground nutmeg
3 tablespoons butter

Rehydrate the dried apples: Pour enough apple juice over the dried apples in a medium bowl to cover. Let stand for 20 to 30 minutes. If using fresh apples, toss with lemon juice.

Make the dough for the pie crust and shape into two rounds. Cover with plastic wrap and refrigerate.

Preheat the oven to 425°F (220°C). Drain the apples and toss with lemon juice. Combine the flour, sugar, cinnamon, and nutmeg in a medium bowl. Sprinkle the flour mixture over the apples, stirring to coat.

Remove the dough from the refrigerator. Roll out the dough on a lightly floured surface to two 11-inch rounds. Roll the dough onto the rolling pin and unroll on top of a pie pan. Fill the bottom crust with the apple mixture. Dot the top of the apples with the butter.

Roll the top crust and cut decorative slits in it to let the steam escape while baking. Roll the dough onto the rolling pin and unroll on top of the filling. Trim the dough to extend ¾ inch over the pie plate rim. Fold the top crust under the bottom crust and crimp the edges together.

Place a 1½-inch-wide piece of foil around the edge of the crust to prevent excessive browning during baking. Bake for 15 minutes. Reduce the temperature to 375°F (190°C) and bake for 25 to 35 minutes, or until the crust is golden. Remove the foil during the last 10 minutes of baking to allow the edge of the crust to brown.

Apple Rhuberry Pie
Makes 6 to 8 servings

If you like rhubarb and apples, you'll be thrilled with this pie. We have a huge rhubarb plant in our yard, and this has become one of our favorites.

Boiling apple juice or water

2 cups dried rhubarb slices, or 3 cups fresh cut rhubarb

2 cups dried apple slices, or 3 cups fresh sliced, peeled apples

2 tablespoons fresh lemon juice

Flaky Pie Crust (right)

½ cup homemade strawberry freezer jam or prepared strawberry jam

3¼ cup granulated sugar

¼ cup quick-cooking tapioca

3 tablespoons butter

1 tablespoon butter, melted

1 teaspoon turbinado or granulated sugar

Rehydrate the rhubarb and apples: Pour enough apple juice over the dried rhubarb and apples in a large bowl to cover. Let stand for 45 to 60 minutes. If using fresh fruit, toss with the lemon juice.

Make the dough for the pie crust and shape into two rounds. Cover with plastic wrap and refrigerate.

Preheat the oven to 400°F (205°C).

Drain the fruit and toss with the lemon juice and strawberry jam in a large bowl. Mix the granulated sugar and tapioca in a small bowl. Pour over the fruit mixture and toss to combine.

Remove the dough from the refrigerator. Roll out the dough on a lightly floured surface to an 11-inch round. Roll the dough onto the rolling pin and un-roll on top of a pie pan. Fill the bottom crust with the fruit mixture. Dot the top of the fruit with the 3 tablespoons butter.

Roll out the top crust, cutting decorative slits to let the steam escape while baking. Roll the dough onto a rolling pin and unroll on top of the filling. Trim the dough to extend ¾ inch over the pie plate rim. Tuck the top crust under the bottom crust and flute the edges. For a crunchy top crust, brush the crust very lightly with the melted butter and sprinkle with the turbinado sugar.

Place a 1½-inch-wide piece of foil around the edge of the crust to prevent excessive browning during baking. Bake in the preheated oven for 20 minutes, and then reduce the temperature to 375°F (190°C) for 20 to 30 minutes, or until the crust is golden. Remove the foil during the last 10 minutes of baking.

Flaky Pie Crust
Makes 1 double 9-inch pie crust

This flaky crust is so tender you won't believe it.

2 cups unbleached all-purpose flour, or 1 cup all-purpose flour and 1 cup pastry flour

1 teaspoon salt

⅓ cup vegetable shortening

⅓ cup butter, chilled

½ cup to ½ cup plus 1 tablespoon cold milk

Add the flour and salt to a large bowl. With a pastry blender or 2 knives, cut the shortening and butter into the flour until the mixture resembles small peas. Sprinkle cold milk over the flour mixture, a spoonful at a time, tossing with a fork until the dough clings together.

Shape into 2 balls and flatten on a lightly floured surface. Cover and refrigerate 1 ball while you are rolling out the other.

Roll out 1 ball on a lightly floured surface to an 11-inch circle. Turn the dough over at least once, lightly flouring the board underneath. Roll onto the rolling pin. Place carefully over a 9-inch pie plate. Do not stretch the dough because it causes it to shrink.

Fill the crust with filling. Roll out the dough for the top crust to an 11-inch circle. Cut decorative slits in the top crust to let steam escape while baking. Roll the dough onto the rolling pin and unroll on top of the filling. Trim the dough to extend ¾ inch over the pie plate rim. Fold the top crust under the bottom crust and crimp the edges.

Bake as directed in recipe.

Almond Cherry Tart
Makes 10 servings

Add a different flavor to this tart by using dried cranberries. Make sure you use a pan with a removable bottom, or you'll never get it out in one piece.

CRUST
1 cup unbleached all-purpose or pastry flour
¼ cup powdered sugar
¼ teaspoon salt
1 teaspoon almond extract
½ cup (1 stick) unsalted butter, chilled

FILLING
1 cup slivered almonds
½ cup sugar
½ cup almond paste

Juice of 1 lemon
Grated peel of 1 lemon (yellow part only)
3 eggs
½ cup whipping cream
1 teaspoon almond extract
½ cup dried cherries, plus extra for garnish

ALMOND CREAM-CHEESE FROSTING
½ cup cream cheese, at room temperature
¼ cup butter, at room temperature
½ teaspoon vanilla extract
½ teaspoon almond extract
2 cups powdered sugar
1 to 2 tablespoons milk

Preheat the oven to 350°F (180°C).

Make the crust: Place the flour, sugar, salt, and almond extract in a food processor. Cut the butter into pieces and drop into food processor, 1 tablespoon at a time. Pulse briefly after each addition. The mixture should be the size of small peas. Press into the bottom of a nonstick 10-inch springform pan with a removable bottom. (If a nonstick pan is not available, grease the pan well.)

Bake for about 12 minutes, or until the sides are very light golden. Remove and place on a cooling rack.

Make the filling: Place the almonds and sugar in a food processor and process until the almonds are finely ground. Add the almond paste, lemon juice, lemon peel, eggs, cream, and almond extract. Process until well blended.

Arrange the dried cherries on the top of the cooled crust. Pour the filling over the cherries. Bake for 25 to 30 minutes, or until a knife inserted in the center comes out clean. Allow to completely cool on a cooling rack. Place in the refrigerator.

Make the frosting: Beat the cream cheese, butter, vanilla, almond extract, and powdered sugar until very smooth. Add enough milk to give it a heavy frosting consistency.

Remove the pan rim. Cut the tart into 10 wedges. Using a pastry bag and decorative tip, pipe the frosting on the top of each wedge. Place a dried cherry on top of each piece.

COOKIES

Pear-Lemon Squares
Makes 36 squares

These moist and chewy bars are a version of traditional lemon bars. The dried pears add a chewy texture and a different flavor. If you want to try something different, substitute dried apricots, dates, pineapple, or light cherries for the pears.

CRUST

1 cup unbleached all-purpose flour

¼ cup powdered sugar

2 teaspoons grated lemon peel

4 tablespoons butter, chilled

FILLING

2 eggs

¾ cup sugar

3 tablespoons fresh lemon juice

1 teaspoon grated lemon peel

2 tablespoons unbleached all-purpose flour

1 teaspoon baking powder

¼ teaspoon salt

1 cup finely chopped pears

Powdered sugar (optional)

Preheat the oven to 350°F (180°C). Grease and flour a 9-inch-square baking pan. Set aside.

Make the crust: Combine the flour, powdered sugar, and lemon peel in a medium bowl. With a pastry blender or 2 knives, cut in the butter until the mixture resembles coarse cornmeal. Press the mixture into the bottom of the prepared pan. Bake for 15 minutes. Remove from the oven and place on a cooling rack.

Make the filling: Combine the eggs and sugar and beat until fluffy. Stir in the lemon juice and lemon peel. Add the flour, baking powder, and salt. Mix well. Stir in the dried pears. Pour the mixture over the baked layer and spread evenly to the sides of the pan.

Bake for 20 minutes, or until the top is bubbly and very lightly browned. Cool on a rack before cutting into 1½-inch squares. Lightly sprinkle with powdered sugar before serving, if desired.

Peanut Butter and Granola Bars
Makes 32 bars

These chewy bars are great for lunch boxes and a nice change from ones you buy at the store.

1½ cups granola

2 tablespoons instant nonfat dry milk

2 tablespoons bran flakes

¼ teaspoon ground cinnamon

⅛ teaspoon salt

¼ cup raisins

1 teaspoon vegetable oil

2 tablespoons honey

½ teaspoon vanilla extract

1½ teaspoons water

⅓ cup crunchy peanut butter

1 egg, well beaten

Preheat the oven to 250°F (120°C). Generously grease and flour an 8-inch-square baking pan. Set aside.

Mix the granola, dry milk, bran flakes, cinnamon, salt, and raisins in a medium bowl. In a large bowl, combine the oil, honey, vanilla, water, and peanut butter. Add the egg and stir to mix well. Gradually stir the granola mixture into the peanut butter mixture.

Press the mixture into the prepared baking pan. Bake for 25 minutes. Cool for 10 to 15 minutes in the pan before cutting into 2 × 1-inch bars.

Filled Drop Cookies
Makes about 36 cookies

Choose the surprise fruit filling from any of the recipes in this book.

Golden Apricot Filling (page 179), Prune-Orange Filling (page 179), Old-Fashioned Date Filling (page 179), or Almond Crunch Filling (page 180)

COOKIES

¼ cup shortening

¼ cup butter or margarine, at room temperature

1 cup firmly packed light brown sugar

1 egg

¼ cup buttermilk

1 teaspoon vanilla extract

1¾ cups unbleached all-purpose flour

½ teaspoon salt

½ teaspoon baking soda

¼ teaspoon ground cinnamon

¼ cup raisins

¼ cup pecans, chopped

Prepare fruit filling; set aside.

Preheat the oven to 400°F (205°C). Lightly grease 2 baking sheets. Set aside.

Make the cookie dough: Beat the shortening and butter and brown sugar in a medium bowl until creamy. Stir in the egg, buttermilk, and vanilla.

Mix the flour, salt, baking soda, cinnamon, raisins, and pecans in another medium bowl. Add to the creamed mixture. Stir until mixed.

Drop the dough from a teaspoon onto the prepared baking sheets. Coat the bottom of a ¼ teaspoon measuring spoon with butter. Press the spoon on each cookie to make a small indentation. Place ½ teaspoon of the fruit filling in each cavity. Cover the filling with a small piece of cookie dough, patting around the edges to seal.

Bake for 7 to 8 minutes, or until the edges are light golden brown. Remove cookies from the baking sheet and place on a cooling rack to cool.

Cherry Chocolate Cookies
Makes about 48 cookies

A surprise dried cherry is in the center of each cookie.

1 cup butter, at room temperature
1 cup granulated sugar
1 cup firmly packed light brown sugar
2 teaspoons vanilla extract
2 eggs
2½ cups unbleached all-purpose flour
¾ cup unsweetened Dutch process cocoa
1 teaspoon baking soda
½ cup chopped pecans

ROLLING MIXTURE
½ cup chopped pecans
1 tablespoon granulated sugar

About 48 dried cherries

Beat the butter and sugars in a medium bowl until creamy. Add the vanilla and eggs and beat well. Combine the flour, cocoa, and baking soda in a small bowl. Add to the butter mixture and blend well. Stir in the pecans. Cover with plastic wrap and refrigerate for 30 minutes for easier handling.

Preheat the oven to 375°F (190°C). Lightly grease 2 or 3 baking sheets. Set aside.

To make the rolling mixture, combine the pecans and granulated sugar in a shallow bowl. With floured hands, shape 1 tablespoon of dough around 1 dried cherry, covering completely. Press one side of the ball into the pecan mixture. Place the balls 2 inches apart, nut side up, on an ungreased baking sheet.

Bake for 7 to 10 minutes, or until set and slightly cracked. Cool for 2 minutes on the baking sheet and then transfer to a rack to cool completely.

Apple-Pear Cookies
Makes about 96 cookies

This refrigerator cookie has a soft texture and a mild fruit flavor. Using apple juice to rehydrate the dried fruits gives a more pronounced fruit flavor.

½ cup apple juice or water, heated
¾ cup dried apples and pears, finely chopped
1 cup butter, at room temperature
1 cup sugar
2 eggs
1 teaspoon vanilla extract
3 cups unbleached all-purpose flour
½ teaspoon salt
½ teaspoon baking soda
½ cup finely chopped nuts

To soften the dried fruit, pour the apple juice over the fruit. Let stand for 5 to 10 minutes. Drain.

Beat the butter and sugar in a large bowl until creamy. Add the eggs and vanilla. Beat well. Mix the flour, salt, baking soda, drained fruit, and nuts in another medium bowl. Add to the butter mixture and mix well.

Shape the dough into 2 rolls, 1¾ inches in diameter. Wrap well in waxed paper. Refrigerate for 4 hours or overnight.

Preheat the oven to 400°F (205°C). Lightly grease 2 or 3 baking sheets. Set aside.

Cut the rolls into ¼-inch slices. Place on the prepared baking sheets. Bake for 7 to 8 minutes, or until the edges are golden. Remove from the baking sheets and place on a cooling rack.

Date Pinwheels
Makes about 80 cookies

This filled cookie is crisp with a rich date flavor. Experiment by using other filling recipes.

Old-Fashioned Date Filling (page 179)
1 cup nuts, finely chopped (optional)

COOKIE DOUGH
½ cup butter, at room temperature
½ cup firmly packed light brown sugar
½ cup granulated sugar
1 egg
1 teaspoon vanilla extract
2 cups unbleached all-purpose flour
¼ teaspoon baking soda
¼ teaspoon salt

Prepare the Old-Fashioned Date Filling. Add nuts, if desired, and stir. Set aside.

Make the cookie dough: Beat the butter and sugars in a large bowl until creamy. Add the egg and vanilla. Beat well. Mix the flour, baking soda, and salt in a medium bowl. Add to the butter mixture and mix well. Divide the dough in half.

Generously flour a large sheet of waxed paper. Roll out each half of dough on the floured waxed paper to a 12 × 9-inch rectangle. Spread with the filling. Starting with the longer edge, roll up tightly to make a 12-inch long roll. Wrap the roll in waxed paper and refrigerate for 4 hours or overnight.

Preheat the oven to 400°F (205°C). Lightly grease 2 or 3 baking sheets. Set aside.

Cut the rolls into ¼-inch slices. Place on the prepared baking sheets. Bake for 7 to 8 minutes, or until the edges are golden. Remove from the baking sheets and place on a cooling rack.

Lunch Box Health Bars
Makes 30 bars

Keep these bars in your lunch box. They're heavy in fruit and fiber, but still satisfy my sweet tooth.

CRUST
¼ cup butter, at room temperature
¼ cup firmly packed light brown sugar
2 tablespoons honey
2 tablespoons light molasses
2 cups quick-cooking rolled oats
¼ cup whole wheat flour

FILLING
1 cup water
1½ cups chopped mixed dried fruits
2 tablespoons butter
½ cup firmly packed light brown sugar
½ cup whole wheat flour
¼ cup wheat germ
¼ cup unprocessed wheat bran
1½ teaspoons ground cinnamon
½ teaspoon salt
½ teaspoon ground cloves
2 eggs, slightly beaten
1 cup chopped walnuts or pecans

Preheat the oven to 350°F (180°C). Generously grease and flour a 13 × 9-inch baking pan. Set aside.

Make the crust: Beat the butter, brown sugar,

honey, and molasses in a large bowl until fluffy. Stir in the oats and flour. Press into the bottom of the prepared pan. Bake for 5 minutes.

Make the filling: Bring the water to a boil in a small saucepan, add fruit and butter, and remove from the heat. Let stand for 5 minutes. Stir in the brown sugar, flour, wheat germ, wheat bran, cinnamon, salt, cloves, and eggs. Add the nuts and stir until well mixed.

Spread the fruit mixture over the baked crust. Bake for 25 to 30 minutes. Cool on a rack. Cut into 3 × 1½-inch bars.

Appledoodles
Makes about 60 cookies

If you're a fan of snickerdoodles, this cookie is for you. These cookies puff up in the oven, but flatten to a crisp cookie as they cool. The little chunks of dried apples give these cookies a chewy texture.

ROLLING MIXTURE

4 teaspoons ground cinnamon

⅓ cup turbinado sugar

COOKIE DOUGH

½ cup butter, at room temperature

½ cup shortening

1½ cups sugar

2 eggs

2½ cups unbleached all-purpose flour

2 teaspoons cream of tartar

¼ teaspoon salt

1 cup coarsely chopped dried apple

To make the rolling mixture, combine the cinnamon and sugar in a shallow bowl and set aside.

Preheat the oven to 400°F (205°C). Lightly grease 2 or 3 baking sheets. Set aside.

Make the cookie dough: Beat the butter and shortening and sugar in a large bowl until creamy. Add the eggs and beat well. In a medium bowl, mix the flour, cream of tartar, and salt. Add to the butter mixture and mix well. Stir in the dried apple.

With your hands, roll the dough into 1-inch balls. Roll the balls in the cinnamon-sugar mixture to coat well.

Place the balls at least 2 inches apart on prepared baking sheets. Bake for 7 to 8 minutes, or until the edges are slightly golden. Do not overbake. The cookies will puff up as they bake and look slightly underdone when removed from the oven. Remove from the baking sheets and cool on a rack.

Nut Butter Cookies
Makes about 60 cookies

Try different nut butters in these cookies. Make your own nut butter (page 113) or use some from the supermarket. Peanut butter is always a favorite, but these cookies are also good with cashews.

1 cup butter

½ cup granulated sugar

1 cup brown sugar, firmly packed

2 large eggs

1 teaspoon vanilla extract

1 cup peanut, cashew, or almond butter

About 3 cups old-fashioned rolled oats

2 teaspoons baking soda

¼ teaspoon salt

½ cup chopped nuts

½ cup dried fruit, chopped, such as apricots, cherries, cranberries, dates, or pears

Make the cookie dough: Beat the butter and sugars in a large bowl until creamy. Add the eggs and vanilla, and beat well. Add the nut butter and mix again.

Grind the oats in the blender until very fine. Measure 2¼ cups oat flour. Mix oat flour, baking soda, and salt in a small bowl. Add to butter mixture and mix well. Stir in the nuts and dried fruit. Cover and chill for 1 hour.

Preheat the oven to 350°F (180°C). Grease 2 or 3 baking sheets.

Drop by rounded teaspoonfuls onto baking sheets. Dough rounds should be about 1 inch in diameter. Flatten with a fork dipped in sugar to form a crisscross pattern.

Bake for 8 to 10 minutes, or until golden around the edges. Cool for about 1 minute on the baking sheet and then transfer to a cooling rack.

Crisp Oatmeal Cookies
Makes about 60 cookies

"These are the best chewy oatmeal cookies in the whole wide world." At least this is what my children all say. You can use all kinds of dried fruits in these. They're all good.

1 cup butter
1 cup brown sugar, firmly packed
1 cup granulated sugar
2 eggs
1 teaspoon vanilla extract
1½ cups unbleached all-purpose flour
1 teaspoon baking soda
1 teaspoon salt
3 cups uncooked rolled oats

½ cup chopped nuts
1 cup chopped dried fruit, such as apples, apricots, cherries, cranberries, dates, or pears

Preheat the oven to 350°F (180°C). Grease 2 or 3 baking sheets.

Make the cookie dough: Beat the butter and sugars in a medium bowl until creamy. Add the eggs and vanilla. Beat well. Mix the flour, baking soda, and salt in a small bowl. Add to the butter mixture and mix well. Stir in the oats, nuts, and dried fruit.

Drop by rounded teaspoonfuls onto prepared baking sheets. Dough rounds should be about 1 inch in diameter. Flatten with a spoon.

Bake for 7 to 8 minutes. When done, cookies will appear slightly moist in the center. Cool about 1 minute on the baking sheet and then transfer to a cooling rack.

BREAKFAST

German Pancake
Makes 4 to 6 servings

This all-time breakfast favorite is puffy and elegant, yet a breeze to make. Serve it with lemons and powdered sugar, fresh fruit, or jam.

½ cup dried chopped apples, apricots, dates, figs, or pears
½ cup apple juice
4 tablespoons butter
6 eggs
1 cup milk
1 teaspoon sugar
¼ teaspoon salt
1 teaspoon vanilla extract
1 cup unbleached all-purpose flour
Lemon juice and powdered sugar, fresh fruit, or berry jam or jelly

Soften the fruit by combining the fruit and juice in a small bowl. Allow to stand for 5 to 10 minutes and drain.

Preheat the oven to 400°F (205°C). Melt butter in a 13 × 9-inch baking pan in the oven, checking frequently to avoid scorching. Remove from the oven.

To mix the batter, combine the eggs, milk, sugar, salt, and vanilla in a blender. Blend until combined. Add the flour. Blend until smooth. With a wooden spoon or rubber spatula, stir in the dried fruit. Pour into the baking pan containing the melted butter.

Bake for 15 to 20 minutes, or until puffy and golden brown. Sprinkle with lemon juice and powdered sugar. Serve immediately.

Creamy Apricot Oatmeal
Makes 4 servings

Oatmeal is always great for breakfast but adding dried fruits really dresses it up. If you're in a hurry, you can use instant oatmeal, but I love making it from scratch. I buy the oat groats in the bulk food section of my supermarket and prefer the flavor of the old-fashioned oats to the quick-cooking kind. You can also use cracked wheat or ten-grain cereal instead of the groats.

3 cups water
¼ teaspoon salt
½ cup steel-cut oat groats
½ cup old-fashioned rolled oats
½ teaspoon ground cinnamon
¼ cup toasted wheat germ
½ cup chopped dried apricots, apples, cranberries, dates, peaches, pears, or raisins
Low-fat milk or yogurt
Brown sugar or honey

Bring water and salt to a boil in a 3-quart saucepan. Stir in oat groats and old-fashioned oats. Return to a boil and reduce heat to medium. Cook until a creamy consistency, 5 to 10 minutes. Stir in the cinnamon, wheat germ, and apricots. Serve warm with milk and brown sugar.

HOW TO DRY FOODS

Good Morning Prunes
Makes 6 servings

I love prunes. Period. I love to have some tucked away in the car for a high-energy, nutritious snack when I'm running errands. When I want to get a little fancy with prunes, I make this for breakfast.

3 cups prunes
1½ cups apple juice or cider
2 tablespoons honey
⅛ teaspoon ground cinnamon
6 fresh orange slices

The night before, place the prunes in a medium bowl, cover with apple juice, and refrigerate. Before serving the next morning, place them in a medium saucepan. Add the honey and cinnamon. Cover and bring to a boil. Reduce heat and simmer for 2 to 3 minutes. Garnish each serving with an orange slice. Serve hot.

Crunchy Granola
Makes about 9 cups

The goodness of homemade is what this granola is all about. It's easy to make and you can vary it with what your family likes in a granola. It's a good snack and a nutritious breakfast cereal.

4 cups rolled oats (not instant)
1 cup wheat germ
½ cup bran flakes
1 cup sweetened flaked coconut
¼ cup sesame seeds
½ cup sunflower seeds
½ teaspoon ground cinnamon
¼ teaspoon salt
2 tablespoons vegetable oil
½ cup honey
½ cup apple juice
½ cup firmly packed light brown sugar
2 tablespoons vanilla extract
2 cups chopped dried fruit
1 cup chopped nuts

Preheat the oven to 350°F (180°C). In a large bowl, mix the oats, wheat germ, bran flakes, coconut, sesame seeds, sunflower seeds, cinnamon, and salt. In a small saucepan, heat the oil, honey, apple juice, and brown sugar until warm, stirring until the brown sugar is dissolved. Remove from the heat and stir in the vanilla.

Pour the oil mixture over the oat mixture, stirring to mix well. Pour the mixture into a shallow 13 × 9-inch or larger baking pan.

Bake for 25 to 30 minutes, or until golden brown, stirring every 10 minutes. Stir in the dried fruit and nuts during the last 5 minutes of baking. Cool and store in an airtight container at room temperature. Use granola within 4 weeks.

Good for You Granola
Makes 9 to 10 cups

Unlike many store-bought granolas, this luxurious blend of oats, coconut, nuts, and fruits is not only good to eat, it's good for you. If you want to vary the flavor, substitute ½ cup chopped pistachios and ½ cup chopped macadamias for the coconut.

¼ cup flaxseeds

4 cups rolled oats (not instant)

1 cup wheat germ

⅓ cup instant nonfat dry milk

1 cup sweetened flaked coconut

1 cup sunflower seeds

1 cup slivered almonds

½ cup butter (1 stick) or ½ cup vegetable oil

½ cup honey

½ cup firmly packed light brown sugar

½ teaspoon salt

¼ teaspoon ground nutmeg

1½ teaspoons vanilla extract

1½ cups chopped dried fruit

Preheat the oven to 300°F (150°C). Finely grind flaxseeds in a coffee/spice grinder or your blender. In a large bowl, mix the ground flaxseeds, oats, wheat germ, dry milk, coconut, sunflower seeds, and almonds.

In a small saucepan, heat the butter, honey, brown sugar, and salt until warm, stirring until the brown sugar dissolves. Remove from the heat and add the nutmeg and vanilla.

Drizzle the butter mixture over the oat mixture, stirring to mix well. Pour into a shallow 13 × 9-inch or larger baking pan. Bake for 25 to 30 minutes, or until golden brown, stirring every 10 minutes. Stir in the dried fruit during the last 5 minutes of baking. Cool and store in airtight containers at room temperature. Use within 4 weeks.

METRIC CONVERSION CHARTS

COMPARISON TO METRIC MEASURE

When You Know	Symbol	Multiply By	To Find	Symbol
teaspoons	tsp.	5.0	milliliters	ml
tablespoons	tbsp	15.0	milliliters	ml
fluid ounces	fl. oz.	30.0	milliliters	ml
cups	c.	0.24	liters	l
pints	pt.	0.47	liters	l
quarts	qt.	0.95	liters	l
ounces	oz.	28.0	grams	g
pounds	lb.	0.45	kilograms	kg
Fahrenheit	F	5/9 (after subtracting 32)	Celsius	C

FAHRENHEIT TO CELSIUS

F	C
90–95	35
110–115	45
130–135	55
150–155	65
170–175	80
200–205	95
220–225	105
245–250	120
275	135
300–305	150
325–330	165
345–350	175
370–375	190
400–405	205

LIQUID MEASURE TO MILLILITERS

¼ teaspoon	=	1.25	milliliters
½ teaspoon	=	2.5	milliliters
¾ teaspoon	=	3.75	milliliters
1 teaspoon	=	5.0	milliliters
1¼ teaspoons	=	6.25	milliliters
1½ teaspoons	=	7.5	milliliters
1¾ teaspoons	=	8.75	milliliters
2 teaspoons	=	10.0	milliliters
1 tablespoon	=	15.0	milliliters
2 tablespoons	=	30.0	milliliters

LIQUID MEASURE TO LITERS

¼ cup	=	0.06	liters
½ cup	=	0.12	liters
¾ cup	=	0.18	liters
1 cup	=	0.24	liters
1¼ cups	=	0.3	liters
1½ cups	=	0.36	liters
2 cups	=	0.48	liters
2½ cups	=	0.6	liters
3 cups	=	0.72	liters
3½ cups	=	0.84	liters
4 cups	=	0.96	liters
4½ cups	=	1.08	liters
5 cups	=	1.2	liters
5½ cups	=	1.32	liters

INDEX

ABOUT THE AUTHOR

Deanna DeLong, a pioneer in home food dehydration, has worked for more than two decades writing, consulting, and teaching about food dehydration. She has lectured to audiences around the world, worked as a food dehydration consultant to major manufacturers in the housewares industry, and written numerous publications about drying.

Deanna has traveled extensively in the United States and abroad teaching food drying. She has taught small-scale, industrial food dehydration throughout Central America as part of a USAID team. She traveled to Poland to assist farmers in developing a food-drying cooperative. With a grant from the Mellon Foundation, she helped develop entrepreneurship in six government-owned food dehydration facilities in Hungary. She taught food dehydration to agricultural students in Mozambique, worked in the Republic of Georgia teaching farmers how to dry persimmons, and consulted with Georgian food processors on dehydration. Deanna's fifteen volunteer projects in developing countries have helped her fulfill her personal mission to help people improve their nutrition by drying foods.

After more than two decades in dehydration, Deanna is now also involved in hydration. Deanna is the owner of Preservation Pantry, a business that carries products for food dehydration, healthful cooking, water filtration, and emergency drinking water.

She and her husband, David Feinauer, live in Beaverton, Oregon. They have eight children and eleven grandchildren.